Birth of the BOXLOCK SHOTGUN

*The Inside Story of
Anson & Deeley, Westley Richards,
Harrington & Richardson,
and the Perfection of the Hammerless Action*

by John Campbell

John Campbell
Birth of the Boxlock Shotgun
Woonsocket, R.I.: ANDREW MOWBRAY INCORPORATED — PUBLISHERS
120 pages

ISBN: 978-1-931464-85-7

© 2020 John Campbell

To order more copies of this book, call Mowbray Publishers at 800-999-4697 or go to www.gunandswordcollector.com

Printed in China

The design and layout of this book was conceived by Jo-Ann Langlois.

Copyright © 2020 by John Campbell

All rights reserved. No part of this work may be reproduced, stored in a retrieval system, or transmitted in any form or by any means, electronic, mechanical, photocopying, recording or otherwise, without the expressed permission from the author.

FRONT & BACK COVERS: This Anson & Deeley boxlock (ser. no. 5056) was the first one ever made by Westley Richards after securing the A&D patent (No. 1756), on May 11, 1875. The gun's lower frame is engraved to this effect. It is a 12-bore with 30-inch barrels, bored cylinder and cylinder, and was presented to John Deeley, Westley Richards' General Manager, as a commemorative gift and display/promotional piece. *Photos — Courtesy of Bonham's. Design concept: Connor Campbell*

1 2 3 4 5 6 7 8 9 10

Dedication

This book is dedicated to the late Clare Stride
and the Anson family of which she is a descendant.
Without Clare's diligent research, this book would not exist,
and without William Anson's genius, the greatest
break-action gun in the world would never have been possible.

I hope this volume helps to commemorate
these two individuals and their life's work.

INTRODUCTION

This isn't just a book about guns. It is a book about three 19th-century English gentlemen, namely, William Anson, John Deeley and William Anson's son, Edwin Anson, and the guns that they made. Because the lives and achievements of these men overlap across similar time frames, I've tried to keep things as comprehensible as possible by dealing with each individual through a separate chapter. In doing so, some minor bits are necessarily repeated, but only for the sake of chronology and biographical continuity.

This format is also best because the story of Anson & Deeley includes a cast of supporting characters who are waiting in the wings to be discovered. Some are known, and others heretofore unknown, but they all played their part upon the stage of shooting history.

While the transcendent Anson & Deeley gun action remains a major focus of this work, there is also a huge trove of other ingenious mechanisms and products to be discovered. This includes latches, safeties, ejectors, target traps, try guns and air pistols, just to name a few. But this host of hardware is part of a larger human story, and that is what I've endeavored to unveil here, along with the tale of how these remarkably creative men sired a shooting heritage that most of us take for granted today. They were amazing craftsmen, businessmen, and even artists. But like all of us, they led personal lives fraught with hope, tragedy, victory and defeat.

Their saga also forms a conduit through history and answers a multitude of questions about the ethos that surrounded Anson and Deeley. How did their lives intersect? How did their famous inventions come about? Who was actually responsible for the concepts? What else did they create? And who may have taken due (or undue) credit for some of those achievements? Then, there's the ultimate mystery of all — What caused the brilliant engineering alliance between William Anson and John Deeley to devolve into a seemingly obscure end? The surprising answers, and more, can be found within the pages of this book, much of its contents previously unknown and unpublished.

Why? Partially because the facts have been scattered to the wind for over a century. But through luck and pluck, the real story can now be drawn together from formerly unavailable sources. These sources include an exhaustive research by Anson family descendant Clare Stride, Anson family documents and letters, U.K. historical records, patents, contracts, licenses, Westley Richards correspondence, and more. There is also key testimony from "men of the trade" who have discreetly withheld their insights until now. It all adds up to a mesmerizing tale of genius, ambition, triumph and travail.

You have my assurance that *Birth of The Boxlock Shotgun* is a story that you never expected...and one that you will remember forever.

TABLE OF CONTENTS

Chapter 1   William Anson
MECHANICAL GENIUS...FATHER OF THE BOXLOCK...VICTIM OF CIRCUMSTANCE ... 9

Chapter 2   John Deeley
A MAN OF MYSTERY, TALENT AND MANEUVERS 39

Chapter 3   Edwin Anson
A HERITAGE OF INVENTION AND DREAMS UNFULFILLED. 79

Epilogue 98

Appendix 99

Index 116

IN APPRECIATION

John Donne once observed that "no man is an island," and without the help and support I've received from some special individuals, this book could not have been created. The first of these is Peter Harris. In the world of U.K. shooting, he needs no introduction. Peter is a master of the shotgun and its use afield. He is not only a BASC clays champion, but also a famed shooting tutor-to-the-stars, including no small number of Royals. Peter is also curator of the surviving records and history of William and Edwin Anson — a vast treasure that was bequeathed to Peter by the late Clare Stride, descendant of Edwin Anson.

That brings me to recognize the late Clare Stride herself. It was her expansive research that formed the foundation of this book and remains a primary resource from which much of the untold story is drawn. A retired BBC film producer, Clare's fascination with her family's history began "...not with a gun, but with a painting that I inherited from my grandfather," she once wrote. "Both William and Edwin painted and exhibited at the Royal Birmingham Society of Artists. The painting I had was by Edwin Anson, 1883, and depicted a man in what I presumed was an English wood, carrying a shotgun. My mother said she thought it was Massachusetts. And since I exhibited at The Royal Birmingham Society of Artists, I was in a position to look into the archives." That move sparked Clare's genealogical passion. Her investigation started at the Society and kept on going. As a result, much of what we know about William and Edwin Anson can be traced to Clare Stride's dogged research and scrupulous records.

The third person I must single out for gratitude is Robert Hodges, descendant of E.C. Hodges, the famed 19th-century London actioner and gunmaker. Robert's skills in media, online research, genealogy and all-round digital magic were invaluable. He uncovered many of the images and personal information contained in this book, and all of it proved key in assembling a more complete story of Anson & Deeley.

A cadre of other individuals and organizations helped as well, and they are listed below:

Brad Bachelder	Michael Foster	Stuart Mowbray
David J. Baker	John Friedman	Andrew Orr
Carol Barnes	John Griffiths	Stephen Quill
Bonham's Auctioneers	Daryl Halquist	Ted Rowe
Connor Campbell	Steve Helsley	Mick Shepherd
Connecticut Shotgun Mfrg. Co.	Holt's Auctioneers	Roscoe B. Stephenson, III
Kristen Figg	Kirby Hoyt	Brian Uprichard
Ernie Foster	Kirk Merrington	Westley Richards & Co. Ltd.

I respectfully salute and sincerely thank each one. They all helped to make this small record of shooting history possible.

Special Disclosure and Notice

Neither this book, its contents, the author, nor its contributors are in any way associated with Westley Richards & Co. Ltd. However, I have received some very helpful cooperation from them, especially with photos and illustrations. For this and more I am most grateful to Westley Richards & Co. Ltd. I also solicited their view on a host of questions and issues regarding their company's history and its relationship with William Anson, Edwin Anson, John Deeley and more. Again, they've helped to the degree that they could.

Still, it is important to understand that this is a completely independent work based on previously published materials, existing public and private documents, personal research by the late Clare Stride, and anecdotal information gleaned from surviving tradesmen and their remembrances. Accordingly, the material in this book has been researched and assembled to the best of my abilities, and I believe its contents to be as even-handed, factual and reliable as possible under the circumstances. Beyond this, I make no claims or allegations whatsoever. My abiding purpose has been to present the information I've uncovered in context with history, then let my readers draw their own conclusions.

Finally, nothing in this book should be construed in any way as to impugn, slight or disparage the character or reputation of any individual or company, past or present.

Original Anson Latch Patent Drawing No. 3791.

Chapter One
WILLIAM ANSON

Mechanical Genius...
Father of The Boxlock...
Victim of Circumstance

Few individuals have had more influence over the double-barrel shotgun than William Anson. His invention of the famous Anson & Deeley boxlock was as pivotal to the advancement of shotguns as Casimir Lefaucheux's break-action concept itself. Even today, the principles of this engineering epiphany stand as the foundation for millions of sporting guns and the yardstick by which all other double-gun actions are judged. In truth, the importance of the Anson & Deeley concept simply defies overstatement.

But, take note, there are two names on this patent, and a question that begs resolution: Was the A&D boxlock primarily a William Anson idea, was it a John Deeley idea, or was it an equitably shared idea? The truth is out there somewhere, and the balance of this story may help you find it. Nonetheless, double-gun enthusiasts must exclusively credit William Anson with one of the most common fore-end latching mechanisms extant, plus an absolutely foolproof boxlock intercepting safety sear and one of the most simple and reliable safety systems ever invented. And this, dear reader, is just the tip of the iceberg.

The root of this story begins with the birth of William Anson on August 2, 1830. He was the second of five children born to Edwin and Helen Anson of Wolverhampton, Staffordshire, England. In the 1841 census, the family was recorded as living in the Snow Hill/Dudley Road area of Wolverhampton. Edwin Anson Sr. was listed in local directories as a locksmith, and Wolverhampton was famous for many types of locks, including gun locks.

At this point in the story, I will make the first of many references to an historic trove of Anson family research compiled by the late Ms. Clare Stride, the great granddaughter of William Anson's son Edwin Anson. She was a retired producer for the BBC and an avid genealogist of the family, who published much of her findings in an article entitled "Anson & Deeley," which appeared in the Spring 2004 issue of *Double Gun Journal* magazine. In her well-researched history, Ms. Stride claims that William's original surname was Hanson and that, not long after his birth, the "H" was somehow lost, to become "Anson."

"William was baptized *William Hanson*," Stride said. "When precisely Hanson became Anson, I do not know."

From one perspective, this could be attributed to 19th-century working class English, in which the habit of "dropping the 'aitches" in the pronunciation of certain names was quite common. For example, "old Harry" might often be referred to as "old 'arry" by his friends and co-workers. Lop the "H" off Hanson in this dialect, and it easily becomes "Anson." However, Clare Stride's research notes, which now reside in our archives, contain another intriguing but unconfirmed possibility:

My mother's cousin Joyce Groves, had said that there were rumours that William had been fostered out to a family in Lichfield, which raised possibilities that he may have been related to the Ansons of Shugborough Hall, but I can find no record of this. Representatives from the Earl of Lichfield's Estate did, however, call on my grandmother to try and ascertain if there were any family connections. The factual (and social) results of that investigation are unknown, and none of the Earl's estate came to the Anson family. So, there was either no connection or none anyone wanted to have known.

Nevertheless, Wolverhampton Library records list the family name as "Anson." Thus, we shall continue under the aegis of that spelling. Records also show that William had at least three brothers: George, John, and Titus. He also had a sister named Ellen. Later directories list both George and William as "locksmiths," like their father.

As a young man, William Anson married Caroline Taylor at the Sedgley Parish Church on April 25, 1858. William

In this undated photograph, William Anson appears somewhat older. Perhaps it was taken after 1883.
Courtesy of the Stride Family

was 27 years old at the time and Caroline was 19. They would eventually have six children together. William may not have been aware of it at the time, but seven years before he and Caroline wed, an especially portentous event occurred that would set the stage for his engineering immortality. It was The Great Exposition of 1851 held in London's Hyde Park. There, in the famous Crystal Palace, gunmaker Casimir Lefaucheux of Paris, France, unveiled a startling design that would change the shotgun trade forever. It was a break-action, breechloading gun that fired a self-contained cartridge. In a world of muzzleloaders, it was like technology from outer space.

The genius of Lefaucheux's idea was instantly recognized by a young gunmaker who had visited the exhibition — one Edwin Charles Hodges. What's more, the soon-to-be-famous "E.C." Hodges also realized how to make Lefaucheux's gun significantly better and potentially establish himself in the trade. So, E.C. wasted no time in creating a vastly improved version with a more mechanically advantageous "bite" and a better opening system.

He presented this prototype to gunmaker Joseph Lang the Elder, who immediately realized its potential. And since the French gun had not been patented in the U.K., Joseph Lang fearlessly introduced the first break-action drop-down breechloader to the British sporting market in 1853. In fact, Lang often touted the fact that he'd inaugurated the breechloader into English sport. An 1864 advertisement in *The Field* claimed as much, in unambiguous language: *Joseph Lang of 22 Cockspur Street begs to inform gentlemen that he has a BREECH-LOADER on an entirely new principle, the simplest and quickest ever offered to the public. It combines strength and durability. J.L. was the first to improve and introduce the breechloader into England...*

Thus, E.C. Hodges' advanced concept became the turning point for English gunmakers. Nevertheless, Lang's gun had traditional hammers that still required manual cocking, as did a plethora of break-open English sporting guns for more than two decades to come. William Anson would help change all of that, but it would take the intercedence of events an ocean away to provide him the opportunity.

Edwin Charles "E.C." Hodges in 1865. His genius helped Jos. Lang perfect the Lefaucheux gun for English sportsmen and set the stage for the A&D breakthrough a decade later. *Photo — Robert Hodges*

William Anson Joins Westley Richards

England's 1861 census shows William and Caroline Anson as living at 27 Zoar Street in Wolverhampton. At the time, William described himself as a cabinet locksmith, but this year was to become very important for William Anson. In March of 1861, the issues of slavery and state's rights finally erupted in the United States of America. Accordingly, seven Southern states broke away from the Union to form The Confederate States of America. This precipitated the U.S. Civil War in April of 1861. Since the agricultural South had scant industrial resources for the production of arms and war material, much of what they so desperately needed was outsourced from England. To be entirely accurate, the North also ordered arms from Britain, and as one might imagine, this sudden demand for guns turned the industrial city of Birmingham into a boomtown almost overnight.

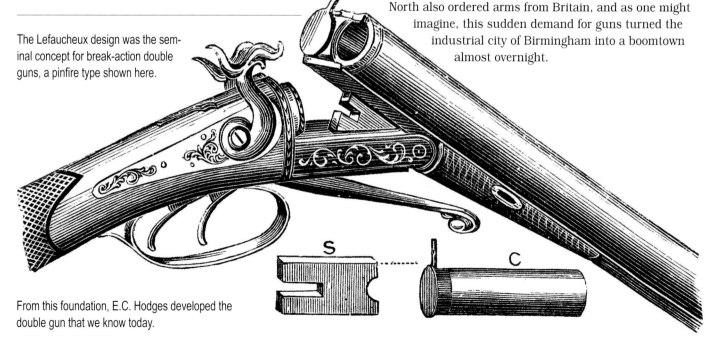

The Lefaucheux design was the seminal concept for break-action double guns, a pinfire type shown here.

From this foundation, E.C. Hodges developed the double gun that we know today.

According to figures cited in his book *The Birmingham Gun Trade*, David Williams reports that Birmingham industries shipped over 730,000 firearms to America, and London makers sent an additional 344,000 before the U.S. conflict ended. Collaterally, English troops and material were in great demand elsewhere around the globe, as conflicts also raged in the southern regions of Africa and in the Far East.

William Anson undoubtedly took notice of all this and realized that the principles of a household lock could be readily transferred to gun lock construction without much ado. Thus, at some point after 1861, he moved directly into Birmingham along with his wife Caroline.

By 1863, William Anson was described in records as a "gunsight maker." This was possibly for (or at) Westley Richards & Co., where he would later become an "action filer" by 1868. Sadly, Clare Stride admits, "I don't know (exactly) when William joined Westley Richards." Unfortunately, Westley Richards & Co. could not offer clarification on this issue. Perhaps such records are lost. So, the best I can deduce from existing information is that William Anson formally joined Westley's sometime between 1861 and 1868.

However, in strict chronology, Birmingham records show that William began his own business at 123 Steelhouse Lane in 1869. In fact, this is the "establishment date" carried through on promotional materials made-up by William and his son Edwin as late as 1917. But what was William making at 123 Steelhouse Lane? In all likelihood, it was his ingenious Anson push-rod fore-end latch. Within his 1872 patent description, Anson states that he makes the parts. So, just maybe, William maintained a side business, even after he'd joined Westley Richards.

The 1871 census records show William and Caroline as living at 75 Ashtead Row, Birmingham. By this time, three daughters had been born as well as two sons, George Edwin (known as Edwin, b.1863 in Birmingham), and John Albert (known as Albert, b.1868).

At some point in 1873, it is certain that William Anson was made foreman of the Westley Richards shotgun action shop. In light of this appointment, it is logical to assume that he had some previous history with Westley's in order to attain such a post, probably as an action filer and perhaps as an outworker. William may also have impressed management with his patented push-rod fore-end release, which he was undoubtedly making on his own.

As an aside, it is worth mentioning that a young Scot named John Robertson was also attracted to the prosperity of Birmingham in those years. He joined Westley Richards in 1862, and as fellow employees, Robertson undoubtedly knew William Anson and John Deeley. It wasn't long before the siren song of London drew Robertson onward. In that city, he would work at James Purdey's, establish his own trade business and ultimately become the famous owner of Boss & Co. But, all that's another story.

Nonetheless, the bloody American Civil War ended in 1865, which left the Birmingham arms industry with a lot of capacity and a suddenly reduced market. But the expansion of the

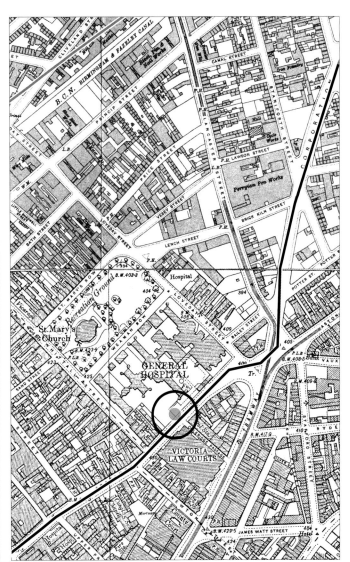

The approximate location of William Anson's Birmingham shop at 123 Steelhouse Lane is circled. The lined street nearby is Steelhouse Lane, with law courts opposite. The line also delineates the old Birmingham gun quarter perimeter. *Map — BirminghamGunMuseum.com*

Empire presented viable alternatives for arms sales. First, there were the British military and colonial markets to supply. Then, there was a burgeoning trade in sporting arms, which was fueled by social and political factors as much as anything else. So, British gunmakers still managed to prosper.

It is at about this same time that William Anson developed a most unexpected outlet for his talents — painting. Perhaps this was a creative diversion from his structured work life, because Anson remained an amateur painter of notable skill creating at least 14 known works throughout his life. Some were even displayed in Birmingham area galleries, with surviving examples treasured by collectors, even today. Anson's passion for painting would later be carried forward by his son Edwin. As part of her research, Anson descendant Clare Stride later discovered that "quite a few gunmakers attended art classes" in Birmingham. But it was mechanical engineering, not art, that would pave the way for William Anson.

The Anson Push-Rod Latch

Throughout his life, William Anson generated a virtual gold mine of mechanisms toward the advancement of double guns. The first of these is one I've already mentioned — the ubiquitous push-rod style fore-end latch, commonly known as the Anson latch. It was recorded as William Anson Patent No. 3,791 on December 14, 1872. It is still in wide use today by a host of English and European gunmakers, virtually unchanged from the original design.

However, if one examines the original patent drawing, three surprising aspects of this design become readily apparent. The first is that the latch is shown fitted to a Jones lever hammer gun, which may seem a bit incongruous to present-day boxlock shooters. With more careful analysis of the drawing, it is noteworthy that the only means for the mechanism's attachment to the fore-end is a single wood screw through the rearward portion of the fore-end iron. The usual small machine screw through the forward section of the latch pipe, which draws against a metal fore-end finial, is missing. Perhaps Anson realized this second point of attachment was necessary after he submitted the patent drawing. Or, maybe it was there all along, but was merely omitted from the drawing.

The third surprise to be found in a careful reading of William's amended 1872 patent is one that has never been noticed, or at least never publicized before. His basic claim was for the pipe and push rod activation of the mechanism, not necessarily the sliding bolt that engaged the barrel lug. The language of his patent on page 4, line 10, makes this very clear (see Appendix):

I wish it to be understood that I do not claim generally the use of a sliding spring bolt for securing the fore-ends of drop down guns to the barrels, but I claim as my Invention... connecting the fore ends of the said small-arms to the barrels and disconnecting them from the said barrels by means of a sliding bolt, such as e, **sliding in a tubular guide such as d, the parts constructed, arranged, and combined substantially as described and illustrated.**

So, why would Anson's latch claim be couched in such a way? Well, according to authors I.M. Crudgington and D.J. Baker, in *The British Shotgun, Vol. One*, it appears as though William Anson did not invent the push-rod fore-end latch! That honour goes to gunmakers Guillaume Lorent Barens and Jean Fructueux Ladougne of Paris, who actually patented the first push-rod latch on July 25, 1867. Crudgington and Baker add this perspective: *This is a forend fastening identical in design to that patented many years later* [1872] *by Westley Richards foreman, William Anson, which is known as the Anson rod forend.*

But wait, there's more. Even before Anson came into the picture, William Spinks Riley of Birmingham, Warwickshire, was granted Patent No. 1825 on June 17, 1872, for a very similar push-rod latch. Six months after Riley's patent, on December 14, 1872, William Anson was granted British Patent No. 3791 for his famous latch. Crudgington and Baker

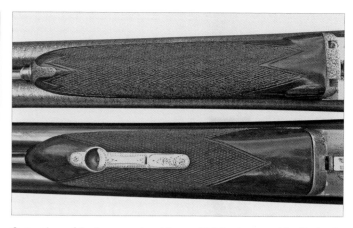

Comparison of the Anson push-rod fore-end latch, above, and the Deeley & Edge latch, below. Most Westley Richards guns utilized the Deeley & Edge system.

point out that Anson's design was actually the third patent of a push-rod/sliding bolt mechanism.

To lend yet another curious perspective to Anson's latch, it is worth noting that Westley Richards' double guns almost always employ the Deeley & Edge forearm latch and not the Anson type. Why would they have such a preference? While it is only speculation, the reason may have been a combination of ego and ambition.

It was less than six months after William Anson patented his push-rod latch when the Deeley & Edge latch was patented in April of 1873 by John Deeley and James Edge, foreman of the Westley Richards sporting and military rifle department. This mechanism not only put money into the pockets of Messrs. Deeley and Edge, but also reserved a very functional latching system for Westley Richards & Co. What's more, it was "the boss' idea."

As a result, it is likely that William Anson's latch assumed a second-tier standing in the company. Thus, William was left to find other takers in order to make any significant money from it, mostly beyond the confines of Westley Richards. Still, a great number of high-end provincial and London guns were fitted with these Anson latches, and many were stamped with the name "ANSON" and his patent.

To add more perspective to the fore-end latch issue, Clare Stride relates this opinion from a well-known contemporary English gunmaker who must yet remain anonymous: *Both invented fore-end catches — the "Deeley fore-end catch" and the William Anson rod fore-end catch. [However] they were wiley enough to manage to get their inventions patented under their own names and not Westley Richards. I would have thought that John Deeley would have undertaken all the monetary and contractual negotiations, with his accountancy background.*

Nonetheless, yet another William Anson idea was waiting in the wings. And it would change the double-gun world forever.

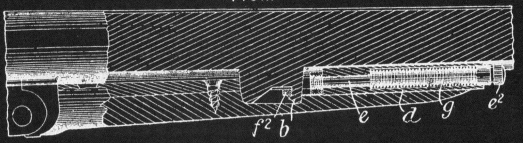

Patent drawing of William Anson's push-rod fore-end latch. Note that it shows only one screw for attachment to the fore-end.

William Spinks Riley was issued Patent No. 1825 for this fore-end latch on June 17, 1872, six months before William Anson's patent.

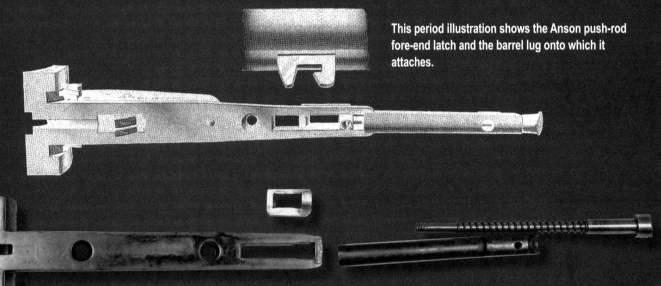

This period illustration shows the Anson push-rod fore-end latch and the barrel lug onto which it attaches.

Basic bits of an Anson latch in exploded view. Includes the fore-end iron, push rod, spring, and the pipe through which the rod and spring work. The rod threads into the rectangular locking slide, above, which engages the barrel fore-end lug.

The first push-rod, sliding bolt fore-end latch was patented in 1867 by Parisians Guillaume Lorent Barens and Jean Fructueux Ladougne. This was five years before Anson patented his famous design in 1872.

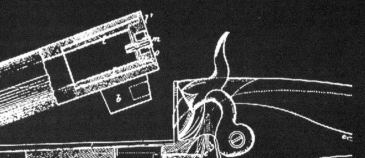

The Anson & Deeley Boxlock Emerges

It is commonly believed that Anson & Deeley's boxlock was the first hammerless, barrel-cocking shotgun ever designed. In point of fact, it is not. That honour goes to Joseph Needham. He patented his barrel-cocking gun in 1874, a year previous to the A&D design. Needham's gun can be examined in British Patent No. 1205.

Messrs. I.M. Crudgington and D.J. Baker substantiate Needham's primacy in *The British Shotgun, Vol. Two*: *What is in no doubt is that the Needham was the first British barrel-cocking hammerless sporting shotgun and its inventor can lay claim to fame surely and squarely on this fact.*

Although ground-breaking in concept, Needham's underlever design was somewhat fragile and inelegant, both in function and appearance. Still, it presented a principle worthy of further development, a fact that undoubtedly had not escaped William Anson.

Thus, it was on May 11, 1875, when Anson's "Big Idea" brought the barrel-cocking shotgun to perfection. On this day, both William Anson and Westley Richards' new Managing Director John Deeley were granted British Patent No. 1756 for the famous Anson & Deeley "boxlock" action. It was light years beyond Needham and featured a stunningly simple and robust mechanism that took brilliant advantage of Archimedes' "Law of The Lever." In other words, the A&D approach used the barrels themselves as a lever to multiply force and cock the gun. At the nose of the action bar, two cocking dogs pivoted near the hinge pin. These connected the forepart and barrels of the gun with the lock work. As the gun was opened, this linkage effectively transformed the barrels into a long, powerful lever with more than enough mechanical advantage to cock two heavily sprung tumbler/hammers housed inside the action frame.

As opposed to Needham's gun, the Anson & Deeley was elegantly straightforward, flawlessly efficient and perfectly suited to cost-efficient mass production. In sum, it was genius. As a result, untold millions of boxlock shotguns have been made on the A&D principle and are still being made today. In *Modern Sporting Gunnery*, Henry Sharp put it succinctly, "Upon its introduction, the Anson and Deeley was perceived to be superior to all other forms of gun-lock." According to Maj. Gerald Burrard, in *The Modern Shotgun*, "...it would be hard to imagine anything much simpler." G.T. Teasdale-Buckell immediately grasped the potential in *Experts On Guns & Shooting*, stating, "It completely revolu-

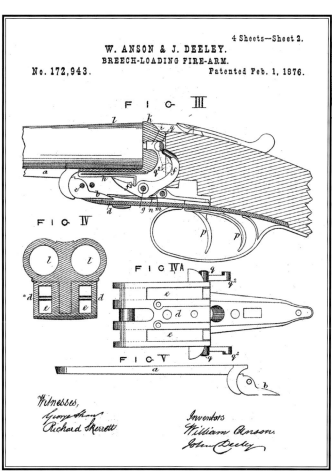

The key illustration from the A&D action's U.S. Patent No. 172,943. Note that it retains the cross-bolt safety of the original British patent. Here, the works are in cocked position.

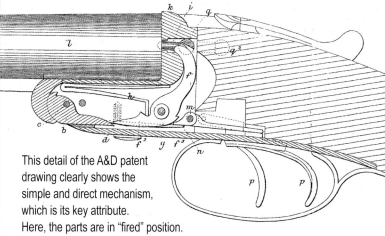

This detail of the A&D patent drawing clearly shows the simple and direct mechanism, which is its key attribute. Here, the parts are in "fired" position.

Below: This inside bottom view of an early A&D action shows the two cylindrical cocking dogs at the action knuckle. They engaged mating cuts in the fore-end iron. The sears, sear springs, and lower limbs of the tumblers are also seen.

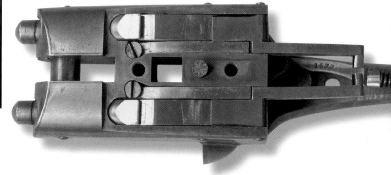

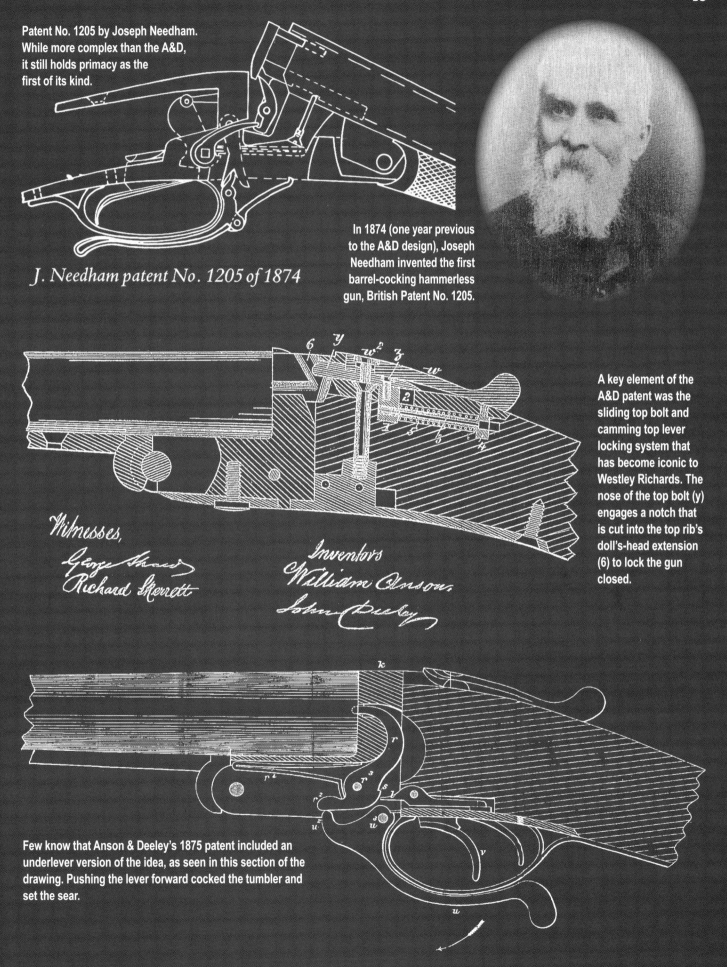

A very early A&D boxlock with Anson's original thumb tab cross-bolt safety arrangement. Experts are still unsure of the purpose behind the milled groove along the bottom edge of the frame.
Photo — Courtesy of Westley Richards

tionized the breechloader." While that praise is certainly well deserved, a few less well-known points about the original 1875 patent are worth calling to your attention.

The first is that it includes the famous Westley Richards sliding top bolt to fasten the action closed. This bolt engaged a notch cut into the doll's-head extension of the top rib and was the only means by which early A&D boxlocks were locked down. The same sliding bolt is still used today on Westley Richards boxlocks, albeit in conjunction with the Purdey underbolt system via William Anson's Patent No. 1833 of 1883. That combination provides three individual bites to lock the gun.

Another fact that has apparently gone without notice is that the original A&D patent also included an "underlever" variation of the boxlock idea. This approach utilized a Jones/Needham-looking lever that wrapped back around the trigger guard, and was pivoted through the frame of the gun just ahead of the guard. By pushing this lever forward, an extension on its front cammed the nose of the tumbler up and backward to cock the gun. It should come as little surprise that this concept was never developed further.

And finally, an obscure but equally noteworthy aspect of the A&D patent was a rotating "crossbolt" safety arrangement. This concept featured a crosspin with a "flat" that rolled into the path of the tumbler, blocking it from moving forward and detonating a cartridge. This safety's intrinsic flaws were (a) it was fairly inconvenient and (b) it served to intercept a motion that had potentially already begun, rather than preventing that motion in the first place. A modest number of A&D guns were produced with these safeties until William Anson came up with his top tang, sliding thumb button design in 1876, Patent No. 4513.

Here's something else to consider for students of 19th-century English double-gun design: There is a fascinating parallel between Anson's original rotating-flat crossbolt safety and the side safety made famous by W.W. Greener. It seems as though Greener may have borrowed and modified the concept by moving it rearward to traverse the stockhead. Greener's safety also has a similar rod/flat approach. But in the Greener version, it is rotated to either block or permit lifting of the trigger blades. This safety was applied to both Greener's *Facile Princeps* (Easily the Best) guns along with many of his A&D boxlocks. While Greener's approach certainly worked, his crossbolt safety is only slightly less inconvenient than Anson's original.

To its enduring credit, very little alteration has taken place in the basic A&D design over the years. The means of actuating the cocking dogs was changed a few times and the locations of the sear notch moved in some iterations. In fact, an entire segment of the February 1912 edition of *Arms and Explosives* was dedicated to the analysis of this sear/tumbler notch alteration (see Appendix).

By the mid 1880s, the Purdey underbolt had been added to most run-of-the-mill A&D actions, actuated by either the Scott or Greener top lever mechanisms. However, Westley Richards camming top lever guns were a bit of a different

This articulated mechanism, Patent No. 1833 of 1883, was William Anson's way of connecting the sliding top bolt of the A&D action to a Purdey underbolt. The result was three individual bites to lock the gun closed.

challenge. So, William Anson devised an ingenious means to connect and coordinate the original top lever and sliding Purdey underbolt. This can first be seen in Anson & Deeley Patent No. 1833 of April 11, 1883. The resulting three-point lock up made the action very robust and quite suitable for double rifles, which would soon encompass powerful big-bore and smokeless powder cartridges.

Many boxlocks were also made with round Greener, or the square-style Scott crossbolts. In whatever combinations, these enhancements brought the A&D lock-up to virtual perfection and served to enhance its basic design, not change it. Still, safety-conscious shooters wanted something more. So, by the beginning of the 20th century, the A&D sear tails were lengthened, and intercepting safety sears were added if the customer desired. Otherwise, the essential A&D action has endured unaltered over the decades.

It is also true that the original A&D patent went a long, long way to put the "rich" in Westley Richards, along with a few other individuals whom I shall discuss shortly. However, there is still some question over exactly who came up with the seminal A&D idea.

Ernest Hemingway used his Westley Richards .577 A&D double to good effect in Africa. Here, he checks the barrels with two cartridges ready in his right hand.

Origins of The A&D Boxlock

According to the book *Westley Richards & Co. In Pursuit of The Best Gun*, author Jeremy Musson states that John Deeley once claimed the A&D boxlock was his idea and that Anson merely worked out the details. G.T. Teasdale Buckell credits the company itself in *Experts On Guns & Shooting*: *The Westley Richards patent hammerless gun, the Anson and Deeley, was the first gun in which the cocking of the tumbler was done by the opening and closing of the barrels.* (Note Buckell's oversight of Needham and that the A&D action cocks on opening, not on closing. But Buckell may have simply been describing the entire action that takes place.)

Nonetheless, more independent historians, as well as the Anson family, have strongly suggested a different scenario. It is their contention that William Anson actually fathered the idea and that John Deeley and Westley Richards simply financed the work and claimed credit as co-patentees. To me, this is the most likely circumstance, and it is underwritten by Donald Dallas in his book *The British Sporting Gun And Rifle*:

In his Centenary address to the [Westley Richards] *staff in 1912, Deeley stated that he had thought up the principle but that William Anson had worked out the actual design. I am skeptical about this statement, appearing to put Deeley in the forefront... It is my belief that William Anson, being a working gunmaker, invented the design. He would not have sufficient funds to patent it on his own and sought the help of John Deeley, who would then want his name upon the patent so that he could claim financial benefit from it... The owners of gunmaking firms often claimed that since a proposed design had most probably been thought out during the firm's time in the working day, the firm had claim over the patent.*

In support of the Dallas position is the fact that original British patent documents always refer to this mechanical achievement as the "William Anson and John Deeley" concept. With their names in that specific order. It was submitted in that format, and it was signed off in the same way by both Messrs. Anson and Deeley, who were in obvious accord with this order of reference (see Appendix).

So, wouldn't it be intuitive to assume that the primary inventor would be listed first in documents intended to preserve the intellectual property? It would seem logical to me.

In any case, one thing is certain. The potential value of the Anson & Deeley action was not lost on its creators. They doubtlessly saw money in their futures — and lots of it. The first hints of what Messrs. Anson and Deeley may have had in mind is evidenced through chronology:

- John Deeley became Managing Director of Westley Richards in 1872 — the same year in which William Anson patented his famous Anson fore-end latch.
- In 1873, William Anson becomes foreman of the shotgun action department.
- In 1873, the format of Westley Richards patent filings is apparently changed. Whereas they had previously been filed under "Westley Richards" (presumably the company name), they were now filed under the names of specific Westley Richards employees — mostly in conjunction with John Deeley, and later Leslie Taylor (Taylor having the highest number).
- In 1875, Messrs. Anson and Deeley patent the A&D boxlock action under their own names, yet maintain an umbilical connection to Westley Richards & Co.
- In 1876, William Anson makes a rather abrupt, yet apparently amicable, departure from Westley Richards and sets up his own shop at 123 Steelhouse Lane. Later, he is listed at Egyptian Hall, 77 Slaney Street.

The order of signatures on the A&D patent might allude to the primacy of the idea. In other words, William Anson is first because the idea was his?

Further Evidence

There is yet more nuance to consider regarding the A&D boxlock. The first actual A&D gun said to be made at Westley's was ser. no. 5056, and even identified on the bottom of its frame as "THE FIRST/ANSON & DEELEY/HAMMERLESS GUN/Patented 11th May/1875." The name of Westley Richards is applied in its usual position — engraved on the sides of the action bars. Furthermore, a period gun case instruction label is reproduced on page 108 of the Westley Richards history book. The label appears thusly:

INSTRUCTIONS FOR USING
ANSON & DEELEY HAMMERLESS GUN
Manufactured By
WESTLEY RICHARDS & CO. LIMITED

Please note the order of reference, terminology and emphasis in both cases. It is first and foremost an "Anson & Deeley Hammerless Gun" as if this were the name of the maker. The subordinate reference is one of mere manufacture by Westley Richards. There could be two reasons for this construction.

First, Westley Richards may have felt it best to promote this breakthrough gun action under a new and captivating brand identity that would enhance its image, desirability, and foster a unique standing in the marketplace. In other words, the public's perception of "Anson & Deeley" should be a step away from that of Westley Richards. And perhaps A&D was even intended as a separate profit center to promote and license this action to the gun trade in general, along with other desirable mechanisms. It's difficult to determine the truth of the matter. For a more contemporary perspective, I cite *The British Shotgun, Vol. Three* by I.M. Crudgington and D.J. Baker: *William Anson was almost certainly the true*

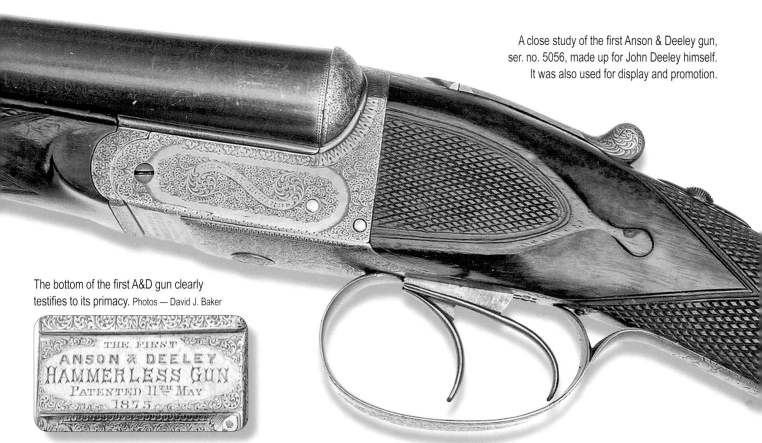

A close study of the first Anson & Deeley gun, ser. no. 5056, made up for John Deeley himself. It was also used for display and promotion.

The bottom of the first A&D gun clearly testifies to its primacy. Photos — David J. Baker

inventor of the action that is now known as the Anson & Deeley, because of the way in which it was patented. [Anson's name first]. There is an oral tradition within the Anson family, however, that William was, in some way, badly treated over the deal.

Through all of this, a niggling issue remains, Just who held primary sway over the A&D boxlock patent, and who were the principle beneficiaries? Westley Richards? Messrs. Anson & Deeley? A firm called Anson & Deeley Patentees? Or all of the above?

Nevertheless, the chronological progression of entities connected to the management, direction and marketing of the A&D boxlock seems to be:

1. Anson & Deeley/Westley Richards & Co.
2. Robert Couchman
3. Anson & Deeley Patentees
4. E. Anson & Co.

And now, we'll explore the fascinating story behind each of these entities.

Anson's Independence & Robert Couchman's License

To continue with the A&D tale, let us return to the year 1876 and ponder an amazing turn of events. William Anson had formally joined Westley Richards and became foreman of its shotgun action shop. In that role, he co-patents a transformational gun design destined to change the sporting arms marketplace forever. And after this historic triumph, Anson abruptly leaves the company.

Yes, indeed, with everything seemingly in his favor, the traditional story is that Anson decides to chuck it all and go off on his own to an uncertain future. At first blush, this appears utterly irrational. Or was it? Recent research gives us some insight.

Anson's departure roughly correlates with what appears to be the first licensing of the A&D patent. This license was granted to a fellow named Robert E. Couchman of No. 6 Waterloo Street, Birmingham. This contract, now in our files, was executed on June 22, 1876, and required Couchman to pay 15 shillings per "sporting gun or rifle" produced with the A&D action, and to number each gun or rifle consecutively, beginning with the No. 1.

It is also important to note that the language of the contract specifies Westley Richards & Co. as the *licensor* of Patent No. 1756, which itself was "granted under the great seal of the United Kingdom of Great Britain and Ireland to William Anson and John Deeley..." An intriguing twist of proprietorship, to say the least.

Additionally, any royalties Couchman owed were to be paid quarterly to the "licensor," namely, Westley Richards & Co. Therefore, one must logically assume that the company would then disburse an appropriate portion of those proceeds to the patent holders themselves based on some still unknown formula.

Of course, the recently separated William Anson was one of those individuals. Thus, he must have retained some level of trust in and/or affiliation with Westley Richards & Co. and its Managing Director John Deeley, who was now serving as his royalty collector and paymaster.

An addendum to Couchman's license was added on November 1, 1876, granting him rights to use William Anson's "dickey bird safety" mechanism, Patent No. 4513, for the sum of three shillings per unit. Later, Couchman licensed this mechanism to lockmakers Joseph Brazier & Sons, probably for reasons of efficient volume production and for use as a component part by Westley Richards and other gunmakers.

Got all that? Good. Now for the curious part — Robert Couchman was not a gunmaker. He was actually a land surveyor and the nephew of Charles Couchman, a Director of Westley Richards & Co. In fact, there are allegations that Robert Couchman may have also become a director himself, appointed by Westley Richards the Younger, at the same time he named John Deeley as CEO. So, the next logical and very intriguing question that arises is: Just why would Westley Richards & Co. issue one of its own (potential) directors a license to manufacture its own A&D gun under a patent held by two of its own employees, e.g., William Anson and John Deeley, especially when the former individual was no longer an employee?

The truth is difficult to know. But William Anson's surprising "departure" begs a certain amount of speculation. This is especially so if he maintained a fiduciary interest in the patent business being managed for him by Westley Richards & Co./Robert Couchman. Anson's newfound independence had to take money, but from where? Did he get a lump sum buy-out from Westley's for the boxlock? Or did Anson strike some kind of cooperative arrangement with John Deeley, who may have financed Anson's independent operation?

Yet another option is possible. Could Anson have been established as a legitimate satellite supplier and/or engineering consultant for Westley Richards?

In her relentless search for clarification, Anson family descendant Clare Stride also wondered about all this:

What was the relationship between William and John Deeley? What I did not understand was that if William formed his own company in 1869 and Deeley was head of Westley Richards in 1872, why were they still collaborating in 1883? The mystery was solved by going through the Kelly Trade Directories for Birmingham, where I found listed the firm of Anson & Deeley Patentees at 78-1/2 High Street, Birmingham. This was near the old premises of Westley Richards.

While the possible scenarios are manifold, evidence for any of them is inconclusive. However, there are hints at what may have transpired:

- In 1869, William Anson was listed as a manufacturer of gun fore-ends at 123 Steelhouse Lane. It would make

John Deeley may have fostered and maintained a rather curious business relationship with William Anson after Anson left the direct employ of Westley Richards. This included an outside firm named Anson & Deeley Patentees.

sense to assume that this was the Anson latch mechanism he later patented in 1872. It might also be assumed that Anson was also an outsource for Westley Richards, which may have included rifle sights.

- At some time around 1863, Anson joins Westley Richards as an action filer, then becomes manager of their gun action department. Soon after, he invents the A&D gun with John Deeley in 1875, then leaves in 1876.
- In 1876, Anson was issued Patent No. 4513. This actually covers two safety mechanisms for the boxlock. One is a grip safety that fell into obscurity, and the other is the highly popular top-tang "dickey bird safety" that became widely used by Westley Richards, by W. & C. Scott and various other makers for untold thousands of British guns. Why was it so popular? Because, like many of Anson's concepts, it was simple, it was reliable and it was easy to make. In fact, you can see Anson's name stamped on many of them when British double guns are taken down to bits.
- William Anson either moved about quite a lot within the Birmingham gun quarter or, much more likely, he established a number of small sub-shops, staffed by other workmen, to keep up with demands from the trade.
- The various Birmingham addresses recorded or reported for William and Edwin Anson are a bit mind-boggling:
  ♦ 78½ High Street (as A&D patentees)
  ♦ Egyptian Hall, 77 Slaney Street
  ♦ 106 Little Greden Lane
  ♦ 123 Steelhouse Lane & Egyptian Hall, 77 Slaney Street
  ♦ 123½ Steelhouse Lane
  ♦ Egyptian Hall
  ♦ 145 Steelhouse Lane
  ♦ 33½ Whittall Street
  ♦ Back of 126 Steelhouse Lane
  ♦ 47 Great Tindall Street
  ♦ 46 Bath Street
  ♦ 55 Bath Street
  ♦ 27 Durham Road

The sheer number of these premises leads me to believe that many, if not the majority of these locales, were actually the shops of outworkers who supplied their various skills to the Anson operation as a whole, and were simply listed in trade records as "Anson" shops.

Oddly enough, some of Anson's independent operations may have been prompted by W.W. Greener. Why? Because Greener had taken a license from Couchman on May 24,

1877, to build sporting guns and rifles on the Anson & Deeley plan. In this endeavor, it would make eminent business sense for Greener to buy rough or semi-finished boxlock units from some existing entity. This could have been Westley Richards, a Birmingham firm called The Braendlin Armoury or perhaps a newly established satellite operation run by William Anson. Greener could then finish these actions up at his own manufactory. In fact, the January 3, 1880, issue of *The Ironmonger* gives us this insight: *Mr. Greener has been one of the largest manufacturers hitherto, of the Deeley & Anson hammerless gun, on which he has paid royalties for nearly 1,000...*

Clare Stride says William Anson was listed as a "gun filer" at 106 Little Greden Lane in 1877, a year after he left Westley Richards. This may well have been a "branch office" of Anson's Steelhouse Lane locale. But here's a curious bit — in 1877, Anson also appears at Egyptian Hall, 77 Slaney Street. In 1881, he is simultaneously listed as a "snap maker" (fore-end snap/latches?) and as a "manufacturer of gun actions for breechloading guns" at 123½ Steelhouse Lane.

In 1882, Anson pops up again as a gun polisher at 33½ Whittall Street. The year 1883 sees Anson listed as a "gunmaker" at 123 Steelhouse Lane, and a "gun manufacturer" at Egyptian Hall. His Egyptian Hall listing roughly coincides with a decision by Harrington & Richardson of Worcester, Massachusetts, to market A&D boxlock guns in the United States, but more on that shortly.

For whatever perspective it may provide, the very first hammerless gun produced by Holland & Holland was built on an Anson & Deeley action, according to Donald Dallas in his book, *Holland & Holland, The Royal Gunmaker*. This particular gun was a 12-bore (Patent No. 5134) completed on August 27, 1878, for a Mr. G. Arbuthnot.

Two aspects of this report are most interesting. The first is that Arbuthnot's H&H boxlock is only 78 numbers past ser. no. 5056, the very "first" A&D gun, made up for John Deeley himself. This juxtaposition would be especially noteworthy if Westley Richards actually made the gun up for H&H (not uncommon in the trade), and the number on Arbuthnot's gun is sequential with Westley Richards numbers. However, if ser. no. 5134 is an H&H number, then all bets are off.

What also makes this boxlock interesting is that it seems to be somewhat of an anomaly. The vast majority of H&H hammerless guns sold in the 19th century were based on other designs — notably, the sidelock design of Thomas Perkes.

But H&H maintained some affinity for the A&D design. Much later, after the Anson & Deeley patent expired in 1889, H&H began to introduce a series of single-shot rook rifles based on the A&D action. Then in the 1960s, H&H introduced the elegant single-barrel "Super Trap" gun built on the A&D action, which continued to be produced into the 1980s.

Anson's Boxlock Intercepting Safety

One intrinsic quality of the Anson & Deeley boxlock is its resistance to being accidentally jarred to fire. This is due mostly to the strong mainspring tension, a very robust sear/notch engagement, and the direction of mechanical forces being exerted. The stout mainspring tends to keep things in very firm engagement, and if the A&D action is properly made and adjusted, accidental discharge is virtually unheard of.

However, shooters tend to be a very conservative lot, especially those of the 19th and early 20th centuries. These fellows were used to a host of sidelock guns that were a bit more liable to go "bang" if brutally mishandled. In an effort to minimize this potential, various English gunmakers devised intercepting safety sears that would engage and block the fall of the tumbler to prevent discharge unless the gun's triggers were deliberately pulled. This gave sportsmen an added measure of safety and psychological calm.

But unfortunately for the worrisome, the first A&D guns had no such safety sear and may have been viewed by shooters as potentially dangerous in a mishap. To address this concern and its potential to derail sales, William Anson applied his genius once more. On March 7, 1879, Messrs. William Anson and John Deeley were issued Patent No. 907, which included two versions of an intercepting safety sear for the A&D action, as well as a thumb safety. Please keep in mind that, although William Anson shares this patent with John Deeley, it is commonly accepted that he left the direct employ of Westley Richards & Co. some three years earlier.

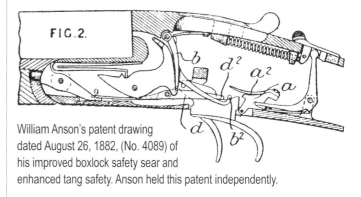

William Anson's patent drawing dated August 26, 1882, (No. 4089) of his improved boxlock safety sear and enhanced tang safety. Anson held this patent independently.

Nonetheless, a significant improvement of one of these intercepting sears would become widely popular with Westley Richards and a host of Continental gunmakers. However, that would have to wait until July 26, 1882, when William Anson alone would be granted Patent No. 4089. This design significantly revamped the shape of the earlier interceptor and added a long tail that would be lifted collaterally by the trigger, along with the gun's sear tail. If things got out of engagement, the tumbler's fall would be halted by the interceptor.

Empirical evidence from a range of English guns suggests that this intercepting sear may well have been an extra-cost option. Why? Because many A&D guns made during the same time frame and by the same makers were not fitted with the intercepting sear feature.

Within this same patent (No. 4089), William Anson also updated his famous rocking "dickey bird safety." This was received enthusiastically by the trade. In fact, it was used on Westley Richards boxlocks as well as untold thousands of other British guns.

Anson's intercepting sear and safeties were granted U.S. Patent No. 305,264 on September 16, 1884. It is of special note and importance to know that William's son, Edwin Anson, signed as witness to this U.S. patent. Ergo, he must have been in the U.S. in September of 1884, (on assignment to Harrington & Richardson). William Anson's next U.S. patent (No. 327,914) of October 6, 1885, was not witnessed by Edwin, indicating that Edwin had most probably returned to England by then, but I digress.

To return to the original patent (No. 907), the second safety sear design, which was hung from a pin across the roof of the frame, gained virtually no traction in the trade. Neither did the cross-frame thumb safety, and little enthusiasm was generated for the second safety design William Anson presented in Patent No. 4089. An examination of the patent drawings might easily explain why (see Appendix).

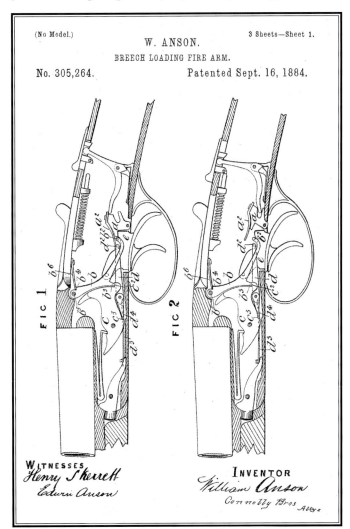

William Anson's U.S. Patent No. 305,264 for improvements to his boxlock safety sear and top tang safety. Note that his son Edwin signed as a witness, indicating that both men may have been in the U.S. at the time.

Harrington & Richardson Makes A&D Boxlocks

About four years after William Anson struck out independently, a relatively young U.S. gun company by the name of Harrington & Richardson licensed the famed A&D shotgun for production in the U.S.A. This firm had been formed just five years earlier, in 1875, by Gilbert Harrington and William Richardson, who were both previous employees of Frank Wesson. It is also enlightening to keep the nascent state of H&R in mind for what follows.

In 1880, H&R was primarily a pistol maker, but may well have been trying to find a more balanced niche in the firearms industry. In that regard, the market for hammerless double guns could have appeared quite attractive. After all, firms such as Lefever and Colt were just introducing their own hammerless guns to the marketplace. So, in this situation, H&R may have seen an opportunity. Through one bold move, they could leapfrog mainstream competition by simply licensing the world's *ne plus ultra* hammerless design from Anson & Deeley, then target upscale double-gun clientele of the U.S. This may have been an especially tempting idea, since U.S. patent protection for the A&D action had already been granted in 1876 and would remain in force until 1890.

At this point, I must endeavor to correct and supplement previously reported time frames for Harrington & Richardson's licensing of the A&D action. The following heretofore unknown facts are from documents held by two individuals: former H&R President Ted Rowe, whose family gained a controlling interest in H&R in the 1930s, and Ernie Foster, who worked in the H&R sales and marketing department until 1963.

They have a letter on file from John Deeley of Westley Richards & Co., dated November 20, 1879. In this correspondence, Deeley offers to license the Anson & Deeley action to H&R. Whether or not there was any prior correspondence between Westley's and H&R is unknown, but at a minimum, we can establish the fact that H&R's licensing negotiations began on that date in 1879. Exactly who at H&R decided to move forward with the project is unknown, but go forward they did.

Harrington & Richardson's license to manufacture A&D doubles was actually issued by Robert E. Couchman of Birmingham, England (see Chapter II for more about Couchman), Westley Richards' agent for A&D patents. The contract was signed by Messrs. Harrington, Richardson and Couchman on February 20, 1880, and was recorded in the Massachusetts state records on April 12, 1880 (see Appendix). These documents are in our archives.

Within this general time frame, Westley Richards & Co. sent four "pattern guns" to H&R, along with some forgings, possibly to serve as patterns themselves. Presumably, the guns sent were meant to exemplify the four grades of doubles that H&R would eventually offer to consumers. This is supported by a March 6, 1880, letter from John Deeley in which he states he is "shipping over some fully made guns." This letter is in the files of Ted Rowe.

One of the guns that Deeley may have sent was a particularly fine one, which could have well been made up as a pattern for what would become the very best grade of double in the H&R line. This gun, ser. no. 303, is presently in the collection of Mr. Rowe. I hasten to add that its serial number may not be a H&R number, but rather one applied by Westley Richards or one if its outworker shops. It is also possible that this is a patent use number.

Parker Loses An Opportunity — But Gains A Classic

Before I continue with the H&R story, a bit of historical perspective is in order. By concluding the Anson & Deeley license agreement in 1880, Harrington & Richardson might well have spurred the creation of an iconic American shotgun — the Parker Hammerless. This intriguing turn of history is strongly suggested in a letter from Robert Couchman to Harrington & Richardson, written at the direction of John Deeley. The full text is in Chapter Two, but here is the relevant portion:

82 High Street
Birmingham, England
Jan. 7th, 1883

Messrs. Harrington & Richardson
Worcester, Mass. USA

Gentlemen:
We have an application from Parker Bros. Meriden, Conn., asking us to give them a license to make our hammerless action. This of course we are unable to do as you are our sole licensee for the whole of the United States...

For elaboration on subsequent events, turn to Chapter Two. This missed opportunity undoubtedly gave Parker Bros. the impetus to create their own hammerless gun, which was introduced to the U.S. market in 1888. In fact, "Old Reliable" soon became an American classic.

H&R Ramps Up For A&D Production

Future events aside, the potential for H&R shotgun sales was bright in 1880. With exclusive manufacturing rights in hand, H&R went ahead with its Anson & Deeley double-gun project. According to documents in our possession, H&R's agreement with A&D formally ran from April 12, 1880, until some indefinite point in late 1884 or early 1885.

Production numbers for these guns have been "guesstimated" by many, but even former H&R executives Ted Rowe and Ernie Foster have no concrete information concerning how many doubles were actually made. "But it wasn't many," according to Rowe. The highest serial number they've seen or heard about was ser. no. 2115. "But that doesn't mean H&R started with No. 1," said Rowe. "They could well have begun anywhere." The lowest serial number that's been observed is No. 50, which is an elegant 12-bore, last known to be in the collection of double gunsmith Brad Bachelder of Grand Rapids, Michigan. However, if H&R followed the typical English format for patent use numbers, they may have indeed started with No. 1 in the patent use sequence. According to Bachelder, the water table of his 12-bore is marked "Anson and Deeley's Patent Feb. 1, 1876 #50." If this gun is really the 50th made under Anson & Deeley's U.S. license, then there may well be 49 earlier H&R guns out there, somewhere.

With regard to actual production, it is generally accepted that these A&D double guns were, in fact, manufactured by H&R in the United States. In *Niles Guide to Affordable Double Barrel Shotguns in America 1875–1945*, the author goes so far as to state that they were made on "machinery imported from England." While this may well be true, it may not be the whole story.

The classic Parker Hammerless double was very likely the direct result of H&R's exclusive 1880 licensing of the A&D action for U.S. production.

Former H&R President Ted Rowe contends that the entire second floor of H&R's Worcester factory was eventually dedicated to the manufacture of these double guns. What's more, he said that some of the necessary machinery was imported from England, but that other machines were acquired locally in the U.S. Rowe added that a cadre of English craftsmen were brought over to help set up the machines and teach necessary skills to the H&R workmen. Exactly who these Britons were is known only in part.

Clare Stride confirms that one of them was Edwin Anson, son of William Anson. Edwin presumably acted as a consultant and very probably a production supervisor. In fact, Edwin painted a rather intriguing fall hunting scene outside of Worcester, Massachusetts, in 1883. This was virtually in the middle of H&R's boxlock production run. It is interesting to note that this painting was also displayed in an exhibition at the Royal Birmingham Society of Artists in that same year of 1883. Even more fascinating is that it was presented in concert with art created by John Deeley.

An artist herself, Anson descendant Clare Stride actually became involved in tracing the Anson family's history through her discovery of an Edwin Anson painting. According to information she subsequently uncovered, Clare learned that "quite a few Birmingham gunmakers attended art classes" and apparently dabbled in painting.

Clare Stride also confirmed that another of William Anson's sons, Claude Alonso Anson, born on July 2, 1875, worked at H&R in the U.S. However, if Claude's cited birth year is accurate, he was most certainly (a) an 8-year-old child worker, or (b) not too heavily involved with H&R guns at the time. However, he did stay in the U.S. and fostered a long line of Ansons who still reside in New England and in Georgia. In fact, one of Claude's grandsons was Ronald George Kingham Anson, who became Vice Chairman of the noted Kenyon & Eckhardt ad agency in New York City. Ronald lived in Darrien, Connecticut, and retired in 1984. Edwin's father, William Anson, must have been in the U.S. for at least a short period of time, since he had his photograph taken at the studio of Louis Oliver, 323 Main St., Worcester, Massachusetts. Unfortunately, the surviving print is not dated.

And while it is only a hearsay recollection passed along by H&R's Ted Rowe, an Englishman named "Baker" is also said to have been on hand at H&R. Unfortunately, the English gun trade is rife with Bakers, and without specific information, it is impossible to know exactly which Baker this might have been.

What is known, however, is that Westley Richards & Co. acquired the bankrupt

Edwin Anson, son of William Anson, traveled to the U.S. in the early 1880s to assist H&R in setting up double-gun production at its plant in Worcester, Mass.

The second floor of H&R's Worcester plant is where double gun production took place. This illustration from the turn of the 20th century.

business of Frederick (F.T.) Baker in the early 1900s and incorporated its clientele and products into their London shop. Westley's still retain rights to the F.T. Baker name, but this does not prove that F.T. Baker helped H&R set up their U.S. gunmaking business a decade earlier.

A January 1883 letter from Robert Couchman to Harrington & Richardson gives more general insight. But first, it is well to keep a few points in mind about the situation extant:
- After a slow start, H&R had just got its U.S. production of Anson & Deeley guns underway in 1883.
- Anson & Deeley/Westley Richards were undoubtedly anxious and had high hopes that H&R would make the production and sale of A&D double guns a success in the U.S., which was obviously a huge market for firearms.
- The patent protection clock was ticking in the United States. Anson & Deeley's exclusive rights to make or license this action had only seven years to run in the U.S.A. They would naturally want to make the most of that opportunity in the face of competition, especially with the help of a licensed U.S. manufacturer whose products were exempt from burdensome import tariffs or duties.

With that, here is the applicable portion of the Couchman/Deeley letter to H&R, (emphasis added): *We have written to* [Parker Bros.] *& asked them to communicate with you. As the sale of this* [A&D] *gun is likely to increase very much in the States,* **we believe it worth your while considering the advisability of supplying actions & barrels to gunmakers in the United States, as by this means you would not only make a very large trade in actions** [and] **barrels upon which you may assure a remunerative profit but keep the said gunmakers from bringing other guns into competition with yours...**

Aside from the fact that Parker Brothers was itself desirous of making A&D guns (turn to the John Deeley chapter for that story), Couchman's suggestion that H&R could make "remunerative profit" from supplying barrels and actions to Parker, *et al.*, must have been based on some actual manufacturing capability. In other words, H&R apparently did have the capacity to make double-barrel A&D guns as well as components, in quantity, at its Worcester facility.

Complete U.S. manufacture is further supported by the fact that none of the A&D guns made by H&R appear to have any sort of English proofs. In fact, they have no proof marks at all. With regard to the barrels, this is especially enlightening. All barrels made and/or bored in England and intended for English-made guns have to pass provisional proof at either the London or Birmingham proof houses. If they pass, they are stamped as such and returned to the submitting gunmaker for additional work. H&R barrels have no stamps. Thus, we might assume that they were obtained as bored

This portrait of a robust William Anson is undated but is said to have been taken by photographer Louis Oliver in Worcester, Massachusetts, most probably between 1880 and 1883. *Photo — Courtesy of Stride family*

blanks, most likely from England or Belgium, and were then finished up at H&R's Worcester plant. Of course, The U.S. has no proof laws and requires no marking of barrels.

Still, there is reason to believe that some early H&R guns may have been made in Birmingham. The basis for this is that a former H&R archivist once told John Friedman, author of *English Shotguns Between The Wars*, that H&R simply "bought them from Anson." In this, he could have been referring to the "fully made" guns Deeley initially sent over or some early H&R doubles offered that were for sale in 1882. He could have also been referring to E. Anson & Co. guns that were sold in the U.S. after H&R ceased production of its own doubles, but I will get to the story of E. Anson & Co. in due course.

With regard to the majority production of H&R doubles, the learning curve for U.S. craftsmen may well have been met, and all guns were made in-house. This seems to be borne out in a Summer 2007 issue of *Double Gun Journal*, which included a feature by Don Hardin. In Hadin's article, he cites a 1909 *Field & Stream* article entitled "The History of American Arms & Ammunition" by James T. Sullivan. In his *Field & Stream* report, Sullivan states that "...H&R double guns were built by a dedicated group of craftsmen on the second floor of H&R's Worcester factory." While Sullivan did not disclose the nationality of the workmen, Hardin makes a rather safe guess based on product quality: *The guns were obviously close copies of the Westley Richards guns of the time and the quality of the guns that were turned out certainly wasn't that of apprentice workers.*

Hardin continues: *The article also stated that the guns were entirely machine made. The almost identical look of the Westley Richards gun to the Harrington & Richardson gun makes one think that the English company helped the new endeavor get its start.*

In my view, this analysis is essentially accurate, especially if one considers Robert Couchman and the Ansons to have been agents of Westley Richards. What's more, Hardin discloses that Richard Littlefield, H&R's historian from 1974–1976, said that "the workmen were from Birmingham, and spent around six months setting up the machinery and teaching the gunmaking." Empirical evidence suggests that H&R workers learned their skills very well, indeed. Either that, or some of their Birmingham gunmaker/instructors stayed on in the U.S. a good bit longer than six months, perhaps throughout the entire production life of the guns or longer. I will expound on that last bit shortly.

Will The Real Mr. Deeley Please Stand Up?

At this point, there is a curious bit of confusion in the H&R scenario. References to a "Mr. Deeley" occasionally crop up as being the individual who came over from England to supervise set-up of the machinery and initial production of double guns. On the other hand, Clare Stride suggests that this work was actually done by Edwin Anson, probably acting as a representative of Couchman/Anson & Deeley. Under such circumstances, reports of the day could have easily misidentified Edwin or William Anson as "Mr. Deeley," especially if they were representatives of Anson & Deeley.

Such a misconception may have originated or taken credibility from a Schoverling, Daly & Gales ad in the November 1882 issue of *Forest and Stream*. This ad for H&R doubles states that the workmanship on these guns was "inspected by Mr. Deeley."

This is almost certainly not correct, even though it is true that H&R was making Anson & Deeley double guns. So, was that bearded English fellow in the shop really Mr. Deeley, or was it Mr. Anson? It's an easy transposition for a 19th-century copywriter to make. After all, Edwin Anson and his father were certainly English. And they were right there in Worcester to arrange for manufacture of Anson & Deeley shotguns, so a misinterpretation is certainly possible.

On the other hand, a career in national advertising leads me to suggest that this copy may have been consciously "enhanced" with its reference to Mr. Deeley. After all, his name was on the mechanism, and his imprimatur on each gun would potentially add some measure of trust and sales value. While I may be prejudiced, this is the scenario I'm betting on.

From a practical standpoint, it seems far more likely that a "working gunmaker" like Edwin Anson and/or his father would be vastly more qualified to set up gunmaking machinery and instruct others in its use than would an administrative CEO like John Deeley. In addition, it is unlikely that John Deeley Sr. would have had the time or inclination to travel to the U.S. and then remain to supervise and inspect such work.

Nevertheless, William Anson may have unknowingly lent some measure of confusion to the issue. As we've already pointed out, one of the few photographs we have of William Anson was taken by Louis Oliver, a photographer whose shop was in Worcester, Massachusetts.

Logic dictates that William's sitting must have taken place during the time H&R was setting up for and/or making Anson & Deeley double guns, probably 1883. At the time, William Anson sported a full beard, very much like that of John Deeley. He also spoke with an English accent, was a principle of Anson & Deeley Patentees and undoubtedly reviewed and approved some of the initial craftsmanship in this American iteration of the A&D boxlock. Thus, it is understandable that the identities of Anson and Deeley could have been easily and innocently transposed in the mind of a copywriter. Or, provided him a convenient excuse for some enhanced "truth well-told."

H&R's Production Window For A&D Guns

How long did production of H&R double guns actually last? A Schoverling, Daly & Gales ad that ran in the April 1886 issue of *Forest and Stream* featured H&R hammerless doubles. This does not mean H&R guns were still being produced in 1886, but it certainly indicates they were still available. It is also of interest that this SD&G ad for H&R guns appears immediately below an ad by James Purdey & Sons of London for their own Frederick Beesley action sidelock doubles. And at the bottom of this ad, Purdey makes a rather uncharacteristic solicitation for U.S. market expansion: *Messrs. Purdey & Sons are prepared to sell the rights, or grant a license (subject to certain conditions) for the sole manufacture of this gun* [the Beesley sidelock] *in the United States.*

Apparently, there were no takers for that offer. Otherwise, the U.S. may well have had a few "American Purdeys" to compete with H&R's American-made Anson & Deeley guns.

With regard to outside competition, it is also a curious circumstance that, although H&R was exclusively licensed to make A&D double guns in the U.S., their franchise did not include exclusive rights to sell and distribute A&D guns. Indeed, contemporary advertising by J. Palmer O'Neil & Co. and Pittsburgh Fire Arms Co., both of Pittsburgh, Pennsylvania, offered Westley Richards branded boxlock doubles through at least 1883. Some guns carried the Westley Richards name outright, while others were branded "Pittsburgh Fire Arms Co.," or "Samuel Buckley," even though they were clearly made by Westley Richards.

So, when did production of H&R Anson & Deeley boxlocks actually come to an end? No one knows for certain, including former H&R executives. But, if one aggregates the best guesses of all concerned, along with what little surviving documentation is available, it appears as though H&R stopped making A&D guns in mid to late 1885. That also aligns with a December 5, 1885, entry in England's *The Ironmonger*, which made its report from an ocean away as well as some months behind H&R's business decisions: *Westley Richards Company reports trade moderate, especially as regards the United States where one of their principal patents, the Anson & Deeley hammerless, is now being produced by machinery at a very low price, under royalty of course, to the owners...*

When H&R finally did cease production of double guns, there was a lot of "fine wood" left over, according to H&R historian Richard Littlefield. And to the certain dismay of double-gun mavens everywhere, Littlefield said it was subsequently used for "high-end pistol grips."

Harrington & Richardson Hammerless B. L. Double Guns.
Can now be had 10-bore, 8½ to 10 lbs.

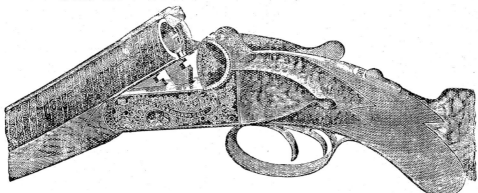

This gun is made entirely by machinery, with all the latest improvements that American skill has produced. The material is the best the market affords, and the workmanship is as accurate as the best appliances and finest workmen can produce. The action is the celebrated Anson & Deeley, of which Messrs. Harrington & Richardson are sole licensees in this country. The rubber butt plate is of most exquisite design. The iron work is entirely of the best wrought metal, and case-hardening and blueing of the finest finish. The hammers, singly or together, can be let down without snapping by pressing the triggers and closing the barrels; by the Harrington system of chambering and choking the best results in pattern and penetration are obtained.

STYLE.—Top snap, double bolt, extension rib, automatic safety catch, English walnut stock, patent fore end.

	12 g. 7⅞ to 8½ lbs.	10 g. 8½ to 10 lbs.
No. 1. Laminated steel barrels, outline engraving	$100 00	$110 00
2. Damascus barrels, good scroll engraving, selected stocks	150 00	160 00
3. Same as No. 2, but finer in all points	200 00	210 00
4. Premier quality, every part made with the most scrupulous care, and of most exquisite finish	300 00	310 00

SCHOVERLING, DALY & GALES, 84 & 86 Chambers Street, N.Y.
MANUFACTURERS' AGENTS (WHOLESALE ONLY).

A Schoverling, Daley and Gales trade advertisement announces that the H&R double was finally available in 10-bore.

---

500   FOREST AND STREAM.   [Jan. 25, 1883.

Don't Be Deceived or Led Astray.

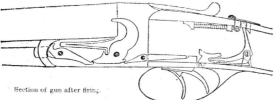
Section of gun after firing.

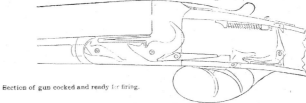
Section of gun cocked and ready for firing.

The Anson & Deeley Hammerless Lock,
AS MANUFACTURED BY
Westley Richards & Co., London, Eng.,
HAS NO EQUAL!

And is the only hammerless gun in the market that is absolutely faultless, being simple, durable, and possessing those wonderful shooting powers, combined with that indescribable symmetry and beauty so characteristic of Westley Richards' product.

Every desirable feature is found in this gun. Superiority of Material and Workmanship. Absolute Safety in Handling. Without Comparison in Durability and Simplicity.

Shooting Qualities Unsurpassed.

The following letters from prominent sportsmen cover the ground exactly:

CLARKSVILLE, Tenn., March 20, 1882.

J. Palmer O'Neil, Esq.:
My Dear Sir—The Westley Richards Hammerless Gun I obtained from you has been the admiration of all my friends. I consider it much the best Hammerless gun, and recommend all sportsmen who can afford the luxury of a perfect gun, to buy a Westley Richards Hammerless. Respectfully, PATRICK HENRY.

BURLINGTON, Iowa, Sept. 20, 1882.

J. Palmer O'Neil & Co., Pittsburgh, Pa.:
Dear Sirs—The Greener and Westley Richards guns arrived safely yesterday A. M., and in the evening I took them both out and targeted them. I like the Greener better for only one reason, and that is it fits me a trifle better. But the Westley Richards made by far the best target, so I have concluded to keep it and return the Greener. The Westley Richards is certainly a little beauty, and makes as fine a target as I ever saw. One of my friends who is a great sportsman went out with me, and before the trial made all manner of fun of the "pop gun," even while he admired its graceful shape and elegant workmanship. But the result of the trial rather surprised him. He shot against the Westley Richards, his 11lbs. Daly loaded with 5 drams of powder and 1¼oz. of No. 7 shot, while I used 3½ drams of powder and 1⅛oz. No. 7 shot. At 30, 40 and 50 yards I beat him badly in distribution and penetration. At 60, 65 and 70 yards fully equalled him. And the difference at 75 and 80 yards could hardly be noticed. I am much pleased with the gun, and as soon as I become a little more accustomed to it I have no doubt my shooting will be greatly improved. I shall take pleasure recommending the Westley Richards Hammerless Gun.
Yours truly, GEO. H. TOUSEY.

J. PALMER O'NEIL & CO., Pittsburgh, Pa.
Agents in the U.S. for Westley Richards' Hammerless Guns.

As H&R was selling its own A&D double, J. Palmer O'Neil & Co. ran this 1883 *Forest and Stream* advertisement in direct competition. It trumpeted nothing less than the A&D hammerless gun made by Westley Richards. Note Anson's dickey bird safety.

H&R Guns: The Prima Facia Evidence

A Shoverling, Daly & Gales catalog page from the 1880–1882 era indicates H&R guns were offered in four letter grades: A through D — with A (or "Premier Quality") being the most ornate and priced accordingly at $300 in 12-bore. Later, SD&G ads used Arabic numbers to roughly identify the same grades. Other distributors used letters or numbers, depending on their preference. Nonetheless, there appears to have been four levels of quality for sportsmen to choose, although the guns themselves were not marked in any special way to delineate that. The SD&G catalog copy describes H&R doubles thus:

This gun is made entirely by machinery with all the latest appliances that American skill has produced. The material is the best the market affords, and the workmanship is more accurate than that of hand-made guns can possibly be. The action is the celebrated Anson & Deeley, of which Messers. H. & R. are sole licensees in this country. The rubber [hard composition] butt plate is of most exquisite design. The iron work is entirely of the best wrought metal, and the case-hardening and blueing [sic] is of the finest finish.

C, Fine Damascus steel barrels, selected quality English walnut stock, fine checking, scroll engraving and fine finish throughout. [12 g.] $150 [10g.] $160

D, Laminated steel barrels, English walnut stock, checked and engraved with a handsome bird's-eye border, finely finished throughout. [12 g.] $100 [10g.] $110

12 g. 7 1/2 to 8 1/2 lbs. 10 g. 8 1/2 to 10 1/2 lbs. ... All the above guns have pistol grip stocks and rubber butt plates.

The Grade A guns also seem to feature beaded and serpentine fences, sculptured top lever tabs, tulip paneled forearms plus checkered stock head "cheeks" with arrowhead drop points. Grade B guns had traditional beaded fences, tulip paneled forearms and checkered stock head cheeks, but without drop points. It is also evident that the grip and forearm checkering was progressively finer and more extensive from Grades D through A. This is particularly noticeable on the grip panels.

The nicely figured buttstock of this Grade C now has a Silver's-type pad installed atop the original composition buttplate, which was ground flat and used as a base to avoid cutting the wood. This scheme increased length of pull but ruined the original plate.

The hammers, singly or together, can be let down without snapping by pressing the triggers and closing the barrels. Unless otherwise ordered, both barrels are choked by the most improved system and are warranted to make the pattern stated on the ticket accompanying the gun.

Style: Top snap, double bolt, extension rib, automatic safety catch, English walnut stock, patent fore end.

No. A, Finest Damascus steel barrels, finest English walnut stock, highly polished, gold name plate, finest checkering and engraving of game scenes and fancy scroll work, together with best workmanship and finish throughout. [12 g.] $300 [10g.] $310

B, Extra fine Damascus steel barrels, extra figured English walnut stock, silver name plate, fine checking and engraving of game and scroll work, and very fine finished throughout. [12 g.] $200 [10g.] $210

With this in mind, it is also important to note that the four levels of quality available in H&R's doubles were apparently not as standardized as shooters have come to expect from other gunmakers. In other words, one Grade A or B gun may be noticeably different in checkering, wood and engraving than another of the same level. And "by any other name," this also seems to apply to Grade 1 or Grade 2 guns. The photographic evidence presented here certainly supports this.

Such proof suggests two things: First, clients for Grade A or B guns may well have been able to request specific features they preferred for their guns. At the price levels that were quoted, this is very likely. The second possibility is that craftsmen who made up these high-level guns may have been allowed special creative freedom, as long as the result met the specified grade of quality. Nevertheless, while the Shoverling, Daly & Gales catalog information is illuminating, it is predictably aggrandizing. As someone who spent a career in the postwar advertising world, it is easy for me to spot some enhancement of the facts in the general description of these guns. Take this passage for example: *This gun is made entirely by machinery with all the latest appliances that American skill has produced. The material is the best the market affords, and the workmanship is more accurate than that of hand-made guns can possibly be...*

Hammerless B. L. Double Guns,

HARRINGTON & RICHARDSON.

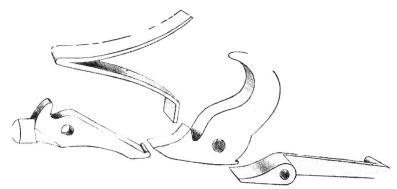

Fig. 4. Showing the strong and simple lock mechanism.

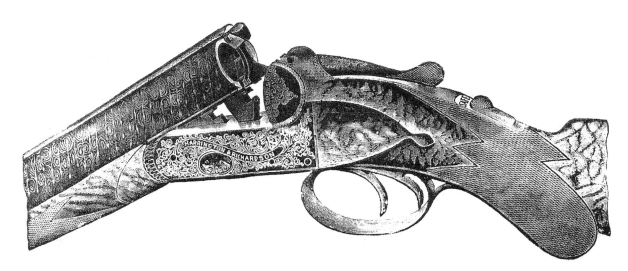

This gun is made entirely by machinery, with all the latest appliances that American skill has produced. The material is the best the market affords, and the workmanship is more accurate than that of hand-made guns can possibly be. The action is the celebrated Anson & Deeley, of which Messrs. H. & R. are sole licensees in this country. The rubber butt plate is of most exquisite design. The iron work is entirely of the best wrought metal, and the case-hardening and blueing is of the finest finish.

The hammers, singly or together, can be let down without snapping, by pressing the triggers and closing the barrels. Unless otherwise ordered, both barrels are choked by the most improved system and are warranted to make the pattern stated on the ticket accompanying the gun.

Style: Top snap, double bolt, extension rib, automatic safety catch, English walnut stock, patent fore end.

	12 g. 7¼ to 8¼ lbs.	10 g. 8½ to 10½ lb
No. A, Finest Damascus steel barrels, finest English walnut stock, highly polished, gold name plate, finest checking and engraving of game scenes and fancy scroll work, together with best workmanship and finish throughout	$300 00	310 00
B, Extra fine Damascus steel barrels, extra figured English walnut stock, silver name plate, fine checking and engraving of game and scroll work, and very fine finished throughout	200 00	210 00
C, Fine Damascus steel barrels, selected quality English walnut stock, fine checking, scroll engraving and fine finish throughout	150 00	160 00
D, Laminated steel barrels, English Walnut stock, checked and engraved with a handsome bird's-eye border, finely finished throughout	100 00	110 00
C. G. Bonehill, No. 15, Top snap, Bonehill Pat. top lever action, Damascus barrels, double bolt, extension rib, treble fastening, D. & E. fore end, choke bored 10 g. 9 to 10 lbs.		87 50
J. P. Clabrough & Bro., No. 25, Top snap, fine Damascus blts, double bolt, exten. rib, automatic safety, choke bored	120 00	125 00
W. & C. Scott & Sons, No. 30, Top snap, Scott improved action, with patent safety lock, laminated steel barrels, double bolt, extension rib, patent fore end, safety crystal indicator. This gun is made with the same care that characterizes all productions of these celebrated makers	173 33	180 00

Charles Daly Hammerless, see page 5.

All the above guns have pistol grip stocks and rubber butt plates.

The first line is sheer double-speak. Virtually all guns are made "by machinery" to some degree or another, but since the 1880s were still within the Machine Age, this attribute could have added potential value in the minds of period sportsmen. What's more, the hand fitting of these H&R guns clearly speaks against "entirely by machine." Whether or not a machine-made gun "is more accurate than hand-made guns can possibly be," is a question open to enduring debate. Suffice to say that such puffery puts some psychological icing on pride of ownership — whether the claims were valid or not.

Regardless, this copy provides some important information as well as validation about the H&R doubles. Here are the apparent facts:

- There were four levels of quality. Sometimes they're referred to by letters, A through D, sometimes by numbers, and sometimes by price: $100 through $300 guns.
- The guns were made in the U.S., with some early guns very likely finished from rough bits sent over from England.
- The guns were offered in 12-bore and 10-bore only.
- Certain custom features were probably available. This may be inferred from (a) the choke reference: "Unless otherwise ordered, both barrels are choked by the most improved system and are warranted to make the pattern stated on the ticket..." and (b) the fact that some guns were delivered with or without stock ovals, varying lengths of pull, unlisted barrel lengths, or with Silver's recoil pads installed.
- The engraving style applied to Grades A through C guns is characteristically English.
- Although the standard "rubber" buttplates were of "exquisite design," empirical evidence indicates these were hard formed material, commonly known as gutta percha in the U.S., not a recoil pad like we would associate with a rubber buttplate today. What's more, it appears as though the same plate was used on all H&R double guns, from Grades A through D.
- All levels had pleasing English walnut stocks, with ascending degrees of figure.
- Stock ovals, or "name plates," were listed as standard on the two top-level guns but are occasionally missing on these grades.
- Damascus barrels were used on the top three guns, with laminated (twist) barrels reserved for the lowest level. However, some base level guns have been observed with Damascus barrels.
- 10-bore guns cost an additional $10, across the board.
- The phrase that "All the above guns have pistol grip stocks" appears to have been strictly applied. A straight-grip H&R has yet to turn up.

Other important perspectives may be gleaned from the Schoverling, Daly & Gales catalog page. The first is market competition. While we have just one page to reference, it does reveal that H&R doubles were in direct competition with English guns made by C.G. Bonehill, J.P. Clabrough & Bros., and W. & C. Scott & Sons. There were also Charles Daly guns collaterally available, but this name was usually applied to firearms sourced from Germany.

The quality and prestige of these competitive guns also varied. The Bonehills were primarily machine made with only light hand-fitting. They were, therefore, relatively affordable and were never considered top end, although Bonehill tried valiantly to saturate the U.S. market with his products. Clabrough guns were a bit better in the hand-finish department, but still toward the lower half of the spectrum. The W. & C. Scott gun described here was a true sidelock with crystal cocking indicators and the Scott patent fore-end latch. This was a mid-level gun and something to be proud of. It is also well known that, if required, Scott could make a gun fully equal to any London product. Their Premier gun was just one example. In fact, J. Palmer O'Neil & Co. of Pittsburgh offered "a few" W. & C. Scott Premier grade guns for just $150 in 1883. Compared to this work of art, a similarly priced Grade B boxlock gun from H&R didn't stand a chance.

While it is difficult to know the precise regard in which sportsmen of the day held the actions of Harrington & Richardson or Anson & Deeley, it is probably safe to assume that the contemporary view of H&R was that of a pistol maker. So, in great part, any credibility they hoped for in the realm of shotguns would necessarily be attached to the trade name of Anson & Deeley and its association with England's Westley Richards.

Our second perspective from this 1880s catalog comes through retail price. Note that the top tiers of these new H&R double guns are far and away the most costly that were offered here. Only the D Grade gun is roughly competitive with the Bonehill or Clabrough, and a consumer's choice between a new C Grade H&R and the established W. & C. Scott gun would have probably been difficult. Beyond that, we enter the rarefied level of big ticket options with the A and B Grade H&R doubles. While this upscale market may not have been very large, it appeared to be fairly consistent, at least according to the September 18, 1880, edition of *The Ironmonger*:

The great problem at present is to find a hammerless gun suited to American wants which may be produced by machinery. The Anson & Deeley patent, which stands very high in the English market, is too expensive a weapon for extended sale in the United States...

There may have been some truth in that analysis. Even as late as 1893, the market for top-tier English guns appeared viable, albeit limited. This, from that year's September 30th issue of *The Ironmonger*:

Only two Birmingham houses have thought it worth their while to exhibit at Chicago — viz., Mr. W.W. Greener and W. & C. Scott & Son. Both of these firms continue to do a good trade in the United States in high-class hammerless and other sporting guns.

The Westley Richards Company, who do a considerable business with the United States in their Anson-Deeley hammerless gun, make a favourable report of their season's experience...

Although a previous owner of this Grade D H&R double added "checkering" on the ball of its grip, this gun exemplifies the bottom tier of H&R double guns. *Photo — Courtesy of Steven Cobb*

In accordance with this, it appears as though customers who bought upscale guns during the late 19th century often went all-in as they say. If they chose a Harrington & Richardson double, they seem to have often opted for the A and B Grade guns. A legacy of C and D guns certainly exists, but from an observed standpoint, they seem less common than the higher grades.

What's more, many of the H&R guns seen in the upper levels are 10-bore. History suggests this makes sense, as the 10-bore was virtually on a par with the 12-bore for popularity during the 19th century. If you had the means to buy a top-end H&R double, you certainly had no qualms about spending an additional $10 for a 10-bore.

Along with price level, it appears as though a paying customer could "mix and match" certain specifications to create a form of bespoke H&R gun. This may have included fitment of an upscale figured stock to a more prosaic level gun. Specific lengths of pull were apparently another option. Various H&R doubles I know of have original pulls of 13½, 13¾ and 13⅞ inches. My own gun has an original LOP of 13¼ inches. Such specifications certainly suggest a made-to-order potential. The late Brad Bachelder's H&R gun ser. no. 50 adds its own testimony to the custom-order possibility. He described the gun thusly:

The gun is a 12 gauge featuring 26-inch uncut barrels, correct rib, .740 and .745 bores with no forcing cones; .007 and .017 constriction; English Damascus; no proofs, only #50. The LOP is 13 7/8; DAC 1 3/4, DAH 3 1/4; gold oval; exhibition-grade wood; Circassian walnut; fine-checkered, not flat at 22 LPI; H&R buttplate. The watertable is marked "Anson and Deeley's Patent Feb. 1, 1876 #50". The engraving is American [and] looks like Nimschke work. There is no case with the gun. I have had the chance to look over two other A's and a couple of B's, but this one is much better work.

While it has been refinished, Bachelder's double could be one of the "fully made guns" that John Deeley sent over from England. And the "No. 50" stamped on it might be a British patent use number, but as yet, there is no way to confirm this.

Although its stock, barrels and color case have been refreshed, Harrington & Richardson's A&D gun ser. no. 50 is an example of that company's 19th-century boxlocks. It was last in the collection of gunsmith Brad Bachelder. *Photo — Brad Bachelder*

The A&D actions H&R made were the early type with cylindrically shaped cocking dogs protruding from the bar knuckle. True cognoscenti will also notice that these guns were made with a larger-than-usual .905-inch-wide top lever cut, and that the top levers are correspondingly larger. This is quite distinctive and correlates with the cut used for the wide Westley Richards camming top lever. In addition, comparison of many H&R top tang safety buttons to those used by Westley Richards will reveal that they are identical. These are just a few features that suggest that similar componentry may have been used to build H&R guns.

For additional perspective, it may be worthwhile to look closely at both the outside and inside of an H&R double from those years. First, there is the checkering. While it is certainly attractive and especially plentiful on the forearms of A, B and C grades, the grip pattern is subtly different. First, it is more "American" and pointed in style. On the lower grades, it fails to extend down into the ball of the pistol grip as you would expect most patterns to do.

The black tip at the apex of the forearm is also noteworthy. An English gun would use buffalo horn here, but even on the upper-tier H&R guns, these finials appear to be some form of black composite, most likely the same gutta percha used for the buttplates. However, the finials of some A and B grade guns sometimes exhibit a bit of sculpting, which seems to vary with the creative whims of the stocker. Evidence suggests the field-grade D guns had no forearm tip inset at all.

Inside, the stock inletting is up to English mid-level standards, which are measurably above the machine cut stocks of American guns. However, the metal fit and closure of these H&R guns is universally precise and primarily British in character. In response to a hypothesis that English craftsmen were involved with these guns, master gunsmith Brad Bachelder gave this assessment of his ser. no. 50 H&R double:

I would agree that the parts may have been made in Birmingham; the total lack of proofs and the fact that the screws are standard, not metric, lead me to believe the gun was assembled in America. L.D. Nimschke was contracted to engrave the H&R pistols during the time this gun was built. Upon close study, the vegetation, dogs, borders, and scrollwork are all American, not English. A comparative study of H&R engraved pistols should support my beliefs.

While Bachelder's analysis may indeed be accurate, there is a certain amount of grace one must grant to the term "American." Nimschke was a German immigrant with taste and skills rooted in that social ethos. He may have also understood that he was working on guns intended to reflect Anglo-American motifs and style. Thus, some compromise may have been involved in his embellishment. There is also the possibility that H&R doubles were engraved by certain of the English craftsmen who helped H&R produce these guns.

In accordance with English gun trade market analysis, there seems to be a pervasively elite nature to these H&R doubles, especially in A and B grades. Consider that the 1971 H&R Centennial Catalog states that they "commanded prices of up to $300 [which was] remarkable for the times."

Left: Ted Rowe, former President of H&R, examines three high-grade A&D doubles from that company's mid-1880s production.

Below, center: H&R Grade A and B guns from the collection of Ted Rowe. All are stunning, yet all different. This strongly suggests that each was bespoke.

Bottom: Fine points of H&R's high-end A&D doubles are discussed by former H&R sales and marketing executive, Ernie Foster, left, past President Ted Rowe, center, and collector Steve Quill.
Photos — Michael Foster

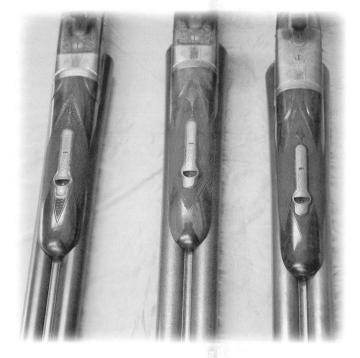

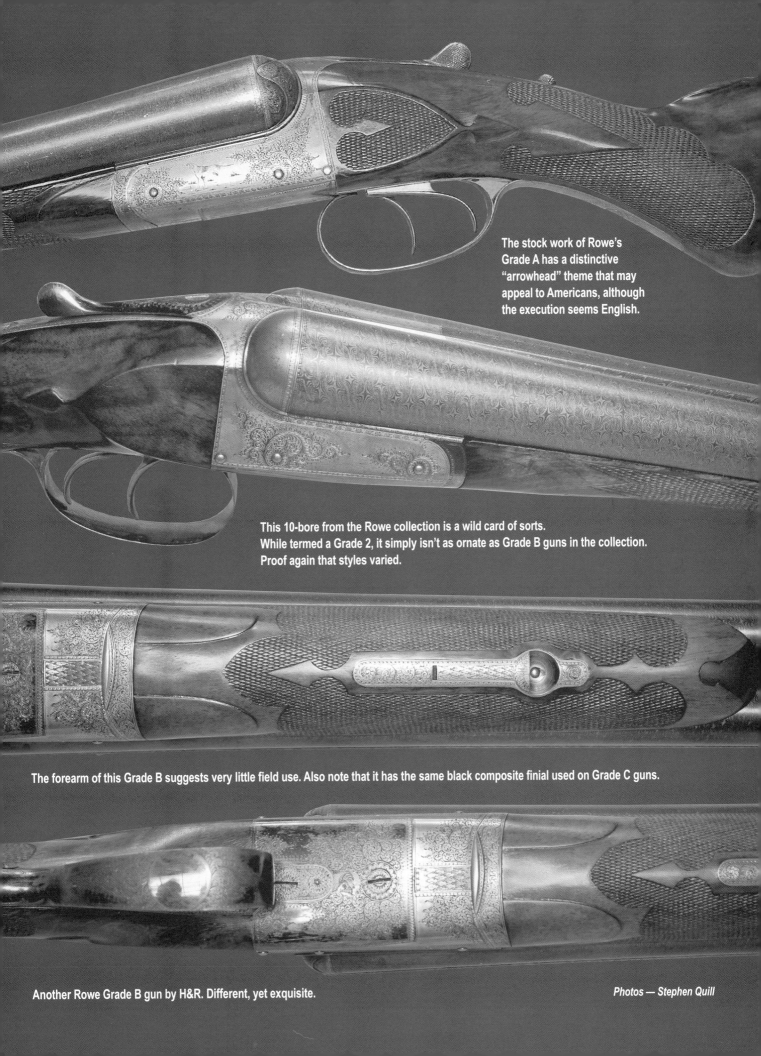

The stock work of Rowe's Grade A has a distinctive "arrowhead" theme that may appeal to Americans, although the execution seems English.

This 10-bore from the Rowe collection is a wild card of sorts. While termed a Grade 2, it simply isn't as ornate as Grade B guns in the collection. Proof again that styles varied.

The forearm of this Grade B suggests very little field use. Also note that it has the same black composite finial used on Grade C guns.

Another Rowe Grade B gun by H&R. Different, yet exquisite.

Photos — Stephen Quill

H&R's 1971 Centennial Catalog includes this reference to the A&D doubles that they made "prior to 1900."

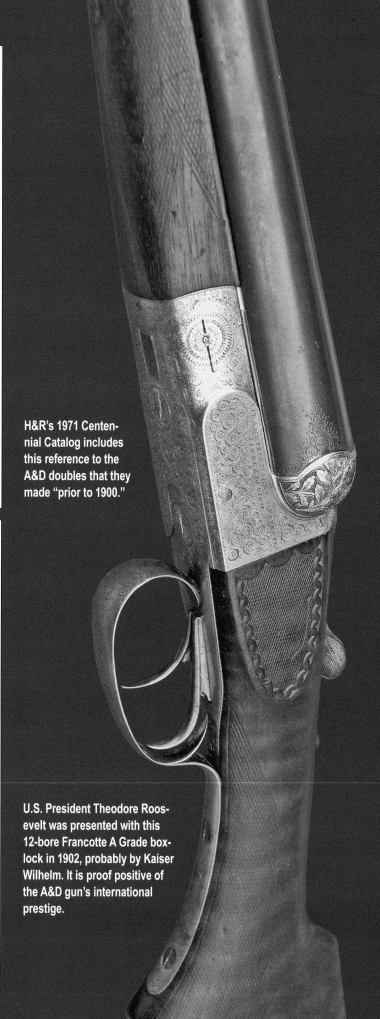

U.S. President Theodore Roosevelt was presented with this 12-bore Francotte A Grade boxlock in 1902, probably by Kaiser Wilhelm. It is proof positive of the A&D gun's international prestige.

This price is confirmed by the Schoverling, Daly & Gales catalog page, which also shows the 10-bore A Grade gun at $310. To put these prices into a contemporary context, $300 in 1880 translates into almost $6,800 U.S. dollars today.

Even more stunning is that the price point of H&R's $100 Grade D "field" gun would still translate into roughly $2,250 in 21st-century money. In light of this, it becomes readily apparent that, either by intent or result, H&R double guns were not targeted toward the 1880s proletariat. Nonetheless, it is noteworthy that production of Harrington & Richardson's A&D-licensed shotgun ceased in late 1884 or early 1885, a year following a fateful House of Lords decision in a legal case regarding the A&D patent.

This verdict effectively gave W.W. Greener the go-ahead to mass produce his own boxlock — the *Facile Princeps*. Officials at H&R undoubtedly knew these guns would soon enter the U.S. market *en masse* and would probably render their license of the A&D action considerably less valuable. Perhaps this, along with C.G. Bonehill's thriving U.S. sales of less expensive machine-made guns comprised even more rationale for H&R to cut their losses and terminate A&D boxlock manufacture. On a positive note, most H&R doubles that have survived are very fine guns indeed, and they remain eminently collectible.

Another result of H&R's failed venture into the A&D double gun was Edwin Anson's return to Birmingham, England, in 1884, which led to a whole new chapter in the Anson family saga.

The Death of William Anson

Upon returning to England, Edwin Anson joined forces with the firm of Cogswell & Harrison, and while Edwin worked with C&H, his father's health began to fail rather prematurely. But William Anson was still inventive, and one of his last British patents brought William full circle and back to his most famous creation — the A&D boxlock.

Studio portrait of William and Caroline Anson. It shows William toward the late 1880s. He has definitely aged in this photo. *Photo — Courtesy of Stride family*

Specifically, Patent No. 7,274 of May 16, 1888, offered yet another means of cocking the A&D action, this time via a single dog in the center of the action knuckle that had two fork-like arms that would lift and cock the tumblers as the gun was opened. Curiously, it came very close to Greener's *Facile Princeps* idea. Nevertheless, a great many Birmingham boxlocks were made with Anson's new cocking mechanism. In the most strict sense, Anson's last patent was U.S. No. 401,101 dated April 9, 1889. This was another improvement of his previous ejector Patent No. 371,118 of October 4, 1887. Yet again, it was not a success.

Little more than a month later, William Anson died at the age of 59 on May 28, 1889, at 6 Church Road, Moseley, Kings Norton, Worcestershire (a Birmingham suburb). His death certificate is dated May 30th. Cause of death was listed as "cirrhosis of the liver, teterus and general anasarca." In yet another twist of irony, Anson died just 17 days after patent protection expired on his transformational Anson & Deeley double-gun action. William Anson was buried on June 1, 1889, at St. Saviour (Catholic) Church, St. Saviour's Road (corner of Hall Road), Saltley, Birmingham, Warwickshire, West Midlands. His headstone has not survived. Anson's wife Caroline, along with their children, inherited his estate, which according to official documents, totaled £1,069 pounds, 13 shillings and 10 pennies, with £471 in cash. That is not very much at all, even in 1889.

It seems an especially meager amount for the man who'd invented the world-standard double-barrel shotgun action and a host of other mechanisms that the British gun trade utilizes even today. So where did all the money go? Was there a lot of it to begin with? If so, was William a bit of spendthrift? Did he have costly vices? Was he heavily burdened with family or business expenses? There is no conclusive answer to any of it, but there are clues.

William Anson's death certificate dated May 30, 1889. His actual death occurred two days earlier on May 28th.

- William Anson's cause of death was listed as "cirrhosis of the liver, teterus [sic] and general anasarca." The usual cause of cirrhosis needs no elaboration. Tetanus (probably the correct medical term) is related to infection via wounds from metallic objects, something a gunmaker would be especially susceptible to. Anasarca (overall swelling) is usually associated with liver failure, linked to cirrhosis.
- Some of this information could suggest psychological factors. Could William have been less than content with his later life or business situation? Could he have resorted to excessive drink in his later years? It's grounds for speculation. But I must also emphasize that there are no facts to establish any of this, nor does it link it to any cause and effect regarding his death.
- On the other hand, William may have simply been unlucky enough to acquire a nasty infection and then died as a result. It could be that simple.
- According to "trade stories," related by author Douglas Tate, plus Anson descendants, and a few not-so-ambiguous letters in the Anson family archives, there was a definite air of animosity between the Ansons and John Deeley by the time of William's death. This was apparently based on allegations that Deeley was less than equitable in his distribution of royalties that were due William and Edwin Anson. All this was undoubtedly tied to the A&D action, plus a number of Anson's other patents he shared with Deeley.

The Ansons' Relationship With John Deeley

Over the course of his career, there is reason to believe that William Anson became less and less intertwined with the business affairs and direction of John Deeley. This was supported by the late Mike Newland, former curator of firearms at the Birmingham Museum of Science & Industry:

There is no doubt that by Edwin's death in 1936 there was a very bad feeling towards John Deeley, and the implication is that both William and his son Edwin did not receive the correct monetary recompense for their inventions. There is no proof as yet to substantiate this fact, and there is no doubt that John Deeley had a keen monetary and business mind, but it does seem a little strange that on her death in 1939, Edwin's widow was reduced to living in a small flat above a shop and left only £125 in her will. Of course this could have been due to Edwin's lack of business acumen and inability to manufacture, market and protect his own inventions.

On that latter count, clarification is highly unlikely. According to Clare Stride: "Dorothy Anson (Edwin's daughter) worked for the [E. Anson] firm in a financial capacity, but unfortunately destroyed all records relating to the firm when she went senile."

It could be reading a bit too much into this, but it is possible that Edwin maintained some sort of limited, yet socially distant business relationship with John Deeley following William Anson's death. And logic would suggest that it was primarily related to royalties generated through Anson & Deeley Patentees.

In addition, the well-respected authors, I.M. Crudgington and D.J. Baker voice their own perspective in *The British Shotgun, Vol. Three* when they wrote: *William Anson was almost certainly the true inventor of the action that is now known as the Anson & Deeley because of the way in which it was patented. There is an oral tradition within the Anson family, however, that William Anson was, in some way, badly treated over the deal.*

So, was it all just business or was it something else?

An Awkward Association

History shows that one of the most ephemeral forms of business arrangement is the partnership. They often start with friendship, devolve into loathing, then degenerate into resentment. And from many indications, this is probably what happened to Anson & Deeley Patentees, which was formed some time around 1884 to shepherd licensing of the Anson & Deeley boxlock design and other Anson & Deeley patents.

Degradation of the partnership is a possibility, because disparate facts, combined with Clare Stride's research, plus the insights of surviving members of the Birmingham gun trade, indicate that sad scenario. The picture looks like this:

- On August 26, 1882, William Anson patented his intercepting safety sear for the A&D boxlock (ser. no. 4089). This was widely used in the trade as an upscale enhancement to the basic A&D design. But curiously, Anson held this patent on his own.
- According to Clare Stride, the painting that Edwin Anson did near Worcester, Massachusetts, in 1883 was also displayed at an exhibition of the Royal Birmingham Society of Artists in 1883. What's more, it was presented in concert with art created by John Deeley. This information suggests two things: firstly, that Edwin Anson made a few trips between the U.S. and England during the period he worked with H&R and, secondly, that he was on reasonable terms with John Deeley at the time. I ask you to keep this latter point in mind.
- After he'd departed Westley Richards, William Anson continued to work with and share patents with his old employer John Deeley of Westley Richards. This lasted for some time. In fact, records indicate that William Anson and John Deeley patented two improvements to their A&D boxlock in 1883, seven years after Anson allegedly left Westley Richards.
- Specifically, William Anson and John Deeley were both issued Patent No. 1,833 on April 11, 1883, for an alternate forked-style cocking dog along with a greatly simplified connecting link between the A&D gun's sliding bolt top lever and the Purdey underbolt. This latter design became the standard mechanism employed in camming top-lever Westley Richards side-by-sides and continues in use even

today. The design was also patented in the U.S. on November 7, 1883, (No. 297,907). There is every reason to believe that Westley Richards & Co. paid Anson & Deeley a considerable sum for the use of these ideas. In addition, this bit of reengineering may well have been a reaction to the ongoing litigation between Westley Richards/Robert Couchman and W.W. Greener over patent infringement of the A&D action.

- One might also view the Anson & Deeley co-patented "hammer top gun" of 1884 as an effort to capture a measure of design security. In connection with this mechanism, Anson's address is still listed 78½ High Street, Birmingham. Once again, this is near the old address of Westley Richards and possibly the business domain of Robert Couchman as Anson & Deeley Patentees.
- To stoke the fires of speculation even more, the protracted legal travail with W.W. Greener might have seriously effected the relationship between William Anson and John Deeley. This litigation turned a corner in 1884, when the House of Lords decided that Greener's *Facile Princeps* action did not infringe upon the Anson & Deeley boxlock patent. This verdict was a serious blow to the earning power of the A&D mechanism, especially because it had five years of patent protection left.
- From 1884 onward, John Deeley appears to have taken a step away from his engineering partnership with William Anson. After 1884, Deeley realigns himself with a Birmingham action maker named Frederick J. Penn.
- As of March 3, 1884, William Anson ceases to share any further patents with John Deeley. In fact, this is the date on which Anson is granted Patent No. 4,292: an improved means of cocking the A&D action — one that eliminates the traditional means of connecting the action with the fore-end iron. This "cocking block" as Anson refers to it, quickly became a standard mechanism in the English gun trade, and thousands of boxlocks were made with it.
- On November 20, 1884, Anson was granted Patent No. 15,299 for a rather curious ejector system. In this, the ejector always acted on both cartridges as the gun was opened, whether they had been fired or not. However, unfired cartridges were blocked from being kicked out by small tabs and were retained. Ejection of fired cases was permitted as normal. "An unduly complicated method of operation which relied on several small and rather fragile parts," according to Geoffrey Boothroyd. Perhaps understandably, this system was not popular. For the record, William tried an improvement with Patent No. 16,138 of December 9, 1886. This one garnered even less enthusiasm in the trade. The same tepid response can be reported for his U.S. Patent of that same idea (No. 371,118 of October 7, 1887).
- Certain questions now arise from previous events: did the patent rights battle with Greener serve to sour the personal and business relationship between William Anson and John Deeley? Was Anson left to manage the remaining products of Anson & Deeley Patentees, plus supply "snaps" and components to the Birmingham gun trade while John Deeley sought greener pastures with F.J. Penn? This may be inferring a bit too much, but then again, maybe not.
- For some reason, the number "7" has always held a mystic value in the Anglo-Saxon ethos. Perhaps this is why British patents expire after seven years, pending renewal for another seven. Thus, the first term of the 1875 patent for the Anson & Deeley boxlock lapsed on May 11, 1883. Interestingly enough, by 1884, a new company called "Anson & Deeley Patentees" had already emerged, ostensibly to grant licensing rights for the A&D boxlock and other A&D mechanisms. Its business address was 78½ High Street, which was near the original premises of Westley Richards & Co. So for the mere cost of renewal, there were seven more years of patent protection available for the most desired double-gun action in the world, and its licensors were now Messrs. Anson and Deeley, via Anson & Deeley Patentees. Collaterally, Robert Couchman fades into obscurity.
- Anson & Deeley Patentees appears to have been set up by John Deeley, with William Anson having a collateral interest. If this was indeed the case, then some level of cooperation must still have existed between the two men in 1884. Perhaps Deeley trusted Anson to continue his gifted inventions, but channel them through A&D Patentees?

Taken as a whole, this series of events simply begs speculation. First, no one knows what the official Westley Richards policy was regarding patents developed by in-house employees (or even if they had a policy). Did the company have rights to the first seven-year cycle? Were inventors free to capitalize on their genius after that time? After all, Westley's required a "cut" of all licensing profits through the Robert Couchman connection, but Anson & Deeley Patentees continued licensing thereafter.

So, who held claim to what? Anson had created the boxlock while he was employed at Westley Richards, but John Deeley presumably financed the work and its legal protection with company money. Yet it is indisputable that the A&D patent was issued in the names of William Anson and John Deeley.

What is also known is that John Deeley was Managing Director at Westley Richards, and by virtue of that post, he could fairly well write his own ticket, indeed. Circumstances lead one to believe that William Anson and John Deeley might have agreed to set up some sort of cooperative or even a shell company to orchestrate the production of firearms sub-assemblies and to license firearms patents to other gunmakers. But, was Westley Richards & Co. Ltd. at the bottom of that rabbit hole, or not?

A perspective on the situation may once again be gleaned from the book *Westley Richards & Co., In Pursuit of The Best Gun*, by Jeremy Musson. In Musson's description of the Anson & Deeley boxlock, it is stated that: *The first really successful hammerless gun was a Westley Richard & Co. patent (no. 1756 of 1875), taken out by Anson and Deeley. John Deeley 'the elder' worked with William Anson, the foreman of Westley Richards Gun-Action department in 1875, who also later set up on his own and took out further patents in his own name... The Anson & Deeley action is the Westley Richards trademark "boxlock."*

That certainly sounds like Westley Richards owned the patent, even though Anson & Deeley are cited on the actual document. What's more, the first license for the A&D gun, which was issued to Robert Couchman, specifies Westley Richards & Co. as the "licensor." As I've already pointed out, patent documents prove that Messrs. Anson and Deeley shared firearms patents up until 1884. It also appears as though Edwin Anson assumed his father's interest in Anson & Deeley Patentees following William Anson's death. Once again, this lasted until 1899 when John Deeley retired from Westley Richards & Co., and Anson & Deeley Patentees was dissolved.

With that move, the Anson family's inventive torch was passed on to Edwin Anson.

Chapter Two
JOHN DEELEY

A Man of Mystery, of Talent... and of Maneuvers

There were more than a few rags-to-riches stories in the 19th-century Birmingham gun trade, but the tale of John Deeley ranks among the most intriguing.

Why? First, because Deeley was very much a self-made man with apparently humble beginnings and very little formal education. Despite these handicaps, he rose to be General Manager of Westley Richards & Co., and registered at least 19 important patents in his industry, not the least of which was the famous Anson & Deeley boxlock of 1875.

What makes these achievements all the more impressive is the fact that John Deeley was not a gunmaker in the traditional sense. He served no apprenticeship at the bench, and he never "made" a gun on his own. Yet, his name is attached to some of the most enduring firearm mechanisms ever conceived.

How did it all happen? To be honest, the full story is difficult to decipher. Little is known of John Deeley's early years, but we do know that he was born in 1825 to Irish working-class parents living in the industrial town of Birmingham, England. Apparently, Deeley was an only child. His father was a steel toy polisher. Young Deeley left school at the tender age of nine to enter the working world as a workshop boy in the brass casting, button and silk trades, but the back shop was not where his natural talents lay. He was a numbers man, but the next decade did little to optimize that gift.

By 1850, 25-year-old John Deeley had married his wife Elizabeth, who was 27 at the time. Soon afterward, Deeley entered the service of a Mr. Henry Edwards as a clerk and bookkeeper in the High Street section of Birmingham. While there, he obtained an introduction to Mr. Westley Richards, who was apparently impressed with Deeley. Perhaps as a result, John Deeley received an appointment to the Westley Richards firm in 1860, which coincidentally had a shop at 82 High Street.

According to the periodical *Arms and Explosives*, "He [Deeley] quickly grasped the true principles of gun making,

John Deeley was Managing Director of Westley Richards from 1872 until 1899. Under his stewardship, it achieved unprescedented greatness.
Photo — Courtesy of Westley Richards

[at Westley Richards] thereafter applying them with a thoroughness that added greatly to the reputation of a firm that already stood high." Deeley initially started by doing menial work in the various Westley Richards sub-shops, but his abilities in accountancy were quickly noticed. Soon, these skills were put to good use in balancing the firm's books, which had apparently been neglected for over three years. This set the pattern for John Deeley's success.

He also resolved to educate himself throughout his early years, and pursued a wide range of academic interests. This included the study of French, a linguistic ability that would pay important dividends later in his career.

Not long after John Deeley joined Westley Richards, another very important individual was hired there around 1863, lockmaker William Anson. By happenstance, this coincided with America's Civil War, which turned Birmingham into a boomtown. After more than a decade of working independently at Westley's, these two men were destined to collaborate on one of the most transformational gun designs ever conceived — the Anson & Deeley boxlock. But I'm getting a bit ahead of myself...

In 1865, Westley Richards the Elder died. The firm he founded then came under the control of his son, Westley Richards the Younger and his half-brother Charles, who handled the business end of things. But these were times when death did not take a holiday. Tragedy would visit John Deeley and his wife the very next year. On October 18, 1866, the Deeley's young daughter Emma died at the age of 6½ years. It was certainly a painful loss.

Five years later, events on the Continent gave John Deeley a chance to prove his financial mettle, and see his star rocket into ascendancy at Westley Richards.

In the wake of the Franco-Prussian War and German unification, Westley Richards' subsidiary, the National Arms and Ammunition Company, was engaged by the German Empire to produce 150,000 units of the new Model 1871 Mauser rifle in 1872.

John Deeley found ways to reduce the per-unit cost of production to such an extent that he saved the company £50,000, a very impressive sum in those days. While the project was not necessarily a complete manufacturing success, since the Germans complained that the quality was not what was required, and the delivered number was reduced to 100,000, this still amounted to putting an extra £50,000 into Westley Richards' coffers by the time the project wrapped up in 1878. For the sake of comparison, that would amount to over £23 million in today's currency — more than enough to get anyone's attention.

Note also that, in 1871, Charles Richards had died at the young age of 47. As a result, John Deeley was appointed Commercial Manager and Director of the company at age 46. Thanks to the Mauser rifle deal, a huge amount of cash was about to flow into the bank account of Westley Richards the Younger, who apparently had felt comfortable enough to retire in 1872.

Westley Richards the Younger at age 40, son of its founder, William Westley Richards.
Photo — Courtesy of Westley Richards

Otto Von Bismarck helped launch John Deeley's career in 1872 by ordering 150,000 Mauser rifles from Westley Richards following the Franco-Prussian War. Deeley reduced production cost to such an extent that he saved the company an extra £50,000.

Below is an illustration of Westley Richards' original shop at 82 High Street, Birmingham. Workrooms were in the back of the premises.

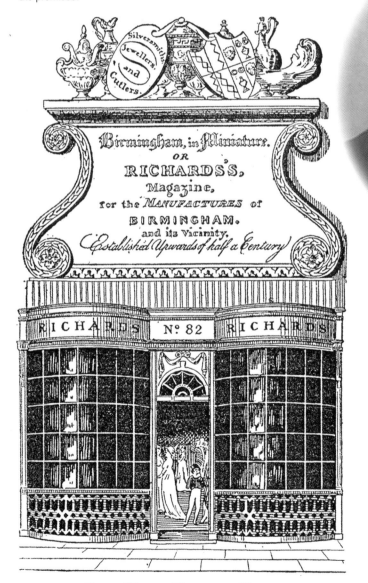

OLD HIGH STREET SHOP.

Richards went off to his home at Ashwell Hall, Oakham, where he raised horses and became a magistrate and High Sheriff of the county until his death in May of 1897. But, even in retirement, Westley Richards did not sever himself from the company. He retained joint chairmanship with his close friend Charles Couchman, who was also on the Westley Richards & Co. Board of Directors. The Couchmans are an important and a heretofore little-publicized dimension of this story, so please keep that name in mind.

Thus, it was Couchman and John Deeley who were effectively left in charge. In fact, Deeley functioned as CEO of Westley Richards & Co. for the next 28 years, and in this role, he was not satisfied with mere managerial and accounting responsibilities — John Deeley wanted more. Apparently, that included enduring business success, prominence in the trade, and income. But not strictly in that order. In any case, he would not follow the course of other accountants or business managers who often appear as stern-faced portraits in a company's forgotten history book. John Deeley had greater things in mind.

To help fulfill this destiny, the stars began to align for Westley Richards & Co. in still other ways. Remember William Anson? Well, he was still a journeyman action filer at Westley's, but his inventive nature had come up with something very important around 1869 — a push-rod style fore-end latch, now commonly known as the Anson latch. This was recorded as William Anson Patent No. 3791 on December 14, 1872, and it is still in wide use today by a host of European gunmakers. From what can be discerned, Anson ginned up this mechanism on his own and made these "snaps" for the trade as a side business.

Perhaps John Deeley was impressed by the ingenuity of this latch and imagined that he could capitalize on the creativity of its inventor. Thus, William Anson's latch could well have prompted his 1873 appointment to foreman of the shotgun action department. But another even bigger idea was churning around in Anson's mind, and it would soon change everything in the double-gun market. Meanwhile, it didn't take long for John Deeley to make his own latch — and his own mark in the company. On April 19, 1873, he worked with James Simeon Edge, foreman of the sporting and military rifle department, to patent two important gun concepts under the same patent (No. 1422). The first was the Deeley & Edge rifle, which some have held was the functional inspiration for the Anson & Deeley boxlock.

The second noteworthy item in Patent No. 1422 was the now ubiquitous Deeley & Edge fore-end fastener for double guns. This became the standard latch for all Westley Richards double guns, and for the vast majority of English doubles as a whole. In fact, it is still the most common fore-end latch in the world, and is used on millions of side-by-side and over/under shotguns.

From a practical standpoint, the Deeley & Edge latch is amply robust to do its job, plus it is easier and cheaper to make and adjust than the Anson latch. On the other hand, Anson's design is probably more elegant. Still, the real mother lode of invention was yet to come.

Birth of The Anson & Deeley Boxlock

Possibly inspired by Joseph Needham's 1874 barrel-cocking patent, an especially fertile idea soon germinated in the mind of William Anson and/or John Deeley. It was so simple yet so straightforward and intuitive that its value was instantly obvious: use the barrels of a double shotgun as a huge mechanical lever to cock its hammers, which themselves would be enclosed within the action body of the gun. The execution of this idea was pure distilled genius. Years later, John Deeley's managerial protégé Leslie B. Taylor characterized the concept as "The ne plus ultra of efficient mechanism."

And so it is was that William Anson collaborated with John Deeley to create the famous Anson & Deeley "boxlock" action, or as John Deeley preferred to call it, the "bodylock." A patent for the A&D action was granted on May 11, 1875, (No. 1756). On February 1, 1876, it was also patented in the United States (No. 172,943).

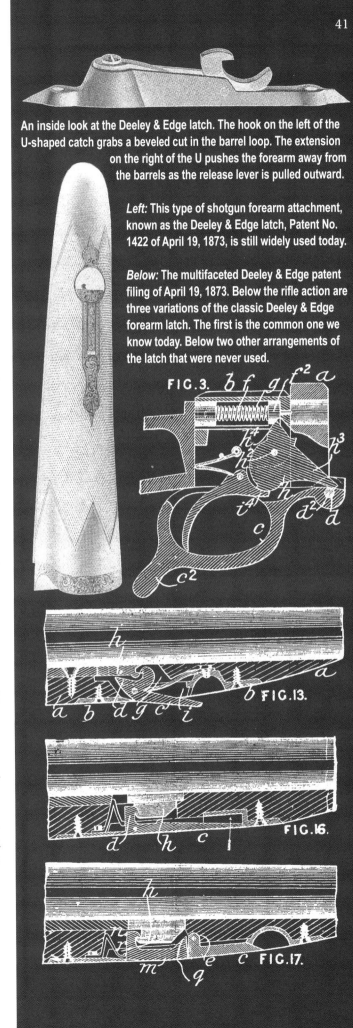

An inside look at the Deeley & Edge latch. The hook on the left of the U-shaped catch grabs a beveled cut in the barrel loop. The extension on the right of the U pushes the forearm away from the barrels as the release lever is pulled outward.

Left: This type of shotgun forearm attachment, known as the Deeley & Edge latch, Patent No. 1422 of April 19, 1873, is still widely used today.

Below: The multifaceted Deeley & Edge patent filing of April 19, 1873. Below the rifle action are three variations of the classic Deeley & Edge forearm latch. The first is the common one we know today. Below two other arrangements of the latch that were never used.

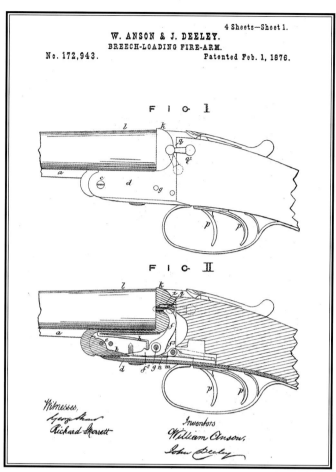
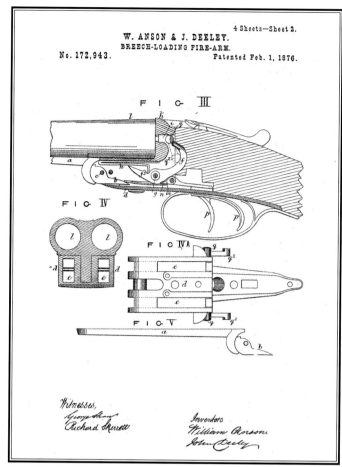

U.S. Patent Drawings of A&D guns.

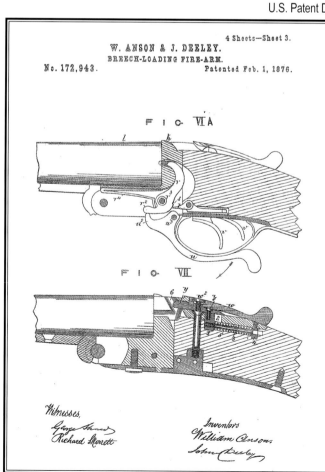
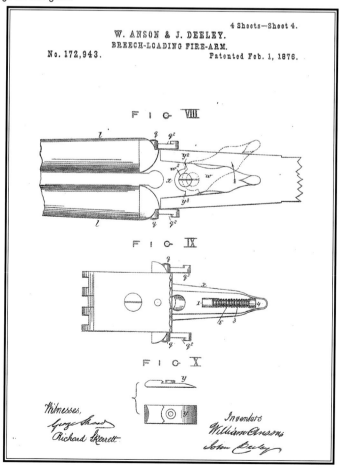

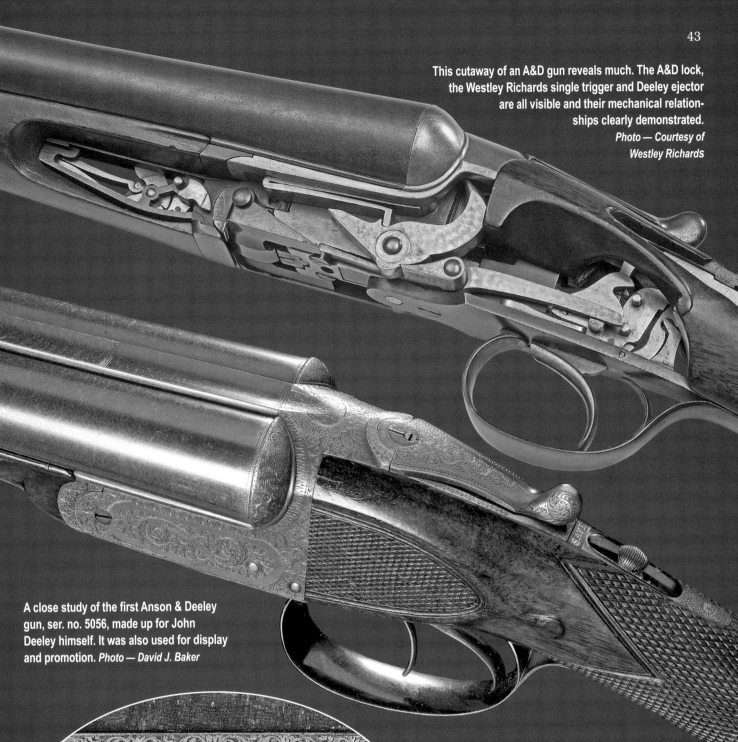

This cutaway of an A&D gun reveals much. The A&D lock, the Westley Richards single trigger and Deeley ejector are all visible and their mechanical relationships clearly demonstrated. *Photo — Courtesy of Westley Richards*

A close study of the first Anson & Deeley gun, ser. no. 5056, made up for John Deeley himself. It was also used for display and promotion. *Photo — David J. Baker*

The monogrammed stock oval of the first A&D gun verifies the identity of its original owner to be John Deeley. *Photo — Bonham's*

The bottom of the first A&D gun clearly testifies to its primacy. *Photo — David J. Baker*

To commemorate this achievement, Westley Richards created the first Anson & Deeley boxlock as a promotional display piece and personal memento for John Deeley. Production on the gun started in 1875 as "Mr. Deeley's gun" according to records, but was actually completed in 1879 (possibly due to engraving time). It is serial no. 5056, a 12-bore, non-ejector with 30-inch barrels, both bored cylinder. The stock oval carries the initials "JD", and the gun weighs 6 lbs., 12 oz. Its length of pull is 14½ inches. The bottom of the gun's frame is engraved with the legend "The First Anson & Deeley/HAMMERLESS GUN."

From that perspective, it is worthwhile to note the order of billing here. This concept has always been called the "Anson & Deeley" action. Not the Deeley & Anson action. Perhaps this can simply be ascribed to the resonance of language and its potential for marketing. Somehow, Anson & Deeley rings in English. Deeley & Anson falls out with a thud.

On the other hand, there may also have been a measure of preeminence in play. Perhaps Anson's name comes first because it was Anson's basic idea, and John Deeley follows in a supportive role because he supplied the money, manufacturing and marketing. Deeley himself apparently had no issue with getting second billing. All of the official patent papers refer to the mechanism as the "William Anson and John Deeley" idea. In that exact order, every time. This includes the last page where both men signed their names. Even there, William Anson comes first.

Still, there are champions on both sides of the issue, and they're all given an opportunity to "strut and fret their hour upon the stage" in the chapter on William Anson.

But should you reference those thoughts, keep in mind that, in a very real sense, John Deeley was Westley Richards in those years. He was the majority shareholder and Managing Director, and he had control of the company purse strings. In essence, he could bloody well do what he wanted.

Deeley's perception of the A&D invention is further illuminated in an interview from *The Sporting Goods Review* of April 15, 1897: *...An improvement in hammerless gunlocks which has had very important effects on the trade. I mean, of course, the Anson and Deeley action introduced by the foreman of our machine shop, and myself, in 1875. Nobody before had succeeded in making an action with so few parts, and of such strength. It was, too, the first gun in which the cocking was done by the dropping of the barrels, and the first really successful hammerless gun... Practically everybody makes it, and, as regards principle, it remains the best today.*

Few could take issue with those points. Except that Deeley seems to have overlooked Joseph Needham, who was actually the first to employ the barrel cocking principal. Deeley also skirts a baffling development related to the Anson & Deeley boxlock, which was William Anson's summary departure from Westley Richards.

Indeed, just months following his A&D gun triumph, it is widely accepted that William Anson left the direct employ of Westley Richards in 1876 and set up his own shop at 123 Steelhouse Lane. But in reality, this may well have been one of the first steps in a far-ranging new venture that had germinated in the mind of John Deeley.

The Couchman Connection

At this point, I must introduce a rather fascinating and little-known piece to the Anson & Deeley puzzle, and that is Anson's apparent departure from Westley Richards seems to coincide with what appears to be the first licensing of the A&D patent. This license was granted to 28-year-old Robert E. Couchman, with offices at No. 6 Waterloo Street, Birmingham (residence at 17 Highfield Road, Edgbaston), and was executed on June 22, 1876. Curiously, this license was granted without William Anson's signature. We have this document in our archives.

However, the odd bit is that Robert Couchman was not a gunmaker. He was a Birmingham land agent and surveyor with a Victorian upper-middle class background that included money and social respectability. So it comes as no surprise that Robert lived and worked in the most expensive areas in and around Birmingham. But key to our interests is that he was also a nephew of Charles Couchman, whom I've made mention of earlier. Charles was a member of the

In April of 1897, *The Sporting Goods Review* published this interview with John Deeley. Today, it remains a special insight into the man and his career in the gun trade.

Above: The September 1882 wedding photo of Charles John Goodman and Amy Harriet Couchman. Here, Robert Edward Couchman (indicated with arrow), first licensee and licensor/administrator of rights to the A&D action, is seen standing in the back row, third from the right.
Below: Another photo from the September 1882 Goodman/Couchman wedding. Seated in the front row are, from left, Mr. and Mrs. John Dent Goodman. Goodman was not only Robert Couchman's father-in-law but also Chairman of BSA. Seated to the far right are Mr. and Mrs. Charles Couchman (Couchman was on the Board of Westley Richards), and Robert Couchman's uncle. Both photos courtesy Mrs. Ann Goodman and Jeremy Archer

Westley Richards Board of Directors and personal friend of Westley Richards the Younger. To make matters even more interesting, Charles Couchman was married to William Westley Richards' niece Annette.

But Charles Couchman held an influence in the community that did not stop with his family tree. He owned a 517-acre estate called Temple House, located 14 miles southeast of Birmingham, which employed 17 workers. He was also a Justice of the Peace and Director of Lloyd's Banking Company Ltd., along with Birmingham politician Joseph Chamberlain (of whom we shall learn more later). Charles Couchman also served as Chairman of the weekly board for Birmingham General Hospital.

A few years before the A&D boxlock came along, Charles Couchman helped Westley Richards & Co. by lending his considerable support to a local licensing application made by his friend, Westley Richards.

Records show that, in 1871, the relatively new Westley Richards Small Arms and Ammunition Company had applied for a license to manufacture ammunition and percussion caps, etc. This was undoubtedly related to the Prussian government's order for 150 million rounds following the outbreak of the Franco-Prussian War. The partners of the Westley Richards Small Arms and Ammunition Company were named as Westley Richards, Thomas Greenwood and John Batley.

This application to manufacture was actually for an extension of a license at Alfred Ludlow's works in Aston, which was a small two-acre urban site owned by Westley Richards. However, Westley's offered to not pursue the Aston license if they could obtain permission to build a completely new works on a 50-acre site at Holdford, which the company had already purchased for £12,000. But even then, they did not want to start a £15,000 factory on this land without first securing a license. The debate at hand centered upon issues of safety.

On that count, Charles Couchman spoke in support of the license, saying the 50-acre Holdford location was the best possible place for a new ammunition factory. Thus, it was concluded that, on public safety grounds, the Holdford site should be approved. By January of 1872, the National Arms and Ammunition Company Ltd. had taken over the business. Lord Lichfield was chairman and John Deeley was a director. The company ceased operations in the late 1880s and was liquidated in 1896.

A decade beforehand, the linchpin of the firm's existence, Charles Couchman, died on August 8, 1886, at Temple Balsall, Knowle, Warwickshire. But, by that time his nephew, Robert Couchman, had reaped a considerable reward from his uncle's connection with Westley Richards & Co. Indeed, Robert had not only been granted proprietary licensing rights for the Anson & Deeley action and Anson safety, but had overseen their secondary licensing to a number of gunmakers, one even in the U.S.

What's more, Robert Couchman may have effectively succeeded his uncle as a Director and Secretary of Westley Richards & Co. In the book *The British Shotgun, Vol. Two*, I.M. Crudgington and D.J. Baker state that he was appointed to that post by Westley Richards the Younger at the same time Richards promoted John Deeley to Director/CEO. But curiously enough, neither Charles nor Robert Couchman are referenced in any official history of Westley Richards & Co. Nonetheless, Robert Couchman was issued the very first license to make Anson & Deeley guns.

From this perspective, the Couchman connection poses a very intriguing question: why would Westley Richards & Co. issue a license to manufacture its own A&D gun, to an outwardly independent party (but probably one of its own directors), under a patent held by two of its own employees, namely John Deeley and the recently "separated" William Anson? One might logically assume that Westley's would hold and manage rights to the mechanism itself as an overarching legal entity.

The particulars of Couchman's indenture (license), which is now in our archives, make these moves even more baffling. It required Couchman to pay 15 shillings per "sporting gun or rifle" produced with the A&D action and to number each gun or rifle consecutively, beginning with the No. 1. The curious thing is that Couchman was in no position to make anything on his own. He was a surveyor, not a gunmaker. And even if he were, he would essentially be paying this royalty to himself as a director of Westley Richards. And just for the record, the language of this contract specifies Westley Richards & Co. as "the licensor" of Patent No. 1756, which itself was "granted under the great seal of the United Kingdom of Great Britain and Ireland to William Anson and John Deeley…"

Additionally, any royalties Couchman owed were to be paid quarterly to the licensor — Westley Richards & Co. Thus, one must logically assume that the company would then disburse part of these proceeds to the patent holders themselves, based on some undisclosed formula. Keep in mind here that one of those patent holders was William Anson, who was now allegedly independent from John Deeley, the other patent holder.

Interestingly, there are some crucially revealing passages in this legal document, and with apologies in advance for bludgeoning you with legalese, I beg to point out these key clauses of the license:

On pages 1 and 2: *The said licensor doth hereby give and grant unto the licensees and their successors, the person or persons for the time being **constituting the company or partnership of the said licensees** the license, power, privilege and authority to make use and exercise and put in practise but in connection with sporting guns and double rifles manufactured by themselves, whole or in part **at or in their present manufactory at High Street Birmingham or in any other premises the licensees may occupy in Birmingham or elsewhere in the United Kingdom** and not otherwise the said invention for which the said letters patent were granted and **to vend sell or dispose of sporting guns and double rifles comprising the said patented improvement or any part or parts thereof** subject to the conditions and stipulations herein after contained…*

The vital nuggets of information to be drawn from this emphasized wording are these:

- Couchman was part of a "company or partnership" potentially in concert with William Anson and/or John Deeley.
- This company and/or "manufactory" was located on High Street in Birmingham. This was near the original Westley Richards shop.
- An allowance for "other premises the licensees may occupy," would certainly cover work done by Anson and sundry workmen at 123 Steelhouse Lane or elsewhere. This could even extend to outworkers installed at other gunmakers' shops.
- The authority to "vend sell or dispose" of guns, rifles or "parts thereof" allowed the Couchman operation to make up complete or semi-finished units for the trade.
- Bottom line, Westley Richards was effectively licensing the A&D action to Robert Couchman, *et al*.

On page 5: *And also that the said licensees and their successors* **shall not nor will without the consent in writing of the Licensor make any assignment of the license** *hereby granted...*

From a superficial reading, this passage might seem to limit Couchman from assigning his A&D license to others, but read carefully — there is the clear ability to assign further rights to the A&D gun with "consent in writing of the Licensor." Thus, Couchman only needed approval from Westley Richards/John Deeley to do so. You will see, in short order, why I make a point of this.

It is also important to point out that Couchman's license was amended on December 21, 1877, granting him rights to use William Anson's "dickey bird" top tang safety mechanism (Patent No. 4513) of November 21, 1876, for the sum of 13 shillings per unit. This simple yet highly effective safety was patented by William Anson in 1876, and now licensed through Couchman, who wasted little time in making money from it. He soon licensed the mechanism to Joseph Brazier & Sons of Wolverhampton, the famous gun trade lockmakers. Nevertheless, it appears highly probable that Brazier was the major outsource for these safeties, which were then installed by Westley Richards and a host of other English gunmakers.

And finally, on page 6, we see this note near the signatures of all parties: *Sealed with the Corporate Commonseal of the said Westley Richards & Company Limited and signed by John Batley and John Deeley, two of the Directors of such Company...* Taken together with a series of other facts, this entire scenario proves especially enlightening. Here is the chronology of events, as they've been uncovered:

- In May of 1875, Anson and Deeley patent the boxlock.
- In early 1876, William Anson leaves Westley Richards to establish his own shop at 123 Steelhouse Lane.
- On June 22, 1876, the first license to produce the Anson & Deeley boxlock is issued to Robert Couchman.
- The Couchman license was executed with the full imprimatur of Westley Richards & Co. as well as John Deeley and Director John Bately.
- Couchman and his company are located on High Street in Birmingham, near the original Westley Richards location at 82 High Street.
- Couchman is very likely to have worked with William Anson, both at Westley's High Street location and 123 Steelhouse Lane, to orchestrate the production of A&D guns and components.

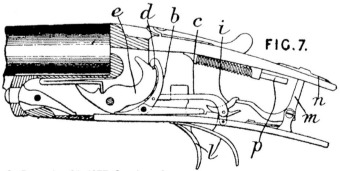

On December 21, 1877, Couchman's license was amended, granting him rights to use William Anson's "dickey bird" top tang safety mechanism, for the sum of 13 shillings per unit. Couchman outsourced it to Joseph Brazier & Sons of Wolverhampton.

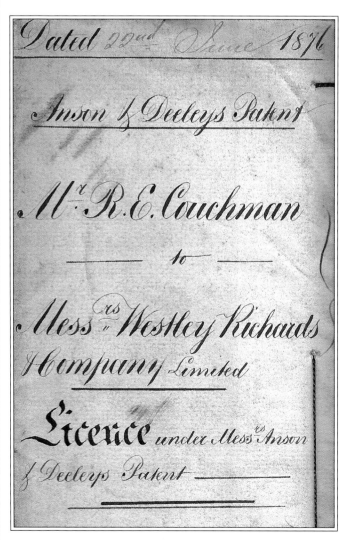

Robert E. Couchman received the first license ever issued for the Anson & Deeley action on June 22, 1876, the cover of which is pictured above along with pages 1 and 6 shown on the following pages. A land surveyor, he was a nephew of Westley Richards & Co. board member Charles Couchman.

This Indenture made the twenty second day of June in the year of our Lord One thousand eight hundred and seventy six **Between** Robert Edward Couchman of No 6 Waterloo Street in the Borough of Birmingham Land Surveyor hereinafter called "the Licensor" of the one part and Westley Richards and Company Limited of Birmingham aforesaid Gunmakers hereinafter called "the Licensees" of the other part **Whereas** the said Licensor is the Proprietor of Letters Patent dated the eleventh day of May One thousand eight hundred and seventy five No 1756 granted under the Great seal of the United Kingdom of Great Britain and Ireland to William Anson and John Deeley therein respectively described for an Invention of improvements in Breech loading Small Arms usually designated drop down guns and pistols **And whereas** the said Licensees have applied to the said Licensor for such license as herein after contained under the said Letters Patent for or in respect of Sporting guns and double Rifles which the said Licensor has agreed to grant on such terms and subject to such royalties stipulations and conditions as are hereinafter contained **Now these presents witness** that in pursuance of the said agreement and in consideration of the payments covenants clauses and agreements hereinafter reserved and contained on the part of the said Licensees he the said Licensor doth hereby give and grant unto the said Licensees and their successors the person or persons for the time being constituting the Company or partnership of the said Licensees the license power privilege and authority to make use and exercise and put in practise but in connection with sporting guns and double rifles manufactured by them in whole or in part at or in their

Page 1 of the first license ever issued for the Anson & Deeley action on June 22, 1876.

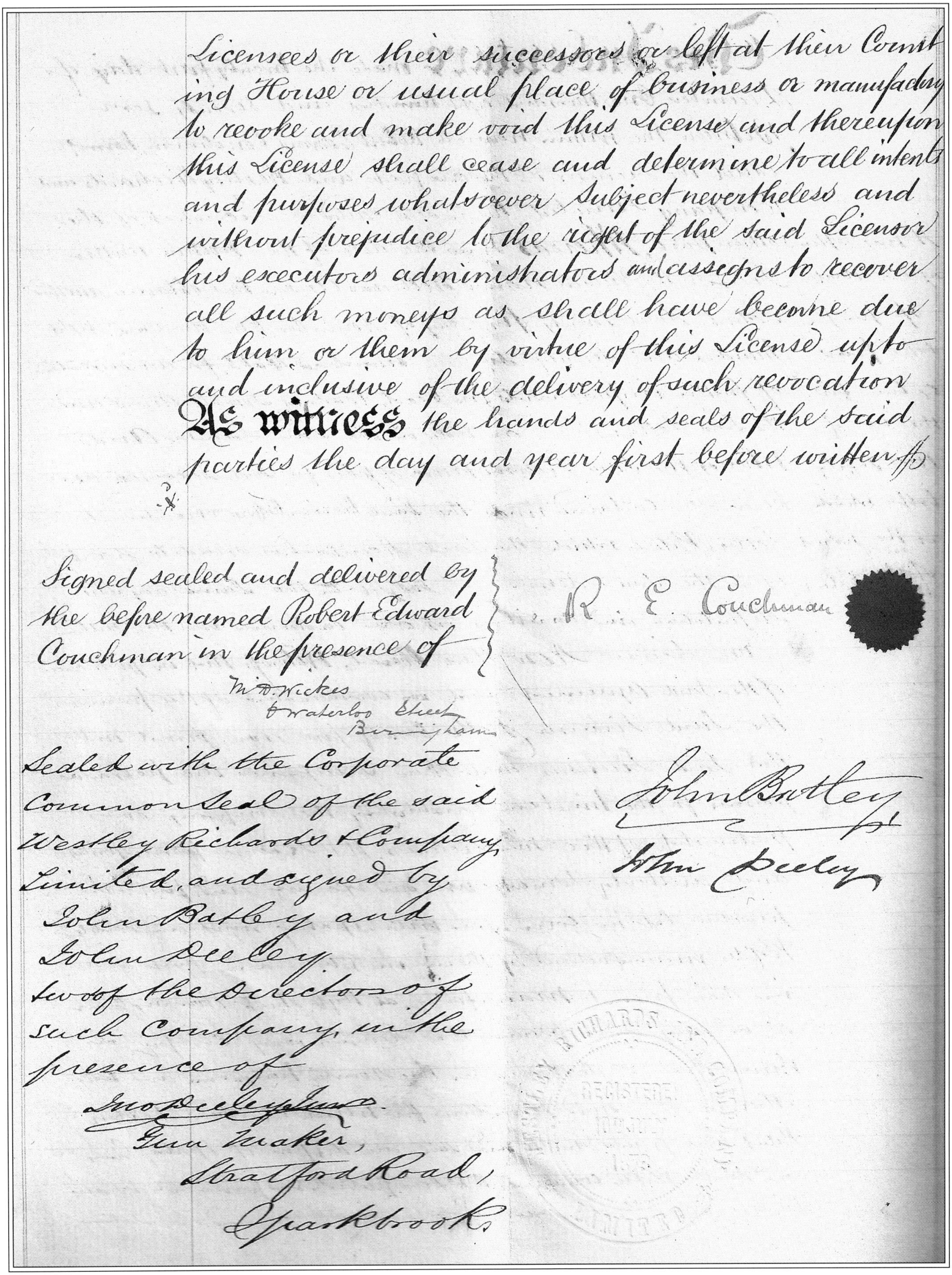

Licensees or their successors or left at their Counting House or usual place of business or manufactory to revoke and make void this License and thereupon this License shall cease and determine to all intents and purposes whatsoever Subject nevertheless and without prejudice to the right of the said Licensor his executors administrators and assigns to recover all such moneys as shall have become due to him or them by virtue of this License up to and inclusive of the delivery of such revocation **As witness** the hands and seals of the said parties the day and year first before written

Signed sealed and delivered by the before named Robert Edward Couchman in the presence of
    T. D. Wickes
    Waterloo Street
    Birmingham

      R. E. Couchman

Sealed with the Corporate Common Seal of the said Westley Richards & Company Limited and signed by John Batley and John Deeley two of the directors of such Company in the presence of
    Jno Deeley
    Gun Maker,
    Stratford Road,
    Sparkbrook

      John Batley
      Wm Deeley

Page 6 of the first license ever issued for the Anson & Deeley action on June 22, 1876 (see Appendix for pages 2–5).

- In November of 1876, Anson patents his dickey bird safety.
- In December of 1877, Couchman is granted license to use Anson's new safety mechanism while Anson was allegedly independent from Westley Richards. Couchman immediately licenses this safety to Brazier & Sons.
- All of Couchman's proceeds from the A&D action and Anson safety business were to be paid back to Westley Richards & Co., a firm on whose Board of Directors he probably sat.
- Couchman could "assign" his license to other gunmakers with the written permission of Westley Richards & Co., a virtual *fait acompli*.
- By 1879, Couchman was termed the "proprietor" of the A&D patent as well as the Anson safety patent.

Put all of this together with the fact that John Deeley was a financial *wunderkind*, as well as a very sharp businessman, and it doesn't take much to extrapolate the following likely scenario: John Deeley probably saw the A&D action and William Anson's inventiveness as his pot of gold at the end of the gun business rainbow. To best attain that treasure, he decided to set Anson up as foreman of a satellite production/R&D facility. On paper, the managerial head of that operation would be Robert Couchman, an effective extension of Westley Richards. And to ostensibly "separate" the licensing of A&D guns (as well as other Anson and Deeley patents) from Westley Richards & Co. proper, the seminal license for these inventions was issued to Couchman.

At this point, the logical question is: Just why would John Deeley want to establish such a separation? The answer is that it could well have been expanded business opportunities.

To understand this, it is well to keep in mind that Westley Richards & Co. was an active competitor in the international gun trade at the time and naturally vied for sales against a host of other Birmingham gunmakers. And now, Westley's had just come up with the *avant garde* gun mechanism of the age. But this achievement was a double-edged sword. On one hand, it imbued Westley's with great opportunity, but on the other hand, that potential also came with a good deal of fear, suspicion and resentment from other gunmakers who were likely to see themselves as being held hostage by a major competitor such as Westley Richards.

In order to maximize licensing opportunities for and income from the A&D action, along with other William Anson creations, John Deeley may have thought it best to create an independent company to represent these breakthrough mechanisms to the trade. This would have to be an entity that was friendly, amenable, and virtually non-competitive, a "middle man" if you will, namely, land surveyor Robert Couchman.

There could have also been a collateral reason for Deeley's separation of the A&D patent license, possibly the establishment of a new income stream from a wide-ranging invention acquisition-and-licensing enterprise. This satellite operation would be managed by Robert Couchman, who would solicit, protect and market the host of arms-related mechanisms being created at the time.

Deeley certainly knew there was an ocean of new ideas out there, but very little of the capital or business acumen necessary to make the most of them. After all, worthy mechanical systems were almost always created by worthy mechanics who were invariably short of net worth, not to mention the connections to make their creations profitable.

On the other hand, an independent broker like Couchman could offer these individuals counsel, financial backing, accountancy, and even a full buyout of their idea if they preferred. And, what better assurance could a gun quarter inventor have for the veracity of such a company than the one representing their own William Anson and his Anson & Deeley boxlock?

While there is no direct evidence for any of these possibilities, there is a series of very public facts in support of such thinking. Much of that is centered on a towering name of the British gun trade — W.W. Greener.

The Greener License of 1877

This story begins just a few months after William Anson leaves Westley Richards, and Couchman is granted a license for the A&D action. While it is impossible to know exactly who it was, it is certain that someone from W.W. Greener's St. Mary's Works approached Couchman in late 1876 or early 1877 regarding a license to make Anson & Deeley guns.

In response, Couchman apparently got approval from Westley Richards and issued Greener a license on May 24, 1877, to build sporting guns and rifles on the Anson & Deeley plan. Oddly enough, the terms of this license specified that Greener was to pay a royalty of 15 shillings per gun or double rifle, exactly the same royalty that was set for Couchman. There was no apparent mark-up to Greener. On the surface, one wonders if Couchman/Westley Richards & Co. made much profit from the Greener license, or if Couchman's per-unit royalty was merely set out for the sake of legal appearances. It appears as though Greener's license to make A&D guns is very likely to have been the first such license issued to a gunmaker outside of Westley Richards & Co.

Keep in mind that negotiations for this license had to have begun well prior to its issuance. In other words, the ink was barely dry on Couchman's own license when Greener appeared in the doorway, asking for his own rights to manufacture. Quite frankly, that smells a lot like Mr. Couchman was operating as a licensing agent for Westley Richards & Co./Anson & Deeley.

With his new A&D license in hand, it appears as though Greener wasted no time in an effort to make the boxlock concept his own. This report appeared in the March 1, 1878, edition of *The Ironmonger*, just 10 months after Greener was licensed to make A&D guns:

We have lately, too, examined a hammerless gun made by Mr. W. Greener, of Birmingham, in which Anson and Deeley's lock is used. The principle of this gun is similar to Mr. Woodward's, that is, the cocking is effected by dropping the barrels, and a safety lever prevents accidental discharge... the ar-

rangements for fastening the barrels to the break-off are also improved. At the end of the rib, between the barrels, there is an eye or staple, which fits into a corresponding slot on the break-off. A bolt concealed in this part of the gun, and worked by the lever, has a simultaneous action with the rest of the mechanism, and passes backwards and forewards through the eye as the breech action is opened or closed....there is also a "safety" on the left side, to prevent the gun going off when cocked.*

To be perfectly candid, this sounds a whole lot like the Greener *Facil Princeps* gun of 1880, which would soon be the focal point of a very famous lawsuit. But more on that later. For now, please consider the time frame of Greener's A&D licensing and the appearance of his own hammerless gun "in which Anson and Deeley's lock is used."

To have such a gun ready for review by the press ten months after being licensed to make the original A&D gun, Greener had to start back engineering efforts and patent avoidance measures almost immediately. While this may not seem kosher, it is not at all unusual. Many companies acquire, disassemble and analyze competitive products and designs. Not many of these companies are sued for adapting the concepts they uncover, but Greener was.

In the meantime, Greener proceeded to make a tidy profit from the original A&D gun. In fact, *The Ironmonger* gave us this perspective into Greener's production, "Mr. Greener has been one of the largest manufacturers hitherto, of the Deeley & Anson hammerless gun, on which he has paid royalties for nearly 1,000..." But the late 1870s were also a harried time in John Deeley's personal life. His wife of 27 years, Elizabeth, died on April 3, 1877. She was only 50 years old. So, perhaps Deeley focused on new business ventures to help defer his grief over the loss.

Toward that end, Deeley knew that, even with Greener's license to make the A&D gun, he was still a long way from actually making it. Production of a gun takes raw forgings, tooling, dies, jigs, and personnel with experience and knowledge of the processes involved. This would have been doubly important for a new concept like the Anson & Deeley action. And even though Greener had his own factory, the obvious shortcut was to obtain semi-finished units from someone who already had the key bits on hand and working knowledge of their production.

Candidly, that could have been William Anson, Westley Richards & Co., or a firm called The Braendlin Armoury Company, Ltd., which operated from 1868 to 1889 at 1–3 Lower Lovejoy Street, Birmingham. The Braendlin Armoury premises and other businesses associated with Augustus Braendlin were actually owned by gunmaker William Tranter, most noted for his pistols. The firms of Bently & Playfair and Charles Reeves were also tenants of William Tranter,

W.W. Greener was probably the second licensee of the A&D action, after Robert Couchman. Later, Couchman and Westley Richards & Co. sued Greener for patent infringment over his *Facile Princeps* gun — Greener won.

but, I digress. Trade records suggest that a combination of Anson, Westley's and Braendlin may indeed have supplied the necessary A&D components.

Clare Stride says Anson was listed as a "gun filer" at 106 Little Greden Lane in 1877. This may well have been a branch office of Anson's already established locale at 123 Steelhouse Lane, not to mention Westley Richards' High Street facilities that he may have had access to. So, it is within the realm of possibility that the guns Anson and his workmen roughed out at any of these locations may well have included some basic units for W.W. Greener. Reports in *The Ironmonger* for January 3, 1880, also hint at Braendlin's role: *The Braendlin Armoury Company are laying down machinery, under the direction of the [A&D] patentees for the production of Powell's modification of the Deeley & Anson patent, by which it is believed the cost may be reduced at least 50 per cent, without any sensible deterioration in the quality or efficiency of the weapon.*

Then, on February 28, 1880, this report appeared in *The Ironmonger*: *By arrangement with the patentees, Messrs. Deeley and Anson, the Braendlin Armoury Company have been for some time past occupied in the mechanical manufacture of the component parts of the hammerless gun already described in your columns, which was the special feature of the recent gun exhibition here, and within the next few days it is hoped that the final process of "assembling," or putting together, will be successfully completed.*

With this stage, a new era will have dawned for the Birmingham gun trade, as it is believed that the mechanical process will effect a saving of quite 40 percent in the cost of manufacture, without affecting he efficiency of the gun.

There is no intention of monopolizing the benefits of the process, which will be freely open to all licensees of the patents, and as the process will be continued to the vital parts of the gun, it will allow the exercise of individual taste and fancy in the general form of the ornamentation of the weapon. In other words, the company are laying themselves out to manufacture for the trade, and as the particular patent chosen is the most popular one in the market — over 2,000 specimens having already been sold, and the demand being still on the increase — there is every prospect of a large business for some years to come.

Cognoscenti will correctly discern that *The Ironmonger's* January 1880 reference to "Powell" is the well-known Birmingham gunmaker William Powell, a very early licensee of the A&D patent. In fact, about 500 of their first guns were fitted with a unique Powell locking system.

William Powell Licenses A&D Guns

Thanks to research by Stephen Helsley, it is now known that the famous Birmingham gunmaker William Powell obtained an early license for A&D guns. Records show that Powell's first A&D boxlock (ser. no. 6524) was finished up on August 1, 1877. Thus, Powell must have approached Robert Couchman and acquired rights to produce guns on the A&D design in 1876 or early 1877, roughly within the same time frame as Greener. The first A&D action, combined with Powell's iconic "thumb lifter"-style top lever, was ser. no. 6707. It was sold on May 27, 1878.

As stated above, these guns were fitted with William Powell's cross-bolt locking system (Patent No. 493) of 1876. This mechanism not only made these guns unique to Powell but avoided additional fees for use of Westley Richards' sliding top bolt locking system.

After 1889, patent protection for the A&D action expired, and as a result, Powell boxlocks were no longer stamped with patent use numbers. For the sake of clarity, it should be repeated that William Powell also made a large number of orthodox A&D guns, without their patented cross bolt.

In addition, William Powell licensed the Deeley & Edge fore-end latch as well as the Anson latch, according to Helsley: "Powell began using the Deeley & Edge fore-end bolt in 1873. The earliest serial number I identified is No. 5484. For the next seven years, Powell used one of four fore-end bolts: the wedge, their provisional patent design, a few Scott's and the Deeley & Edge. In 1880, at about SN 6800, a rapid transition began to the Anson design. The Anson [is still] used for the majority of Powell guns to this day. Somewhere, the spirit of William Anson is undoubtedly smiling."

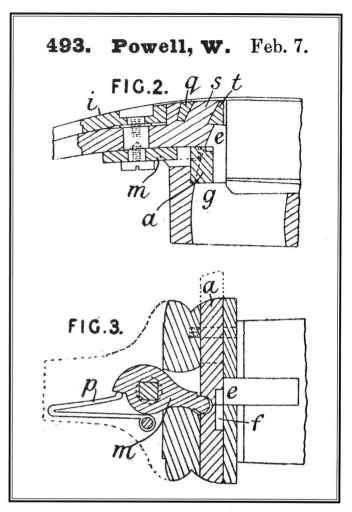

Patent illustration of William Powell's crossbolt system, Patent No. 493 of 1876.

The Charles Osborne & Edward Wilkinson License of 1879

While Greener and Powell were busy making A&D guns, two other Birmingham gunmakers decided to cash in on the Anson & Deeley technology. So, on November 3, 1879, Charles Osborne Ellis and Edward Wilkinson were granted a license to make A&D boxlock guns incorporating the Anson safety.

While this is another very early A&D license, its language is especially revealing. To quote from the Osborne/Wilkinson document, now held in our archives, this phraseology is noteworthy (emphasis added):

Robert Edward Couchman *of No. 6 Waterloo Street Birmingham in the County of Harwick, Land Surveyor, herein called* **the licensor** *of the one part and Charles Osborne Ellis and Edward William Wilkinson gun makers, trading under the style of Charles Osborne & Co., of Birmingham aforesaid gun maker herein after called the licensees of the other part.* **Whereas the licensor is the Proprietor of letters patent dated the eleventh day of May one thousand eight hundred and seventy five No. 1756**, *granted under the Great Seal of The United Kingdom of Great Britain and Ireland to William Anson and John Deeley...*

At this point, it is inarguable that Couchman had officially become the agent and *Proprietor/Licensor* of the A&D action and Anson safety, not Westley Richards & Co. directly. At least, this was the formal, legal face presented to potential licensees.

In addition, the cost of entry had gone up a bit since Greener was licensed. Osborne and Wilkinson had to pay 20 shillings per A&D gun or rifle made up at their Nos. 12 & 13 Whittall Street shop, and another 20 shillings for each Anson safety. Used together, that would be a royalty of 40 shillings for each gun, a considerable amount. This suggests there may have been enough margin in the deal to make things even more profitable for Mr. Couchman.

There's also a new and rather interesting twist in the A&D contract for Osborne and Wilkinson — they had to send the firearms or components they made to Westley Richards & Co. for inspection. Indeed. Here is the precise contract wording:

...And also that they the said licensees and their successors shall send to the offices of Messrs. Westley Richards and Company the sporting guns and double rifles or parts thereof made by them under or by virtue of the license hereby granted...to be viewed and marked by such person or persons as the said licensor shall from time to time appoint.

So, not only did Osborne and Wilkinson pay a pretty penny for the rights to these patent mechanisms, they also had to deliver their products to Westley Richards & Co. for inspection and marking, presumably with a sequential use number. This not only amounted to strict quality control, but a rather overt effort on the part of Couchman/Westley's to keep track of exactly how many A&D guns Wilkinson made and owed royalties on. Altogether, it resulted in a hefty price in money, time and trouble. And once again, this codicil strongly implies that there was a distinct business connection between Couchman and Westley Richards & Co.

Even so, there was a goodly number of quality A&D boxlock guns made with either the Osborne or Wilkinson names on them, many of which survive today.

The Birmingham Gun and Sporting Implement Exhibition of 1879

In 1879, an exhibit was held in Birmingham to showcase that city's gun and sporting goods industry, and a great part of it focused on the latest products of various gunmakers.

For the trade press, the run-up to this event was centered on a wealth of exciting news, especially that of Westley Richards' new hammerless boxlock. This report appeared in the August 9, 1879, issue of *The Ironmonger* in which the journalist curiously transposes the key names involved:

The hammerless gun, Deeley & Anson's patent, has had a great run this summer, and... promises to extend under the fostering influence of reduced prices and improved methods of manufacture. Licenses for the manufacture of this gun, with slight modifications, have been taken out by nearly all the leading Birmingham and London gunmakers, most of whom produce it in two or more grades, representing different qualities of finish at corresponding prices. For the first or highest quality the price is £40. That is the Westley Richards Company's price...

And so it was. The runaway star of the firearm exhibition was indeed Westley Richards & Co. and its Anson & Deeley gun. As evidence, I present this portion of a correspondent's report in *The Ironmonger* of December 6, 1879:

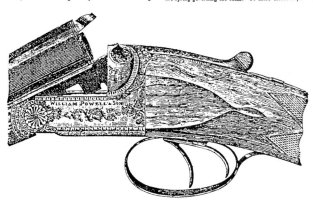
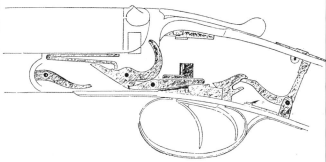

The Ironmonger ran this review and evaluation of the new Westley Richards A&D action at the time of the 1879 Birmingham Exhibition. Curiously, the first gun illustrated carries William Powell's identification, and the second shows Powell's new crossbolt.

[The] *Westley Richards & Co...hammerless gun — Deeley & Anson's patent — which is generally admitted to be "the gun of the future," and was certainly the gun of the Birmingham Exhibition. As this is the parent of most of the hammerless varieties now before the public, the principles embodied in it being licensed to no less than fifteen different makers...*

It is a light, well-proportioned and admirably-finished weapon, which prepossesses by its symmetry and perfect balance and abundantly justifies the prepossession by its shooting qualities and advantages in the field.

It differs from all hammerless guns previously introduced, firstly in the greater strength and simplicity of its lock mechanism, which contains only about half the average number of parts and secondly and chiefly by the novel arrangement of the levers and safety bolt, by means of which the simple action of opening the gun to put in the cartridges effectually locks as well as cocks both the triggers. Thus the sportsman and his friends are guarded against the common danger in cover-shooting of premature discharge through the accidental contact of the triggers either with some projecting twig or branch, or with the clothes or person of the sportsman himself.

From his description, it appears as though this particular correspondent may not have been too familiar with the inner workings of an A&D gun, and as in the December report, the patent names are again transposed as the "Deeley & Anson's patent."

However, it is especially enlightening to read that there were at least fifteen contemporary gunmakers that were licensed to make guns made on the A&D action. This certainly included W.W. Greener, Charles Osborne, Edward Wilkinson, William Powell, Bentley & Playfair and some ten others. After the A&D design fell into public domain in 1889, the tally of gunmakers and ironmongers offering it to sportsmen rose exponentially.

Continental A&D Guns

At some point in the late 1870s, certain Continental gunmakers began to produce A&D guns, apparently under license from Couchman/Westley Richards. These included Auguste Francotte, F.W. Heym, William Schaefer & Son, Georg/H.A. Lindner, (a.k.a., the "Charles Daly" brand sold through Schoverling, Daly & Gales of N.Y.C.) and possibly others. A good many of these guns also featured the Deeley & Edge fore-end latch and William Anson's intercepting safety sear.

Little is known about the exact licensing arrangements concerning these A&D guns, but many do carry the Anson & Deeley Patent (or "Brevete") licensing stamp along with a serialized use number. What is known is that Westley Richards & Co. and Auguste Francotte were on especially good business terms. Westley Richards also employed the services of an agent in Brussels, Belgium, to facilitate patents and legal business with that nation. His name was M. Kirkpatrick, and he lived/worked at 5 Rue de Pepiniére.

Therefore, it seems eminently logical that Deeley and Couchman arranged to license the A&D action to Francotte,

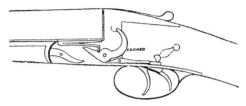

Page three of *The Ironmonger* review and evaluation of the new Westley Richards A&D action at the time of the 1879 Birmingham Exhibition.

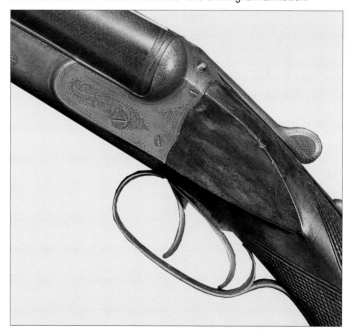

A licensed Charles Daly boxlock. The basic action undoubtedly came from the Francotte works.

who also served as their primary European production facility. Thus, it is highly likely that Francotte forged and roughed out the actions, applied the patent and use stamps to identify rights and track royalties, then sold the basic bits off to gunmakers throughout the Continent.

After May of 1889, the English A&D patent expired, but the Belgian patent may have remained in force for a bit longer. After that, Continental gunmakers could use the action without restriction or royalties to anyone. Nonetheless, they undoubtedly sourced a lot of basic actions from Francotte.

The Harrington & Richardson License of 1880

In 1879, the same year Osborne and Wilkinson were licensed, yet another opportunity to expand A&D gun profits presented itself, this time from across the Atlantic.

In those years, the U.S.A. represented one of the largest sporting firearms markets on the planet. And until the latter part of the 19th century, hammer guns had been a staple of U.S. sportsmen. But new hammerless designs from Colt and Lefever were just starting to change that norm and compete directly with hammerless sidelock guns being imported from England.

This development, and more, did not go unnoticed by British gun trade analysts, who injected a sobering note of caution in the September 18, 1880, issue of *The Ironmonger*:

The great problem at present is to find a hammerless gun suited to American wants which may be produced by machinery. The Anson & Deeley patent, which stands very high in the English market, is too expensive a weapon for extended sale in the United States, where the prime cost is nearly doubled by freight, duty and importers' profit.

For contemporary sportsmen, characterization of the A&D gun as "too expensive" may seem a bit surprising, especially since it is employed in so many affordable double guns on the market today. But keep in mind that the A&D action was cutting-edge technology at the time. In the same

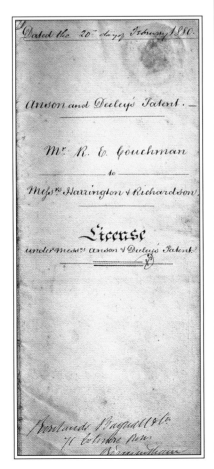

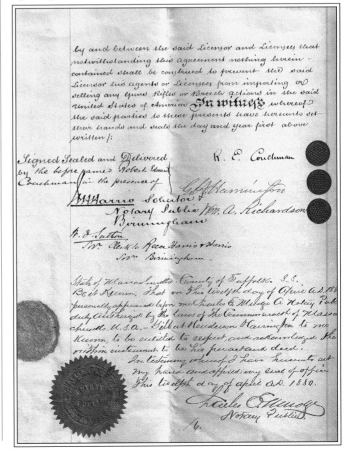

The cover, signature page and page six of Harrington & Richardson's 1880 license to produce A&D guns in the U.S. Note that it was granted and signed by Robert Couchman.

article, *The Ironmonger* also raised the spectre of competition from within the English gun trade itself:

A new hammerless gun, which promises to prove a formidable competitor of the Anson & Deeley pattern, at all events in the Unites States, has been newly patented in this and other countries by Mr. Bonehill, and arrangements are in progress for producing it wholesale by machinery…the inventor claims for his gun, among other recommendations, that it contains fewer parts than the Anson & Deeley, is simpler in construction, and stronger, the stock being less cut away. The cocking is effected by a top lever, which is said to be preferred in the States to the under-lever principle.

While this synopsis contains a good deal of optimism for the Bonehill gun, it also contains two incorrect claims. First, the Bonehill lever-cocker actually has more parts than the Anson & Deeley gun. And secondly, there is absolutely no evidence for the claim that a top-lever cocking gun was the preferred style in the U.S. Still, Bonehill enthusiastically embraced machine-made production and sold a huge number of guns in the United States. In fact, he was one of the strongest competitors to Westley Richards/Anson & Deeley.

In response to this situation, it would not be out of character for John Deeley to imagine a way in which he could claim his share of the U.S. double-gun market by avoiding the abhorrent "freight, duty and importers' profit." His solution? Why he'd simply arrange for the guns to be made in the United States!

Toward this end, it appears as though John Deeley played something of a long shot. It is unknown whether he was responding to a prior inquiry or simply making a judicious cold call, but Deeley did send a letter to the owners of Harrington & Richardson of Worcester, Massachusetts, on November 20, 1879. This letter is still in the files of former H&R President Ted Rowe, whose family has held a controlling interest in H&R since the 1930s. In this letter, Deeley offers to license the A&D action to H&R.

It didn't take long for the owners of this fledgling U.S. gun company to see opportunity, or that opportunity was being thrust upon them. In any case, Deeley's offer worked, and on February 20, 1880, Gilbert A. Harrington and William A. Richardson licensed rights to make Anson & Deeley guns in their Worcester, Massachusetts, manufactory under the Harrington & Richardson brand. And once H&R had pulled the licensing trigger, it didn't take long for John Deeley to stoke the fires of enthusiasm.

In a letter to H&R dated March 6, 1880, (currently in the files of former H&R exec. Ted Rowe), John Deeley states that he is "shipping over some fully made guns." These could have easily come from Westley Richards & Co., William Anson or from the Braendlin Armoury. A month later, on April 12, 1880, H&R's license was notarized and sealed in Massachusetts. And once again, the licensor named was none other than Robert Couchman of Birmingham, England.

The parameters of this agreement generally coincided with earlier A&D licenses. However, H&R agreed to pay Couchman the U.S. equivalent of 15 shillings (about $84 USD today) for the first 1,000 guns made in any one year and a discounted fee of 12 shillings, 6 pence for any number beyond that made within the same year. This was essentially the same as the seminal rate in Couchman's 1876 contract of 15 shillings per gun.

Another interesting aspect of this license is that it included a production/sales challenge to H&R. Specifically, if H&R made *fewer* than 500 A&D guns in any year, then the licensor (Couchman) had the option of offering a similar A&D license to any other U.S. gunmaker he cared to. But there was also a small "out" written in. From the original document in our archives, I quote the precise language of this codicil, with emphasis added: *…it is hereby agreed between the licensor and licensees in order to insure the proper working of the said inventions in the United States of America that **if in any one year the number of guns rifles or breech actions made and sold by the licensees do not amount to five hundred then the said licensor is to be at liberty to grant licenses for the manufacture and sale of guns rifles or breech actions to any other company firm or person he may think fit in the said United States.** But in order to give the said licensees time to prepare for the setting up of machinery and tools for the production and manufacture of such guns rifles or breech actions **the number required to be made within the first twelve months after the date of this agreement may extend over two years.***

In plain language, this last clause allowed H&R to make as few as 500 guns (250 per year) within the first two years of the contract, with their production bogey being 500 for year three, and each year thereafter. Previously, this clause has been misconstrued, misinterpreted or misunderstood to mean that H&R was *allowed* to make 500 guns per year — or *did* make 500 per year. Neither of these conclusions are correct. They were *required* to make 500 guns per year, by year three, or face the possibility of expanded U.S. competition.

Finally, there is one more important provision of the license regarding competitive A&D guns within the U.S. marketplace: *…**nothing herein contained shall be construed to prevent the said licensor his agents or licensees from importing and selling any guns, rifles** or breech actions in the said United States of America.*

In other words, even though H&R had a license to make Anson & Deeley guns, they did not have exclusive U.S. marketing rights. Their products would still be in direct competition with A&D guns imported from England and sold through other U.S. firms. Indeed, this was yet another incentive and a challenge for H&R. Westley Richards and Westley Richards-produced doubles were marketed in the U.S. at the very same time by firms such as J. Palmer O'Neil & Co. and Pittsburgh Fire Arms Co., both of Pittsburgh, Pennsylvania.

Given that the H&R license was not finalized until April 12, 1880, and that importation and set-up of machinery and tools at H&R's plant had to have taken at least 12 months, as suggested by the license language, one projection seems fairly safe, which is that H&R most likely delivered its first A&D double guns to U.S. customers no sooner than late 1882.

A glimpse at the H&R set-up process is also provided in the July 17, 1880, issue of England's *The Ironmonger*:

The Braendlin Armoury Company, which had laid down new and costly machinery for the production of Deeley & Anson's hammerless gun have now completely surmounted all mechanical difficulties, and are sending in to be marked for royalty, by the patentees, some excellent completed specimens. In America, also, machinery is being laid down for the production of the same gun [at H&R], under arrangement with the patentees...

But timing is everything, and as H&R began to roll out its own A&D gun in 1882, other U.S. firms were already doing a brisk business in British boxlocks, according to the July 8, 1882, issue of The Ironmonger:

The American [H&R] machine made hammerless gun (Anson & Deeley's) is reported to be a very superior article to that produced in Birmingham by the same process, and the difference in price is not very considerable. It was first supposed that the manufacture of these guns by machinery would interfere very much with the sale of the hand made article, which is produced here by a number of firms under license from the patentees, but I understand from the parent firm, the Westley Richards Company, that they were never busier than at present on the Anson & Deeley gun, and that the American orders in particular are especially satisfactory.

Well now...the American gun was "very superior to that produced in Birmingham?" A great compliment indeed! In addition, this correspondent then goes on to add a rather intriguing spin to the business situation: *Mr. W.W. Greener, whose impending law-suit with the patentees of the Deeley & Anson hammerless gun is looked forward to by the trade with great interest, continues well employed...*

But while Greener's lawsuit moved forward, U.S. marketers kept boxlock orders flowing back to England, and amidst these sales and opportunities, a famous American gun company apparently missed the boat.

Parker Loses An Opportunity — But Gains a Classic

Before we continue with the H&R saga, a bit of historical perspective is now in order. By concluding the Anson & Deeley license agreement in 1880, Harrington & Richardson might well have spurred the creation of an iconic American shotgun — the Parker hammerless. This intriguing turn of history is strongly suggested by a letter penned to H&R by Robert Couchman at the direction of John Deeley. The original remains in the files of former H&R President Ted Rowe, but a copy is reproduced in this book (see Appendix).

As noted, this letter was completely handwritten and without scrupulous regard to paragraphing or grammar. But to advance the historical record and its understanding, I provide the text here, broken into paragraphs for easier comprehension:

82 High Street
Birmingham, England
Jan. 7th, 1883

Messrs. Harrington & Richardson
Worcester, Mass. USA

Gentlemen:
We have an application from Parker Bros. Meriden, Conn., asking us to give them a license to make our hammerless action. This of course we are unable to do as you are our sole licensee for the whole of the United States.

We have written to them & asked them to communicate with you. As the sale of this gun is likely to increase very much in the States, we believe it worth your while considering the advisability of supplying actions & barrels to gunmakers in the United States, as by this means you would not only make a very large trade in actions [and] barrels upon which you may assure a remunerative profit but keep the said gunmakers from bringing other guns into competition with yours.

We shall have some improvements to bring under your notice shortly as we have patented a great improvement in the present hammerless gun, dispensing with the dogs. It is of course on the same lines as the old one, exactly the same lockwork, the same principle of leverage, but one central lever instead of two dogs. With this invention the gun can be put together with perfect ease when the hammers are down. We hope your trade is increasing & wish you a happy and prosperous New Year.

Yours Very Truly
Anson & Deeley
Per John Deeley
Robt. E [Couchman]

There are a number of revelations to be gained from this letter. The primary one, as we've already disclosed, was a desire by Parker Bros. to license the A&D action as the basis for its own hammerless gun. Also note the date involved, January 7, 1883. Since Parker had already contacted Anson & Deeley about licensing the A&D boxlock, the possibility of doing so had to have cropped up at Parker Bros. sometime in 1882.

With Couchman's regrets, Parker's missed opportunity undoubtedly left that company in a quandary. The American double-gun market was quickly moving away from hammer guns like their current Parker and toward modern hammerless designs like the Colt or Lefever. Unfortunately, H&R had shut Parker out of the A&D action.

The second nugget of information contained within the Anson & Deeley letter is that Parker was encouraged to contact H&R to potentially arrange for a cooperative business arrangement. In this, H&R might supply Parker with barrels and A&D actions in order to facilitate the introduction of a

Parker A&D hammerless gun. This could potentially expand H&R's market for A&D guns in the U.S. and minimize competition at the same time. It is unknown whether Parker Bros. made any such contact, but subsequent events suggest they did not. Instead, Parker Bros. apparently decided to create their own hammerless gun.

Either collateral to this effort or previous to it, there is some evidence that Parker experimented with a sidelock hammerless design. This is supported by at least a half dozen actual guns that have cropped up. These appear to be modifications of Parker hammer guns and follow the general mechanical principles of the Lefever. If these are indeed Parker prototypes, their development was apparently abandoned.

Nonetheless, in 1884, Parker's Charles A. King was tasked to design a unique Parker hammerless action, which was eventually introduced to the U.S. market in late 1888. But under the legal circumstances extant, King's job was no walk in the park. In creating the new Parker action, King had to be very careful not to infringe upon any key aspects of the Anson & Deeley design, which enjoyed U.S. patent protection until 1890. This was especially prudent since W.W. Greener was being sued over this very issue.

King's engineering mandate could well be the reason why the Parker gun's mechanism is curiously complicated and even mechanically pained in some respects. This characteristic extends to the fore-end latch, which outwardly appears to be a Deeley & Edge mechanism, but isn't. Here, King used a cam-and-bevel lever interface to lock the fore-end in place. It works well enough and narrowly avoids patent issues, but it isn't as direct and robust as the Deeley & Edge latch. In summary, the resulting Parker hammerless gun looked attractive, functioned well enough and apparently drew no infringement litigation from Anson & Deeley. By the time the Parker hammerless appeared, the A&D design had fallen into public domain anyway. Still, "Old Reliable" became an American classic.

We know that King's inspiration for the Parker hammerless was indeed the Anson & Deeley boxlock. According to the book *The Parker Story: the most successful, and most copied* [hammerless gun] *was an 1875 patent by Messrs. Anson and Deeley (A&D) of the Westley Richards & Co. for a "box lock" design… The basic design that Charles King eventually chose to develop for the new Parker Brothers hammerless gun was the boxlock action.*

Even to the casually trained eye, there can be little argument that the resulting Parker hammerless gun is a boxlock at its foundational core. But it was never intended to be an improvement of the A&D design. Instead, it was deliberately designed to be different — different enough to avoid litigation. However, what if the timing had been reversed between H&R and Parker? What if Parker had captured rights to the A&D action ahead of Harrington & Richardson? Could U.S. sporting gun history have been very much different? It's an interesting possibility to contemplate.

The final revelation of the Anson & Deeley letter is that the benefits of Anson & Deeley Patent No. 1833 of 1883 would soon be offered to H&R as the sole U.S. licensee. This enhancement did away with the dual cylindrical cocking dogs that protruded from the A&D frame knuckle and replaced them with a single extension on the forearm that activated both internal cocking limbs as the barrels opened. This also allowed the gun to be assembled after the tumblers had been snapped down, something that could not be done with the original A&D design. Apparently, this improvement was never adopted by H&R, as every H&R double that has appeared so far has the original-style dual cocking dogs.

It is also important to note that Patent No. 1833 connected the Purdey underbolt to Westley Richards' existing sliding top bolt via an ingenious linkage devised by William Anson, but such enhancements may well have come too late in the production life of H&R's double gun. Patent No. 1833 would not have been ready to incorporate until late 1883 or 1884, and by that time, H&R had apparently seen the handwriting on the wall and decided to stop making double-barrel shotguns. That was a bit down the road, however.

H&R Gears Up to Manufacture the A&D Boxlock

Four years earlier, the future for H&R seemed much more promising. With exclusive production rights in hand, H&R went ahead with its Anson & Deeley double-gun project in 1880. According to documents in our archives, H&R's agreement with A&D officially began on April 12, 1880, and probably ran through to late 1884 or early 1885. Production numbers have been "guesstimated" by various sources at between 2,000 and 3,000 guns, but the only basis for this has been observed serial numbers, as H&R records have been lost.

Even former H&R President Ted Rowe and marketing executive Ernie Foster have no information concerning how many doubles were made. "But it wasn't many," according to Rowe's assessment. The highest serial number they've seen or heard about was 2115. "But that doesn't mean H&R started with No. 1," said Rowe. "They could well have begun anywhere." The lowest serial number known so far is ser. no. 50, last known to be in the collection of double gunsmith Brad Bachelder of Grand Rapids, Michigan.

Again, documents in our archives reveal that H&R was authorized to make 500+ A&D guns per year for four years. If that rate of production were realized for the entire term of the agreement, then a total output of 2,000-plus guns might be expected. However, various sources quote slightly different time frames for the H&R branded doubles. For example, the *Blue Book of Gun Values* stipulates this information: "…10 or 12 ga., 28, 30, or 32 in. damascus barrels, hammerless boxlock action, 4 grades of European walnut stock and fore-end, 4 levels of engraving, Anson & Deeley markings on lockplate, H&R markings on barrels, ser. no. 01-3000+. Mfg. 1883–1887."

Another resource, *Niles Guide to Affordable Double Barrel Shotguns in America 1875–1945*, states that "H&R doubles [were] made from 1882–1886."

John Deeley • CHAPTER 2

To add its own perspective, the H&R website says that, "In 1880 the firm [H&R] was named sole North American licensee for England's Anson & Deeley double-barrel hammerless shotgun," but it does not specify an end date. Finally, the *Harrington & Richardson Sporting Arms 1871–Centennial Catalog–1971*, references Anson & Deeley doubles on page 19 but only provides a time frame of "prior to 1900."

Once H&R finalized the contract on April 12, 1880, it would have taken a certain amount of time for production to start, for stock to be built up and for market introduction to take place. While it is difficult to know exactly when the first public announcement was made, former H&R President Ted Rowe has an 1881 document on file that shows H&R asked

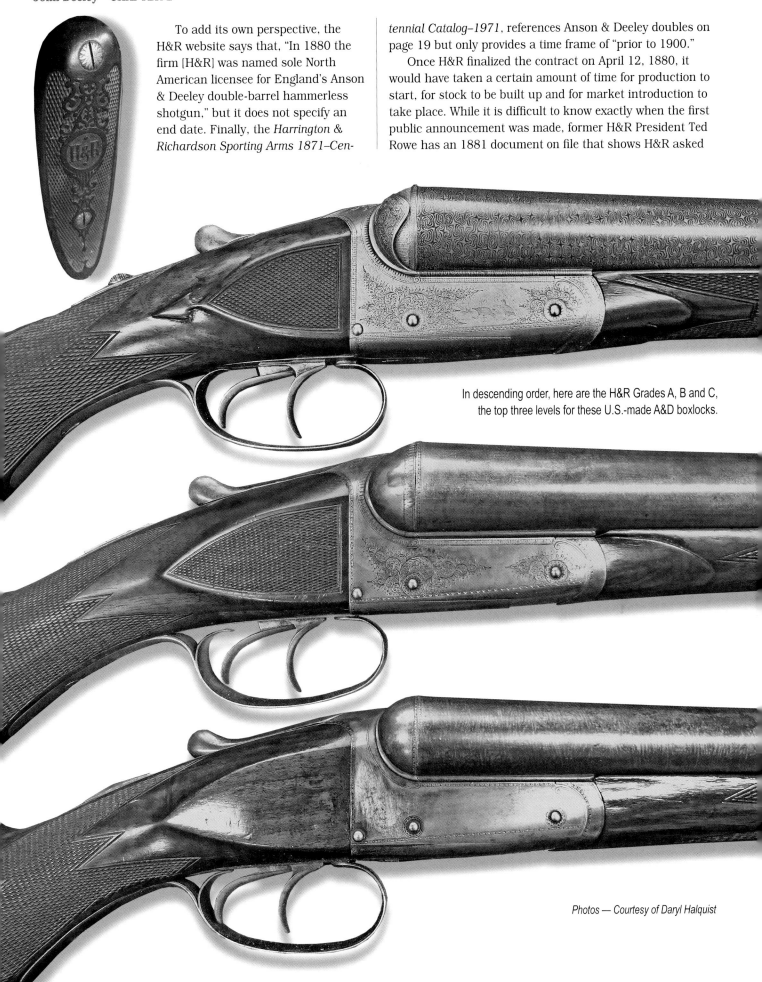

In descending order, here are the H&R Grades A, B and C, the top three levels for these U.S.-made A&D boxlocks.

Photos — Courtesy of Daryl Halquist

John Deeley for an "extension" on its production start-up schedule. One can only assume that it was granted.

Such benevolence may have been easy for Deeley. There was a spirit of ebullience in the British arms trade at the time, and according to the July 22, 1881, issue of *The Ironmonger*, this optimism included U.S. production of the A&D gun:

Among the busiest firms are Mr. Bonehill, Messrs. Hollis & Son, Messrs. Scott & Son and Mr. Greener. The Westley Richards Company are also doing a large business with the States just now in their hammerless gun (Anson & Deeley), which is also being made in considerable quantities for the same market by other makers under license from the patentees.

This business excitement continued in the November 12, 1881, issue of *The Ironmonger*: *The Westley Richards Company, Mr. Greener, Messrs. Scott, Messrs. Powell, Mr. Brunn, Messrs Bland & Son and Mr. Bonehill are at no loss for orders for hammerless guns for these [US] and other markets.*

Then, in November of 1882, *Forest & Stream* carried an ad for H&R doubles, which were offered through sporting goods retailer Schoverling, Daly and Gales. Other distributors eventually included the E.K. Tryon Jr. Co. of Philadelphia, C.E. Overbaugh & Co. of New York, Meacham Hardware, William Read & Sons of Boston, and more.

If we accept late 1882 as an approximate date of introduction, then a two-year "lag time" between agreement and product introduction seems plausible, considering the circumstances under which the guns were made.

This 1880–1882 prep time also tends to align with Clare Stride's research of 1883 Birmingham trade records. These list William Anson as a "gunmaker" at 123½ Steelhouse Lane and as a "gun manufacturer" at Egyptian Hall, Slaney Street. In reality, it would have taken some amount of time for the H&R agreement to initiate model and prototype production in Birmingham. We also know that a small number of fully made guns were sent to H&R by John Deeley. In addition, Anson may have been making semi-finished guns for H&R for some period of time in order to help facilitate introduction.

But all good things must come to an end, including H&R double guns. So, with a host of disparate facts taken into consideration, the best guess as to the end of production is late 1884 or very early in 1885. But this should be tempered with the potential that some in-stock H&R doubles may have remained on hand to be sold at a later date. It is impossible to determine exactly when the last of those guns went out the door.

Why did H&R stop making doubles? More than likely, the reason is that there was no money in it. The cost of production was expensive, the retail price was high, their market segment was small, and domestic competition was robust. In addition, H&R apparently saw a more lucrative market for affordable pistols, which their company was well-positioned to make.

The Greener Flap of 1880

While H&R was preparing to make A&D guns in the U.S., things were getting a bit sticky back in England. As already mentioned, W.W. Greener was apparently not content with making double guns built on a patent held by one of his competitors, much less paying 15 shillings each for the privilege.

While there is no direct evidence in support of it, there is an extremely high likelihood that at least one of the A&D guns that Greener processed through his St. Mary's works manufactory served a purpose beyond profit. Odds are, it was analyzed and back-engineered to advance Greener's own research and development project, that of a new barrel-cocking hammerless gun of his own. The upshot was that Greener patented his famous *Facile Princeps* hammerless gun on March 2, 1880.

John Deeley was not amused. Deeley felt the *Facile Princeps* mechanics clearly infringed on the A&D patent. As a result, Deeley directed Robert Couchman to file suit against Greener for infringement. In fact, the court action itself is officially listed as Couchman vs. Greener, not Westley Richards & Co. vs. Greener, or Anson & Deeley vs. Greener. Thus, by virtue of the suit's filing, there's little doubt that plaintiff Robert Couchman was a legal surrogate for Westley Richards as well as John Deeley and William Anson.

For more detail, here is I.M. Crudgington and D.J. Baker from *The British Shogun, Volume Two: The importance of this*

> November 26, 1881.] THE IRONMONGER
>
> **Paris Electrical Exhibition.**—A net profit of 16,000*l.* is stated to have resulted from the recent Paris Exhibition.
>
> **Alleged Infringement of Patent in Birmingham.**—In the Court of Exchequer, the case of Couchman *v.* Greener, which was an action to recover royalties from the defendant, a manufacturer of small-arms at Birmingham, was recently decided by Baron Pollock without a jury. Mr. Joseph Smith, gunmaker, Loveday Street, Birmingham, said he had been in business as a gunmaker for upwards of 39 years, and was a director of the Birmingham Small Arms Company. He had made himself acquainted with hammerless guns, including Anson and Deeley's patent. The peculiarity of that patent was the mechanism and the raising of the hammers by means of an extension of the fore-end of the barrels. Such a result was not obtained in the same manner before the patent was taken out. The entire cocking was begun and finished by the depression of the fore-end of the barrels. Mr. Anson, an action-filer, of Birmingham, said he was a co-partner with Mr. Deeley in the patent in question, and corroborated the evidence given by Mr. Smith. Mr. Webster, in opening the defendant's case, represented the case for the plaintiff as being the extraordinary question whether or not an action was within the licence. The defendant had paid royalties to the extent of 745*l.*, and was willing to pay upon 200 and 300 more guns at the present time. The defendant now believed he had discovered a gun which, achieving a similar result to that of the plaintiff's patent, was outside that patent, and hence the reason for the present action. Sir F. Bramwell, on behalf of the defendant, said there was no doubt whatever of the utility, novelty, and value of the plaintiff's patent. In the result his lordship gave judgment in favour of the defendant, with costs.

This notice in *The Ironmonger* publicized Greener's initial win in the legal battle over the alleged A&D patent infringement.

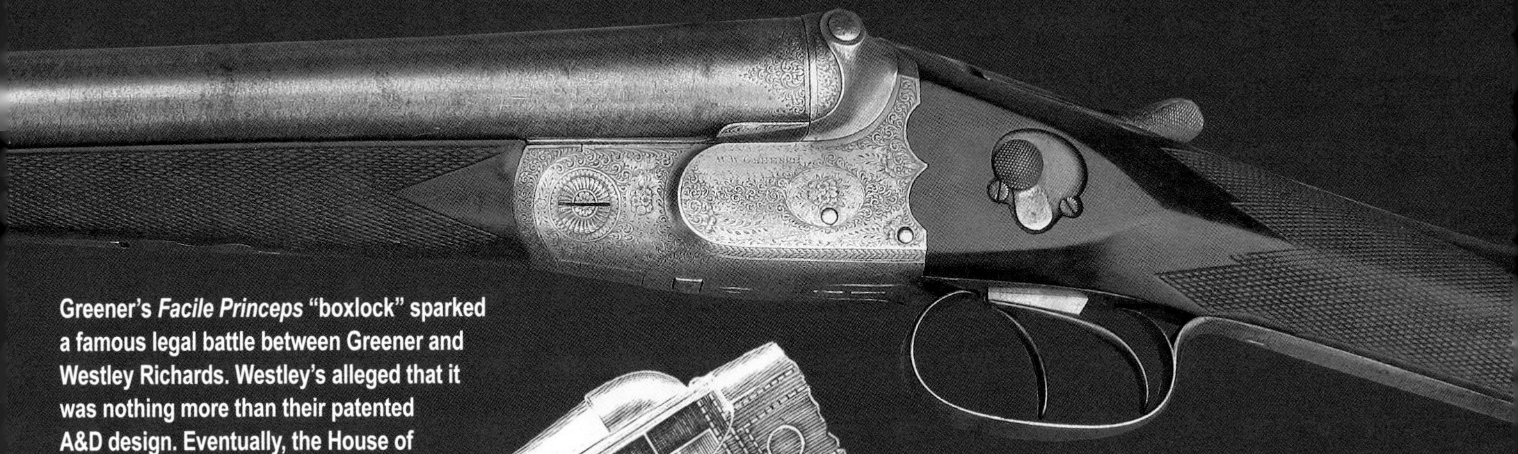

Greener's *Facile Princeps* "boxlock" sparked a famous legal battle between Greener and Westley Richards. Westley's alleged that it was nothing more than their patented A&D design. Eventually, the House of Lords decided the case in Greener's favor.

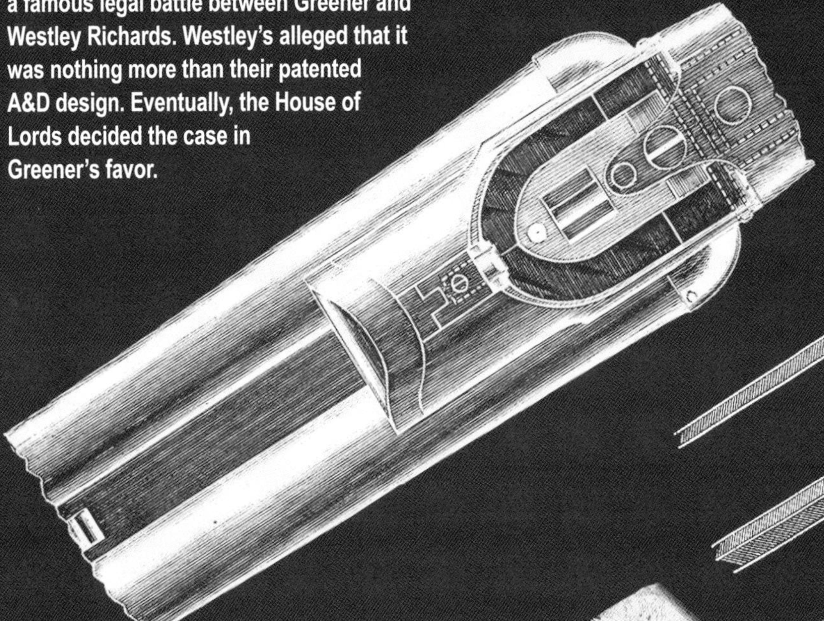

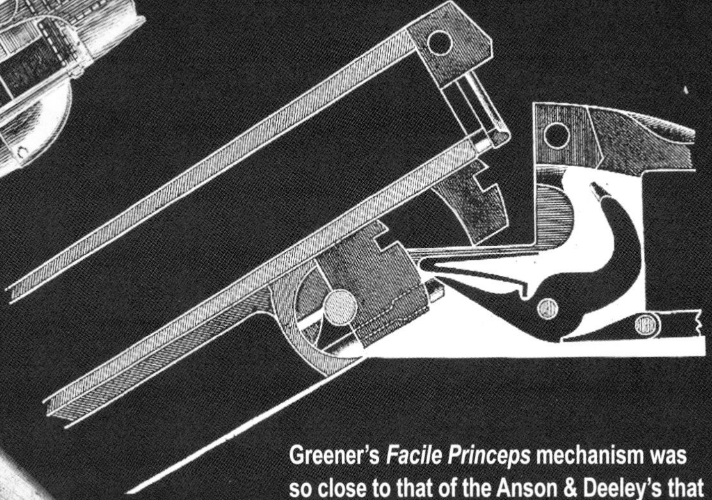

Greener's *Facile Princeps* mechanism was so close to that of the Anson & Deeley's that Greener was sued for infringement.

The unique bits of Greener's *Facile Princeps* are seen here. The "fork"-style cocking arms and the single (black) cocking dog that forces them upward to set the tumblers.

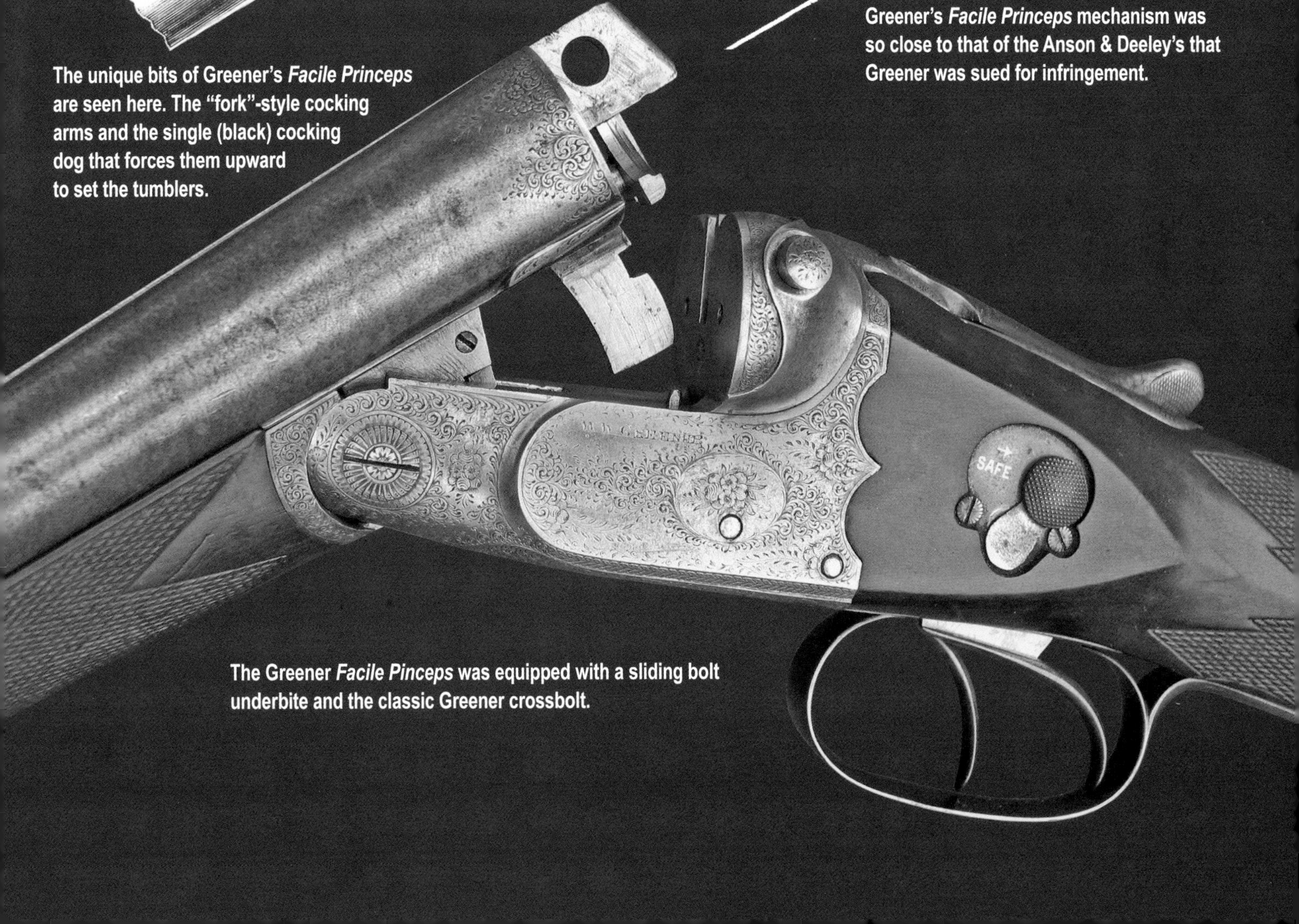

The Greener *Facile Pinceps* was equipped with a sliding bolt underbite and the classic Greener crossbolt.

gun [Facile Princeps] lies in the fact that it precipitated legal action between the patentee [Greener] and Robert Edward Couchman, who was a director of Westley Richards & Co., and a close friend of Westley Richards himself. Greener had taken out a license on 24 May, 1877, from Couchman to build sporting guns and rifles on the Anson & Deeley plan. Under the terms of the license Greener agreed to pay a royalty of 15 shillings per gun or double rifle... Couchman's claim was that Greener's Facile Princeps action infringed the Anson and Deeley patent. He claimed £15,000 damages and, in addition 15 shillings per Facile Princeps gun.

As John Deeley claimed an infringement of intellectual property against Greener, cruel fate dealt him a deep personal loss at the same time. His eldest daughter Elizabeth died on May 19, 1881, at the age of only 30 years. It had to be a terrible blow to him, as well as Elizabeth's husband, Arthur Parker. So, perhaps it was just as well that a few months elapsed before the legal battle with Greener heated up.

The first hearing of the Greener case was held in the Court of Exchequer in November of 1881. For a summary of the details, I turn to a report published in the November 26, 1881, edition of *The Ironmonger*:

Alleged Infringement of Patent in Birmingham. — In the Court of Exchequer, the case of Couchman v. Greener, which was an action to recover royalties from the defendant, a manufacturer of small arms at Birmingham, was recently decided by Baron Pollock without a jury.

Mr. Joseph Smith, gunmaker, Loveday Street, Birmingham, said he had been in business as a gunmaker for upwards of 39 years, and was a director of the Birmingham Small Arms Company. He had made himself acquainted with hammerless guns, including Anson and Deeley's patent. The peculiarity of that patent was the mechanism and the raising of the hammers by means of an extension of the fore-end of the barrels. Such a result was not obtained in the same manner before the patent was taken out. The entire cocking was begun and finished by the depression of the fore-end of the barrels.

Mr. [William] Anson, an action filer, of Birmingham, said he was a co-partner with Mr. Deeley in the patent in question, and corroborated the evidence given by Mr. Smith.

Mr. Webster, in opening the defendant's case, represented the case for the plaintiff as being the extraordinary question whether or not an action was within the license. The defendant had paid royalties to the extent of £745 and was willing to pay upon 200 and 300 more guns at the present time.

The defendant now believed he had discovered a gun which, achieving a similar result to that of the plaintiff's patent, was outside that patent, and hence the reason for the present action. Sir F. Bramwell, on behalf of the defendant, said there was no doubt whatever of the utility, novelty, and value of the plaintiff's patent. In the result, his lordship gave judgment in favour of the defendant, with costs.

In other words, Greener admitted that the A&D patent was good but that his gun was different. Pollock agreed and Greener prevailed.

Westley Richards/Couchman appealed this ruling, and in April of 1883, the Appeals Court also ruled in Greener's favor, but John Deeley and Westley Richards/Couchman were still not ready to give up. The case was deemed to be quite important at the time, and it was turned over to The House of Lords in 1884 for ultimate resolution.

It is interesting to note that, in presenting his case to the House of Lords, Greener allowed his licensing of the Anson & Deeley gun to work against him. In *The British Shotgun, Vol. Two*, I.M. Crudgington and D.J. Baker describe Greener's *faux pas*: *Greener had attempted to counter Couchman's claim by citing the Walsh self-cocking action of 1874, but this tack was ruled inadmissible in that by taking out a license [for the A&D gun] he had accepted the goodness of the Anson and Deeley patent.*

Nonetheless, Greener won again, "...but not unanimously" according to Leslie B. Taylor in his book, *A Brief History of The Westley Richards Firm*. For a rationale and summary of Greener's triumph, I turn again to I.M. Crudgington and D.J. Baker:

The House of Lords ruled that the two patents different [sic] *fundamentally because, whereas the fore-end was essential to the working of the Anson and Deeley, it was merely desirable in the case of the Greener. On this point Couchman's case was dismissed. Greener was awarded costs, as had happened at the two previous hearings, so the total bill for Westley Richards & Co. must have been considerable.*

In *The British Sporting Gun And Rifle*, Donald Dallas adds additional perspective from one of the judges: *...Lord Justice Lindley remarked 'the scheme is different, the idea is different; that is to my mind so plain, when you look at the guns and mechanism that it presents to me no difficulty in the matter; in other words, I say the two guns are worked upon different ideas altogether.*

W.W. Greener could not have agreed more: *...The introduction of my Facile Princeps hammerless action caused much jealousy... Fortunately after a lengthy trial, lasting some years, judgment was given in the House of Lords in my favour when it was ruled that my system did not infringe the plaintiff's patent...*

John Deeley Regroups

The House of Lords verdict in Greener's favor was a body blow for John Deeley, William Anson and Westley Richards. They had essentially been denied a virtual "master patent" on the idea of using the fall of a gun's barrels to cock the action. What's more, Greener had effectively been given a green light to build as many *Facile Princeps* guns as he could sell, and with Greener's established market share and highly capable St. Mary's Works manufactory, that could be a lot of guns.

Indeed, Greener did make thousands of *Facile Princeps* guns and sold them all around the world. But unlike the Anson & Deeley action, no other maker ever licensed Greener's *Facile Princeps*, although a few were sold under other trade names, notably that of E.M. Reilly. But perhaps Greener wasn't interested in licensing the gun, preferring instead

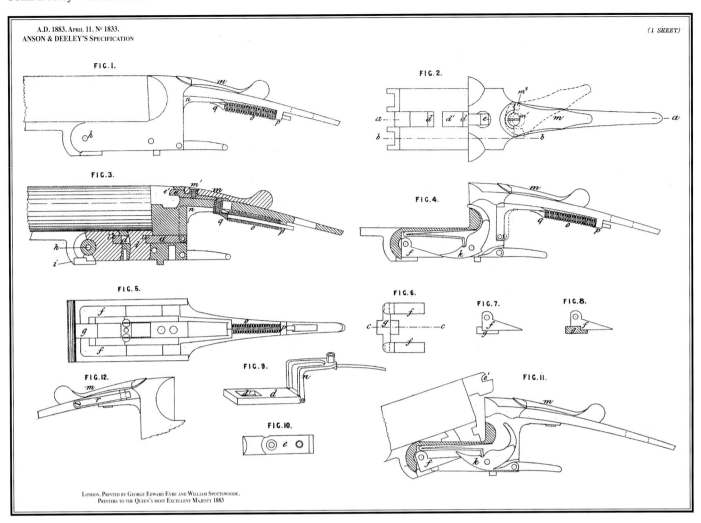

to keep it an exclusive in-house product. Regardless, this containment allowed the A&D design to become the world standard of boxlock guns. Surely, there must have been some amount of satisfaction in that for John Deeley and William Anson.

Still, by the time the Greener suit was resolved, there were only five years of patent protection left on the Westley Richards A&D action. After 1889, it would lapse into the public domain and lose its power to generate income. Doubtlessly, John Deeley thought he had to do something to regain an advantage, and he had to do it fast.

Toward that end, patent records show that he may have tried to refine and enhance the primacy of the A&D action during the Greener litigation. This is exemplified in Anson & Deeley Patent No. 1833 of April 11, 1883. Instead of two cylindrically nosed cocking dogs protruding from the action knuckle, this concept used a central extension on the fore-end that engaged and rotated the two dogs inside the action. These pivoted on the hinge pin. In truth, this was the new aspect of the gun that Robert Couchman had used as an enticement to H&R executives. This improvement was patented in France, exactly six months later, on October 11, 1883. The document is in our archives. In fact, the A&D No. 1833 system can be found on a number of boxlocks made at Francotte's works in Belgium.

Anson & Deeley's Patent No. 1833, which incorporates the Purdey underbolt system into the A&D action. Here, the Purdey bolt is activated by the "drop leg" connector between the top lever and bolt (Fig. 9). This design retains the original A&D sliding top bolt, which engages the rib extension.

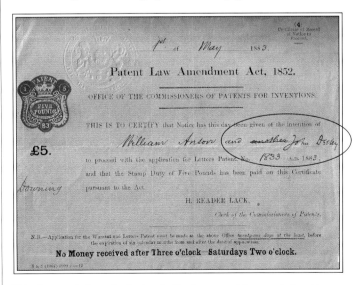

This document allowed patent protection to proceed for a central cocking dog of the A&D action. Notice that it was issued to William Anson and "another," which was subsequently crossed out to be replaced with the name John Deeley.

After patent protection lapsed, a limited number of Anson & Deeley-inspired boxlocks were made up by an obscure French firm sometime in the 1890s. These guns were St. Étienne proofed and identified with the name *Mistrál a Marseille*. The cocking and lock mechanisms followed the A&D concept but with pivot point variations for the tumblers, cocking dogs and sears. Their frames also featured sideplates to cover the works, making them appear as boxlocks but with a sidelock — *je ne sais quoi*. Regardless, they were essentially boxlocks, as was Greener's, lawsuits aside.

On the other hand, John Deeley's No. 1833 patent gained little enthusiasm in the British trade. To quote Crudgington & Baker: "That neither of these improvements is at all widely used merely serves to emphasize the quality of the original [A&D] invention." Perhaps this is why it had absolutely no effect on the House of Lords decision in Greener's favor.

Nonetheless, John Deeley was undeterred. At this juncture, he appears to have taken a two-pronged approach to recovery. The first was to formally restructure the issuance of A&D/William Anson Patents by establishing Anson & Deeley Patentees at 78½ High Street in Birmingham in 1884. In partnership with William Anson, this entity seems to have continued Couchman's licensing and administration of Anson & Deeley guns along with other William Anson patents. Trade directories show Anson & Deeley Patentees remained in operation until 1899, the same year in which John Deeley retired from Westley Richards & Co. But, concurrent with the rise of Anson & Deeley Patentees, Robert Couchman seems to disappear from the scene. Subsequent licenses in our archives are simply issued by functionaries at the Birmingham firms of Waterlow and Saylor Ltd., Rowlands and Co., or Deeley & Hill.

Another apparent result of Greener's 1884 triumph is John Deeley's undiminished attempts at advancing the Anson & Deeley action, but without the engineering acumen of William Anson. Why? Well, it may have been that the extended legal fight with Greener took something out of the creative relationship between these two men.

Thus, after Couchman/Westley Richards lost their case in the House of Lords, John Deeley appears to team up with a different outside consultant, a Birmingham action maker named Frederick J. Penn of Frederick Villa, Linwood Road, Handsworth.

Not surprisingly, the first Deeley/Penn effort appears to have been Patent No. 5049 of 1885, which was an attempt at "improving" the Anson & Deeley boxlock. This cocking arrangement used a stirrup link between the cocking dog and the tumbler's forward arm, but this idea was not a success, especially in the diplomatic sense.

Why? Because one can easily imagine that such a unilateral "enhancement" of the A&D action by Deeley and Penn did not sit well with co-patentee William Anson, who still shared a fiduciary interest in the design as well as Anson & Deeley Patentees. In addition, William Anson's slow fade into obscurity seems to begin during this time frame, and the star of Frederick J. Penn begins to rise.

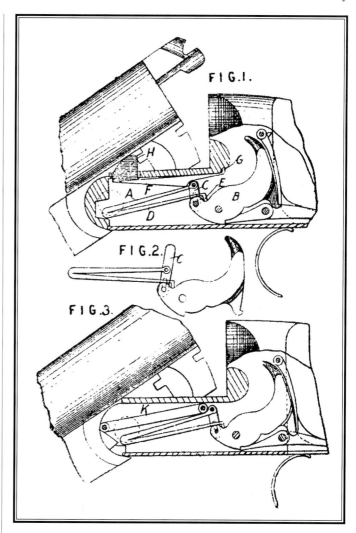

In response to the Greener decision, F.J. Penn and John Deeley came up with a new way to refresh the A&D design: Patent No. 5049 of 1885, a cocking arrangement with a stirrup link between the cocking dog and tumbler.

The Deeley Box Ejector

In the wake of this realignment, John Deeley's name began to appear on a host of new firearms patents. One of the more noteworthy of these was Patent No. 14,526 of 1884, and applies to the first iteration of the fore-end "box" ejector used on virtually all Westley Richards boxlocks and a host of other guns. However, it is not widely understood that this simple ejector was not patented by John Deeley, but rather by John Deeley's son, John Deeley the Younger.

However, while John Deeley the Younger may well have conceived of and designed this mechanism, it is worthy of note that he is involved in no other subsequent Westley Richards & Co. patents, and that improvements to this same ejector were later made by his father, John Deeley the Elder and F.J. Penn.

In fact, John Deeley the Elder created the first improvement with Patent No. 4289 of March 1886. Then, two years further on, this ejector was enhanced yet again via Patent No. 6913 of 1888. However, there are two names on the 1888 patent. One is John Deeley the Elder. The other is our friend F.J. Penn, who may have also become a Westley Richards employee by this time.

For additional support, I offer this per Donald Dallas in *The British Sporting Gun and Rifle*: *...two ejector patents were taken out regarding the Anson & Deeley boxlock...by employees of the Westley Richards firm, John Deeley (Jnr.) in patent no. 4289 of March 26, 1886 and Frederick J. Penn and John Deeley (Snr.) in patent No. 6913 on 9 May, 1888.*

It appears as though this latter date refers to the issuance of a provisional patent, however. A document in our archives dated June 11, 1888, quite clearly specifies "provisional protection," and asks Messrs. Penn and Deeley "when [they] wish the patent completed."

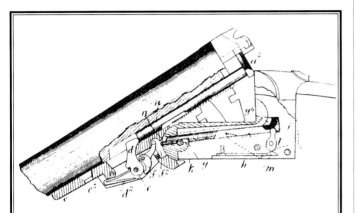

J. Deeley patent No. 14,526 of 1884

The original fore-end "box" ejector, Patent No. 14,526 of 1884, used on virtually all Westley Richards boxlocks and a host of other guns. It was held by John Deeley's son, John Deeley The Younger.

John Deeley the Elder created the first improvement with Patent No. 4289 of March 1886.

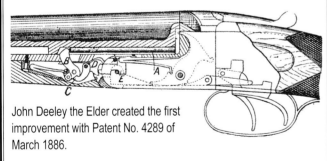

6913. Penn, F. J., and Deeley, J.

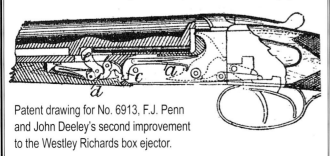

Patent drawing for No. 6913, F.J. Penn and John Deeley's second improvement to the Westley Richards box ejector.

In any case, the salient advantage of the Deeley box ejector is that it is essentially a self-contained unit. This allowed it to be made up separately as an individual component as well as off-site by outworkers. Installation merely required that it be pinned into place and regulated to the gun at hand. Compared to virtually all other ejector mechanisms, this unit was convenience and simplicity combined. With such utility as an obvious advantage, there was quite a bit of anxiety in the trade over the general release of this improved ejector. The April 9, 1887, issue of *The Ironmonger* put it this way: *One of the best* [ejectors] *perhaps, is that attached to the Westley Richards gun, for which the owners at present decline to grant any license to the trade... their Anson & Deeley hammerless is going remarkably well.*

Fortunately, the wait was soon over, and even if John Deeley Jr. really did conceive of the original ejector, it appears as though his father, and that shadowy figure, F.J. Penn, were the two fellows who perfected it. The ultimate result was a very good ejector that is utterly reliable and is still used today. But this invention was not without cost or controversy. I will relate that story shortly.

A decade after the box ejector appeared, John Deeley described the brilliant concept in the April 15, 1897, issue of *The Sporting Goods Review*: *The principle is simply an adaptation of that employed in a gun lock, a mechanism perfected by centuries of mechanical ingenuity and skill. It has very few parts, and they so strong that it is almost impossible for the ejector work to get out of order; in short, we contend that ours is the best ejector which has yet been introduced; that it combines the greatest simplicity with the highest mechanical efficiency, and that the parts cannot be reduced without additional friction.*

A Changing of The Guard

As the Deeley/Penn ejector gained a foothold in 1886, Charles Couchman died. As you may recall, he was Robert Couchman's uncle, Robert being the original A&D licensor. Henry Richards, Westley's cousin, was appointed to replace Charles Couchman.

It is also noteworthy that, by 1886, William Anson's son Edwin had wrapped up his business in the U.S. with the firm of Harrington & Richardson and had returned to England. There, Edwin Anson collaborated on designs with Edgar Harrison of Cogswell & Harrison. Whether or not this alliance was prompted by John Deeley's association with F.J. Penn is difficult to say.

Nonetheless, Edwin Anson and Edgar Harrison went on to design and patent a new boxlock cocking mechanism that featured a good many A&D characteristics. It is Patent No. 14,444 of 1887 and employs a rather pained arrangement in the fore-end to activate the cocking dogs and tumblers of what would otherwise be a close copy of the A&D set up.

From a competitive viewpoint, this Harrison connection could have been a none-too-subtle attempt at balancing the scales with John Deeley, but we can only speculate on that.

Still, it made little difference in the end, as the Anson-Harrison patent found virtually no enthusiasm in the trade.

Meanwhile, in another section of Birmingham's gun quarter, the November 3, 1888, edition of *The Ironmonger* reported that W.W. Greener was not only doing a land office business, but was scooping up new manufacturing assets: *Mr. W.W. Greener reports favourably of his experience in high-class guns for the leading home, foreign and colonial markets, and especially his improved hammerless* [Facile Princeps], *which can hardly be produced fast enough to meet the demand…*

The old Braendlin Armoury, which has been chiefly occupied for some time past in making [A&D and Martini] *gun actions for the trade, has lately passed into new hands, the principle purchaser being Mr. Greener.*

Actually, Braendlin had gone into voluntary liquidation. A major outsource producer of A&D guns had been snapped up by W.W. Greener, inventor of the *Facile Princeps*, its primary competitor. From 1889 to 1915, Braendlin was managed by Charles Greener.

With only a year left on the A&D's patent protection, Greener's move certainly didn't please John Deeley. It may even have prompted him to develop another primary income stream.

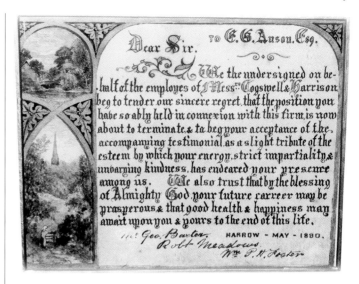

This heartfelt certificate was presented to Edwin Anson upon his departure from Cogswell & Harrison. He must have been especially liked and admired during his time there. *Photo — Stride family*

Below: Patent drawing of the Anson/Harrison ejector mechanism Patent No. 14,444 of 1887. It employs a rather unusual arrangement in the gun's fore-end to achieve cocking.

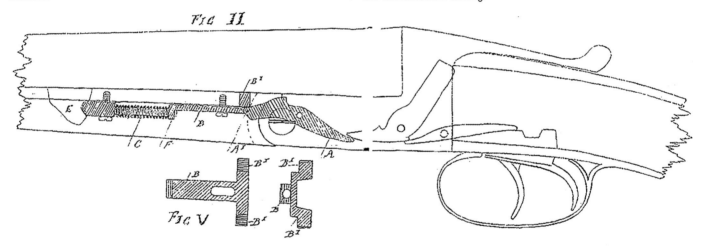

1889: A Season Of Ejector Licensing

The summer of 1889 must have been particularly hot. Especially for the licensing of Westley Richards/John Deeley ejector patents. As a matter of fact, July 23, 1889, saw no less than four licenses issued to four separate Birmingham gunmakers who were already licensed to produce A&D double guns. These licenses are in our archives, and they were all issued by Westley Richards & Co. under the collective stewardship of a small group of Birmingham professional firms.

These included Waterlow Bros. Saylor Ltd., Rowlands and Co., and apparently the accountancy firm of Deeley & Hill, undoubtedly where John Deeley's son, George Dawson Deeley, worked before joining Westley Richards in 1897. In fact, the May 25, 1889, issue of *Britain's Land & Water* magazine carried an advertisement inviting anyone who wished to use the A&D action to contact Deeley & Hill. Concurrent with this evolution in the issuance of licenses, Robert Couchman's name seems to vanish from the gun business landscape.

As a further perspective, it is worthwhile to keep in mind that patent protection for the vaunted Anson & Deeley action had just expired in May of 1889, after 14 years of proprietary control by Westley Richards/Robert Couchman/Anson & Deeley Patentees, *et al*. And while the A&D boxlock faded as an income stream, the Deeley ejector appears to have risen in prominence to become a patent license darling and a new profit center.

One of these ejector licenses was issued to Thomas Pryse and Lewis Pryse of the firm T. & L. Pryse of 80 Bath Street, Birmingham. This license was actually granted for two Westley Richards ejector mechanisms: Patent No. 14,526, held by John Deeley the Younger, as well as John Deeley the Elder's improved version, patent ejector, (No. 4289). Thus, it is almost certain that only the "improved" ejector (No. 4289) was ever made up.

However, the contract states that Westley Richards & Co. were to actually make these ejector units and supply them to T. & L. Pryse, who would then pay Westley Richards 45 shillings per ejector unit — a tidy sum in those days. After Pryse installed the ejectors, the guns would then have to be sent back to Westley Richards & Co. to be inspected, approved and stamped with a use number.

A similar license was granted to Thomas Turner of Fisher Street in Birmingham and James L. Turner of 19 Brook Street, Middlesex, on the same day, July 23, 1889. This was also for use of the ejector patented by John Deeley the Younger, No. 14526 as well as John Deeley the Elder's improvement, No. 4289. This contract also required Westley Richards & Co. to actually make the ejectors and for the Turners to pay 45 shillings apiece for the units. And like Pryse, they had to send guns fitted with these ejectors to Westley's for inspection and marking.

On July 23, 1889, an identical license was also issued to Thomas W. Webley and Henry Webley of Weaman Street, Birmingham, operating as gunmakers Webley & Son. The price per unit and the requirement to present guns or rifles for inspection and marking by Westley Richards were the same.

Finally, July 23rd saw the issuance of yet another license to Thomas Bentley, Charles Playfair, Thomas Charles Bentley and Charles Playfair the Younger, trading as Bentley & Playfair. The royalty and conditions specified in this contract were identical to the others.

However, the summer of fortune was not yet over for Westley Richards. On August 27, 1889, they issued a similar ejector license to W. & C. Scott & Sons, one of the largest gunmakers in Birmingham. Specifically, it was issued to James C. Scott and Martin Scott, and required payment of 45 shillings per ejector unit.

But this license was different from the others in a small but important way. It allowed Scott's to assign the license to other makers with Westley Richards' permission. I point this out because it may well have been a tripping point in the contract later on. But for the first few years, things apparently went well. In fact, the Scott license was updated in 1891 to include a reduction of the per-unit fee to 30 shillings, a hint that a lot of ejectors were being produced.

Under this aegis, ejector licensing proceeded apace through 1890. On February 28, 1890, Westley Richards licensed Richard Redman of 40 & 41 Vauxhall Street, Birmingham, for Deeley ejector Patent Nos. 14526 and 4289. Once again, Westley Richards was to make the units, and Redman was to buy them for 45 shillings each. This contract is in our archives and is interesting in that it is typed, not written out in long hand. This suggests that the terms of these agreements had been fairly well codified by that time.

George Dawson Deeley

On June 30, 1890, a virtually identical license was issued to Richard Hill and John Smith of Price Street, trading as Hill & Smith. This firm was notable for their bar-in-wood boxlock actions. Still, they had to pay Westley Richards 45 shillings for each ejector they used.

And, just to tidy up ejector licenses on hand, allow me to temporarily spring forward to February 4, 1892. This was the date on which gun and rifle maker William Lee of 28 Lancaster Street, Birmingham, was issued a license to utilize Westley Richards-supplied Deeley/Penn ejectors, Patent Nos. 14,256, 4289, 6913 and 1281. His fee per unit was somewhat lower than for previous licensees, being only 30 shillings, but Lee still had to send ejector-fitted guns to Westley's for inspection and approval.

The McKinley Tariff : A Crippling Blow

While British gunmaking prospects appeared bright in the late 1880s, the United States decided to put some severe taxes on imported goods. This came in the form of the reviled McKinley Tariff, which struck a particularly hard blow against imported English shotguns. According to the February 9, 1889, issue of *The Ironmonger* its business hampering effects could be clearly seen on the horizon:

The duty on English guns is already high enough to practically double the price of the arms when landed in the States, with freight and middlemen's charges added, and the new duty, it is calculated, will nearly treble the cost; that is to say, a breechloader which may be bought in this country for something under £2 will cost the American user, if any are found to buy it, nearly £6.

At that price, however, it will come into competition with American machine-made guns, that must in their own country always command the preference, and the consequence is that our gun trade with the United States appears doomed.

It will be observed that the new duty, $10 per gun and 25 per cent ad valorem, presses with peculiar severity upon guns of the cheaper description. Upon high-class guns, worth in this country from £20 to £30 each, the new duty represents a reduction. The result is that while English gun makers are nearly all as busy as they can be shipping guns for delivery before the new duty comes into operation they are almost in despair about the future.

Their fears and despondency were well founded. The tariff became law on October 1, 1890, and its effects were immediate. The December 6, 1890, issue of *The Ironmonger* had this to report:

The McKinley Tariff has practically closed the United States market for cheap guns, but the increase of duty on high-class guns is too small to affect their sale, and makers of established repute do not anticipate any contraction of their business with the States. It must be borne in mind that the advance in the price of American-made guns is at least commensurate with the advance of duty, so that the relative cost of imported arms remains the same as before the change of tariff.

This may have been premature optimism. By the early months of 1891, the situation had not improved much for mainstream English guns. In fact, it appeared as a mixed bag according to the May 16th issue of *The Ironmonger*:

The McKinley tariff has gone far to extinguish the English trade with the United States in cheap guns, though the Belgians, who make a cheaper article, are reported to be busy for that market, and our makers of best guns who are scarcely affected by the change of tariff, report very favourably of American demand.

Americans themselves are able to meet all the requirements of their market, as the Colt Company are now producing a capital machine-made gun... Mr. Greener reports United States orders for high-class hammerless guns have been especially satisfactory.

Westley Richards Acquires The Smallman Patent

On June 22, 1891, a rather curious agreement takes place between Westley Richards & Co. and William Middleditch Scott/William Wilkinson. It is both unusual and salient to our story, because in this instance, Scott and Wilkinson transfer one of their properties to Westley Richards & Co.

In simple terms, Thomas Smallman had assigned (sold, or transferred) his Patent No. 1281 of 1887 to both Scott and Wilkinson on October 29, 1888. This patent describes a form of V-spring double-gun action as well as an ejector system that relied on the mainspring's tension/release, forward-and-back movement to operate the ejectors. This ejector activation is most likely the aspect of Smallman's creation that represented the most value.

In that regard, Scott and Wilkinson, assigned or sold this patent to Westley Richards & Co. on June 22, 1891. The full purchase price of the patent, which had only four more years of legal protection remaining, was 10 shillings.

However, this patent acquisition prompts a fascinating question under the circumstances extant. With a very popular ejector unit of its own already in play throughout the trade, why would Westley Richards pay even 10 shillings for an ejector patent with little protection left, and that they had no apparent intention of using? The most obvious rationale is to "get it off the market" so their own ejector could become more viable. And for 10 shillings, it was probably worth that effort.

On the other hand, this odd transaction may have constituted a crafty bit of maneuvering on the part of Westley Richards & Co., John Deeley, *et al*. How so? Well, in light of

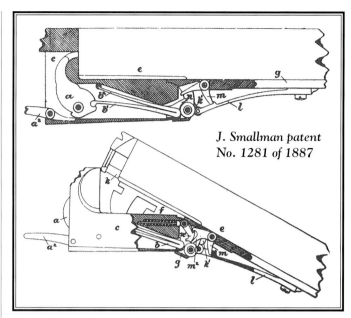

Westley Richards' June 22, 1891, acquisition of Smallman's ejector Patent No. 1281 cost only 10 shillings, but it helped establish a defense for Westley's own ejector system.

subsequent litigation, Westley's new ownership of this patent established these legal facts:
- The patent was good, and that Scott and Wilkinson previously owned it.
- Scott and Wilkinson had undoubtedly "worked the patent," i.e., made ejectors based on it.
- Westley Richards & Co. now owned the patent outright.

While all this seems obvious, the importance of these facts might have soon been worth their weight in pounds sterling. In fact, it wasn't long before John Deeley and Westley Richards launched a one-two punch of high-profile legal actions that could well have rested on their ownership of this patent and its intellectual property. The first of these suits arose in 1891 and was targeted against Thomas Perkes for infringement of the original Deeley ejector Patent No. 14,526 of 1884.

The Deeley/Perkes Ejector Flap

This was a rather unpleasant dispute over the Deeley box ejector that could have easily included two subsequent improvements by John Deeley the Elder, Patent Nos. 4289 and 6913. But, as in their dispute with Greener over his *Facile Princeps* action, things did not end well for Westley Richards & Co. A description of the Deeley/Perkes ejector case is well summarized in *The British Shotgun, Vol. Two* by I.M. Crudgington and D.J. Baker:

Perkes admitted that he had used part of the specification, but claimed in his defense that the 1884 Deeley patent was invalid by reason of being anticipated in all its claims [the patented concepts having been created earlier by others]. *This point he was able to sustain in the original hearing and in the Court of Appeal...* [Deeley's claim was even anticipated by] *Perkes own patent, No. 1968 of 1878...*

Not content with demolishing the 1884 Deeley patent, Perkes next applied to have this patent [Deeley's] revoked and this started another and more complex legal process during which Messrs. Westley Richards sought to amend their specification to produce from it a valid patent... While he won the battle, in a sense Thomas Perkes lost the war; in 1898 he was declared bankrupt, largely as a result of the expense of this litigation...

This prompts us to echo the sentiments of William Wellington Greener as to the "cruel fraud" of the Patent Office taking from inventors their hard-earned money in exchange for 'Patent Rights' which could prove to be as dubious as John Deeley's patent.

Deeley Sues W. & C. Scott

Less than a year after he purchased Smallman's ejector patent from Scott and Wilkinson, John Deeley's litigious crosshairs fell upon his former benefactor, W. & C. Scott. In May of 1892, Westley Richards & Co. sued Scott over alleged infringements of the Deeley ejector patent license. Speculation is that this involved some aspect of the Smallman ejector patent. Then again, Scott had rights to the Needham ejector, so that may have been in play as well. Regardless, this case dragged on for years, cost a lot of money and, like the Greener flap, ended up in The House of Lords, but this time, Westley Richards and John Deeley emerged triumphant.

William Middleditch Scott

Surprisingly, this litigation did not impair business relations between the two firms, at least at its onset. In July of 1892, Scott's ejector contract with Westleys' was updated to allow W. & C. Scott to forego the return of guns to Westley Richards for inspection and allow Scott to mark and keep track of the number of ejector use numbers themselves. It was certainly a trusting business arrangement on the part of Westley Richards. Especially since Westley's had just filed suit against them only two months earlier.

But from an overall financial perspective, the 1890s must have looked especially bright for both Westley Richards and John Deeley. There were now at least five Birmingham gunmakers (and probably more) that were fitting Westley Richards-produced ejectors to their guns, and most of them were paying Westley's 45 shillings for every ejector. This was more than most earlier licensees paid to use an A&D action. Westley's had certainly found a pot of royalty gold here, and they had to be collecting a tidy number of shillings in the process.

But profits for the coming decade had just started to flow for Westley Richards & Co., and like their patent ejector, the next wave of significant cash could also be traced to John Deeley the Younger.

The Lee-Metford Rifle Fix

As events transpired, John Deeley Jr., developed into a very keen rifle shot and competed with The English Eight against Scotland and Ireland for the Elcho Shield, which they won in 1881 and also in 1885. Fortunately, John Jr.'s talents on the target range led him into an association with William Metford, inventor of the famous Metford rifling system.

As a result, Westley Richards was able to use this advanced rifling years before the British government employed it in the new Lee-Metford military rifle. However, there was one major problem with this arm, and it wasn't the rifling. By 1890, it was discovered that the pin holding its separate bolt head in place would fail after sustained use. This breakage rendered the rifle useless — a less than desirable combat condition.

Somehow, John Deeley and/or John Deeley Jr. arranged for Westley Richards to address the problem, probably through their personal association with William Metford. As a result, it is widely held that John Deeley Sr. managed to redesign the bolt head to eliminate the pin and have the rifle work reliably. But a glance at the patent itself (No. 19,145 of November 25, 1890) reveals something quite interesting: This patent was actually shared with none other than F.J. Penn. In fact, Penn's name comes first on the patent, suggesting that it was essentially his idea.

Nonetheless, the British government was pleased with this corrective work, and after a bit of persistence on the part of John Deeley along with some political leverage from Sir William Harcourt of the Royal Treasury, Westley Richards was awarded the princely sum of £3,000. Some sources say this money went directly to John Deeley, but in no case is it revealed how much, if any, went to F.J. Penn, whose involvement has been almost universally overlooked. In addition to this lump sum boon, Westley Richards received a royalty from BSA for every improved Lee-Metford rifle made. But that didn't last for long. The new Lee-Enfield rifle began to come into service in 1895. Still, £3,000 was nothing to sneeze at in 1890. To put this sum into perspective, the entire new Westley Richards manufactory, which was built in Bournbrook in 1898, cost a total of £4,600.

Through all of this, John Deeley the Younger was not in good health. He retired from Westley Richards in 1888. He died of illness in 1893. But this did not curtail the Deeley family's involvement with Westley Richards. John Deeley's second son, George Dawson Deeley, was also a shareholder in Westley Richards and had attended board meetings since 1888, possibly to fill the vacancy created by his ailing brother's retirement in that same year.

Then, on July 2, 1892, John Deeley and F.J. Penn patented an "improvement" to the original Anson intercepting safety sear (No. 12,324). It wasn't a very worthy modification, and the situation may have been made worse through the Anson family's disgruntlement with issues regarding William Anson patent royalties. A few years later, in the April 15, 1897, edition of *The Sporting Goods Review*, Deeley himself would admit that the original A&D action was innately safe, even without a safety sear:

I remember when the A and D Hammerless first came out I showed it to a well-known Birmingham maker. He was not quite satisfied as to its absolute safety I could see, so I suggested a test to him. 'Hold it up at arm's length in the air,' I said, 'and let it drop butt down on the floor.' He took me at my word, and did it. The fourth time the stock broke across but even then the locks remained absolutely unaffected... If it would stand that, " said I, with conviction," it ought to stand anything.

Above: The "fix" for the Lee-Metford bolt problem, Patent No. 19,145 of November 25, 1890. Virtually all references credit this to John Deeley, but a fellow named F.J. Penn played a preeminent role.

Right: The Lee-Metford rifle had a seriously defective bolt head design, which was corrected by F.J. Penn and John Deeley.

Such confidence was a bountiful commodity in the Deeley family. John Deeley's son, George Dawson Deeley had become a certified accountant and was a principle at the Birmingham accountancy firm of Deeley & Hill, which also managed A&D patent licensing for a while.

Then, in the summer of 1897, George decided to refocus his career and was appointed to the Westley Richards board of directors in a role we would view today as the Chief Financial Officer. This was two years before John Deeley would retire in 1899.

William Metford, inventor of Metford rifling and ally of Westley Richards. John Deeley the Elder managed to fix Metford's flawed military rifle with the help of F.J. Penn.

The Westley Richards Single Trigger

If we back up just a bit to November 11, 1895, yet another product of the Penn/Deeley engineering collaboration comes to the fore — the Westley Richards single trigger. Yes, F.J. Penn once again gets top billing on this patent, suggesting that the mechanical scheme may well have been his primary concept. Two years later, this trigger was protected in Belgium. The certificates for this are in our archives (see Appendix).

However, the 1897 Belgian document contains an intriguing revelation about John Deeley and/or Westley Richards & Co. Specifically, it offers the following information as part of the patent application entered by Westley's Brussels patent agent M. Kirkpatrick: *I have the honor to ask you to grant to my applicants, Frederick James Penn of Handsworth, England and **John Deeley of Birmingham, England and being resident in Brussels, 5 Rue de Pepiniére**, an import license for improvements made to double-barrel shotguns and rifles with a single trigger English patent of 11, November 1895...*

The salutation and Brussels address of this document are a typeset form, while the balance of this application is handwritten. To us, this indicates that Deeley employed M. Kirkpatrick as a representative in Brussels to facilitate patents and legal business with Belgium. The 5 Rue de Pepiniére address was apparently Kirkpatrick's. However, a casual translation might easily be construed to suggest that Deeley was a resident of Brussels, which was not the case.

Meanwhile, down in the tip of Africa, two Boer Wars still hadn't settled the political hash extant. Thus, the South African Republic (ZAR) suddenly felt the urgent need for thousands of Martini-Henry rifles in 1896/97. In this, Westley Richards and the Belgian firm of Auguste Francotte were only too willing to fill the order. However, a dispute soon developed between Francotte and Westley Richards over certain Martini-Henry patents held by the British firm.

So, because John Deeley had made himself fluent in French, he traveled to Liège and managed to resolve the issue in favor of Westley Richards. While there is no proof of it, one might logically presume that Mr. Kirkpatrick helped Deeley to iron out this sticky business with Francotte.

21,346. Penn, F. J., and Deeley, J. Nov. 11.

Single-trigger double-barrelled guns.—The right-hand sear a carries a sliding plate c having projections c^2, c^3, and the left-hand sear b carries a spring-operated sliding plate d having projections d^2, d^3. When the hammers are at cock the plates c, d are in the position shown, and are retained therein by the pressure of the right-hand hammer k on the part c^4 of the plate c. When the trigger h is pulled the projection h^1 acts on the part c^3 of the plate c and discharges the right-hand barrel. The fall of the hammer k allows the plate c to move forward under the action of the plate d and its spring g. In this position the projection h^1 on the trigger is under the part d^3 of the plate d ready to discharge the second barrel. In a modification, the sliding piece of the second sear is replaced by a cranked lever. In another modification, the spring g is replaced by a spring placed in advance of the sears and acting on a pivoted lever which operates the right-hand slide plate c. In another modification, the plate c has but one projection, which is engaged by a spring pin passing through the left-hand sear b. In a further modification, a pivoted lever is provided for enabling the left-hand barrel to be first discharged when so desired.

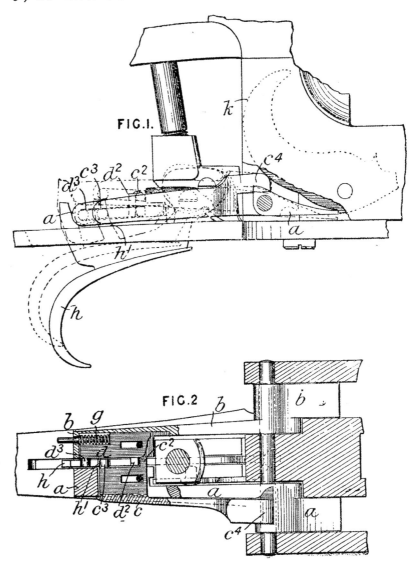

Illustration and details of the Penn-Deeley single trigger, Patent No. 21,346. It became ubiquitous on Westley Richards guns.

The Hand-Detachable Lock

The year 1897 brought another signal achievement for Westley Richards, namely the hand-detachable lock (or "droplock") version of the Anson & Deeley action. Although John Deeley and Leslie B. Taylor share official credit for this innovation, the issue remains open as to just how large a role either one really had in its development.

Consider a curious revelation from the book *Westley Richards & Co., In Pursuit of The Best Gun*, wherein it is stated that the hand-detachable lock was "ginned up" by Leslie Taylor along with an unidentified "foreman" of the back shop. Even more intriguing is that the same book credits Leslie Taylor and John Deeley with the detachable lock's invention, with Deeley entering the picture from the sidelines, as it were. So, just who really created the hand-detachable lock?

Was it Leslie Taylor? Was it John Deeley? Was it Shop Foreman X? Or perhaps it was all three of them in some form of contorted collaboration?

Leslie B. Taylor

10,567. Deeley, J., and Taylor, L. B. May 7.

Breech actions, drop-down barrel.—Relates to drop-down guns with detachable lock-plates as described in Specification No. 17,731, A.D. 1897, and consists of constructions of lock-mechanism intended to secure the minimum weight of pull-off, of means for enabling the hammers to be readily cocked by hand when the lock-plates are detached, and of means for securing the detachable lock-plates. In the construction shown in Fig. 1, the sear is in the form of a bell-crank-like lever b, b^2, the nearly vertical arm b of which occupies a recess a^2 in the head of the cocked hammer a and engages a bent a^1 near the top of the head of the hammer. The horizontal arm b^2, upon which the trigger acts, is made considerably larger than the vertical arm b. The bent may be formed in a separate piece fixed in the recess a^2 of the hammer. In a modification, shown in Fig. 7, the arm b of the sear b, b^2 engages a bent a^1 formed in the back of the hammer, the trigger acting to depress the arm b^2 of the sear by means of a pivoted lever g^2. In another construction, the hammer is retained in the cocked position by an arm h, Fig. 8, with a hooked end engaging with a fixed projection i until the arm is pushed forward by a bell-crank lever b, b^2 acted upon by the trigger. The weight of the pull-off is still further reduced by placing the

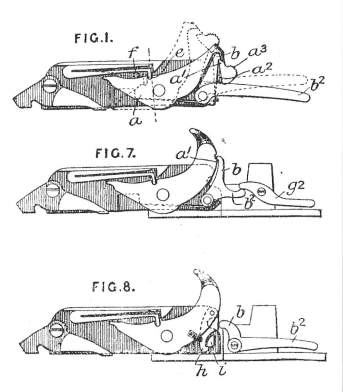

Above: In 1907, the hand-detachable lock was updated through this patent, No. 10,567. The key rationale here was to make trigger pulls a bit lighter. The approach seen in Fig. 1 required a separate firing pin in the gun frame. Patentees are listed as John Deeley and Leslie Taylor.

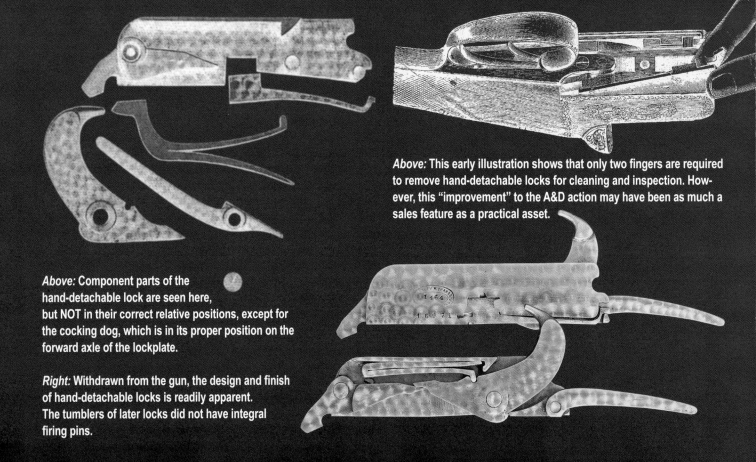

Above: This early illustration shows that only two fingers are required to remove hand-detachable locks for cleaning and inspection. However, this "improvement" to the A&D action may have been as much a sales feature as a practical asset.

Above: Component parts of the hand-detachable lock are seen here, but NOT in their correct relative positions, except for the cocking dog, which is in its proper position on the forward axle of the lockplate.

Right: Withdrawn from the gun, the design and finish of hand-detachable locks is readily apparent. The tumblers of later locks did not have integral firing pins.

To help answer that, allow us to quote directly from Jeremy Musson's book, *Westley Richards & Co., In Pursuit of The Best Gun*. On page 122, Musson states: *Leslie Taylor had asked the then shop foreman if it was possible to conceal the various pins on which the Anson and Deeley lock work hung, which showed through the side[s] of the action body... The foreman came up with the inspired suggestion of fixing the lock work to internal plates which in their turn were [hung on trunions, and] concealed in their positions by the action floorplate.*

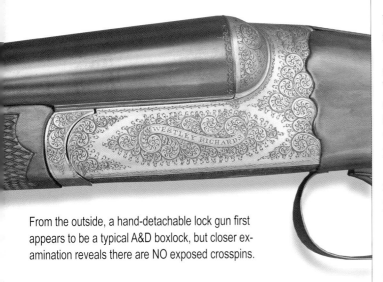

From the outside, a hand-detachable lock gun first appears to be a typical A&D boxlock, but closer examination reveals there are NO exposed crosspins.

If this were testimony in court, it would certainly seem to credit "the foreman" with the intellectual property for hand-detachable locks and would leave Leslie Taylor with little more than an expressed desire for aesthetic improvement. What's more, John Deeley is not brought into the picture at all. However, in *Experts On Guns & Shooting*, G.T. Teasdale-Buckell credits hand-detachable locks this way: *The new improvement, [is] the invention of Mr. Leslie B. Taylor and Mr. John Deeley...*

In *British Gunmakers, Volume 2*, Nigel Brown also attributes invention of the "droplock" to Taylor and Deeley. What's more, the names of Taylor and Deeley are specified on the 1897 patent itself. But if a shop foreman did indeed work out the detachable lock, why not name him on the patent? William Anson and James Edge were both Westley Richards shop foremen, and both got due credit for their inventions. Still, for whatever reason, it appears as though the identity of the fellow who actually conceived of the hand-detachable lock had to remain obscure. Until now.

For the record, the Internet Gun Club contends that this foreman's name was Howard A. Davies, of the gun action department. Davies later worked for Westley's in London.

By 1927, he left Westley's and set up shop in Colchester in the basement of Halladay's gunmakers at 63 Cannon Street. It was there that he trained Peter Radcliffe, the son of gunmaker K.D. Radcliffe. In 1932, gunmaker Bernard Chaplin purchased premises at 6 Southgate Street, Winchester, and started trading as "Howard A. Davies." Thus the Davies name must have held some measure of prestige. Nonetheless, in 1955, the company was renamed B.E. Chaplin.

Although Davies may have had great skill and applied it to the hand-detachable lock, his name does not appear on the Westley Richards patent. Neither is he mentioned in Leslie Taylor's book *A Brief History of The Westley Richards Firm*, and he is mentioned only once in the book *Westley Richards & Co., In Pursuit of The Best Gun*, where he is referred to as a viewer of .303 military rifles during WWI. What's more, Davies does not appear in the book's list of patents.

Even though its patent protection has long expired, the hand-detachable lock is not an easy thing to make up. Still, it may interest collectors to know that Italian gunmaker FAMARS cataloged a revival of the droplock in 2001. This double gun was available in 12- or 20-bore, and was called the "Tribute" for understandable reasons (see illus. at left).

The Deeley/Penn/Taylor Ethos

Beyond the Howard Davies enigma, the precise relationship between F.J. Penn, John Deeley and Leslie Taylor remains a bit foggy. Was Penn involved in the hand-detachable lock? Was he an employee of Westley Richards? Or was he a semi-independent craftsman — much like William Anson allegedly became after he left Westley Richards in 1876?

Then there are the collateral factors of marketing and those of ego to consider. The detachable lock concept may have been so brilliant and incisive that it simply had to be

Model:	Tribute
Description:	Anson & Deeley smooth barrels side-by-side with removable mechanisms.
Calibers:	12 and 20 bore.
Action:	Anson & Deeley system, Westley Richards version. Automatic ejectors, with manual safety.
Trigger:	Single or double trigger, with forward trigger articulated.
Barrels:	Demibloc, soft welded.
Stock:	Select Grade 3 walnut is standard, made to client's specs., with 0,8mm step checkering.
Engraving:	Classic English Scroll, on standard version.
Weight:	3000 gr. (12 bore) 2700 gr.(20 bore).
On request:	Spare lock mechanisms with different settings.

Smoothbore side-by-side with removable mechanisms.

The "Tribute" is a Westley Richards version of the Anson & Deeley hunting model side-by-side. The lock mechanism can be easily removed through an opening under the action. A plate is lifted after depressing a checkered latch button recessed in the forend thus exposing the locks for easy removable.

This particular feature of the Tribute, is quite unique and mechanically very difficult to manufacture. Also difficult to engrave, match and hide the joining.

The advantage of a spare set of lock mechanisms is obvious. They are also easily cleaned and maintained, allowing better functionality under extend field conditions. The Tribute side-by-side is available in 12 and 20 bore.

View the Pricing Guide

Request a Quote on a Custom Firearm

First National Gunbanque Corp. P.O. Box 6719 Colorado Springs, Colorado 80960
Tel: 719.444.0786 Fax: 719.444.0731 Email: info@fngbcorp.com

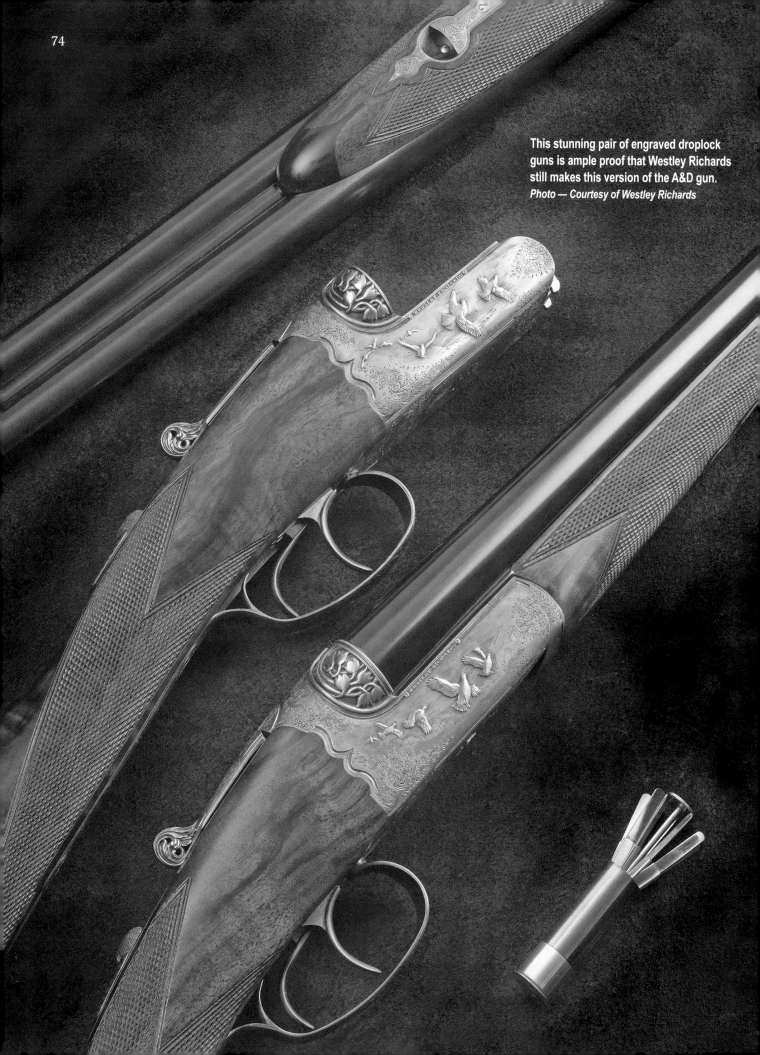

This stunning pair of engraved droplock guns is ample proof that Westley Richards still makes this version of the A&D gun.
Photo — Courtesy of Westley Richards

credited to Westley Richards' luminaries for the sake of company prestige, and not to be publicly shared with shopmen like Davies or Penn. In the end, we may never know the truth.

According to I.M. Crudgington and D.J. Baker in *The British Shotgun Vol., Three*, F.J. Penn collaborated with John Deeley on a single-trigger design in 1898, a year after the hand-detachable lock was patented. At that time, Penn's address was listed as 117 Linwood Road, Birmingham, not as an employee of Westley Richards in Bournbrook. Also, consider this — beyond his listing in its roll of patent holders, Penn is otherwise not mentioned in Musson's book on Westley Richards & Co. Although this proves little one way or another, it does tend to suggest that Penn remained as some form of consultant to the firm.

With the foregoing in mind, it might seem imprudent for Westley's to credit John Deeley and Leslie Taylor as co-patentees of the hand-detachable lock when, in all probability, neither of these men likely had much hands-on involvement with the mechanism at all. Of course, a shaky rationale for their primacy can be easily constructed — John Deeley was one of the original patentees of the Anson & Deeley action, and thus deserved extended credit for this new lock-mounting technique. In addition, it was Leslie Taylor who realized that the visible pins of the A&D gun were aesthetically gauche and suggested that they be somehow done away with. Ergo, Taylor and Deeley deserve patent rights to, and royalties from, the hand-detachable lock.

The party who was apparently overlooked in all of this is the late William Anson, and his estate. Since William Anson was co-inventor of the original Anson & Deeley action, one might logically assume the Anson family had cause to expect consideration in this droplock modification as well as a share of remuneration. After all, the works of the hand-detachable A&D action did not change, only the means by which these bits were installed into the frame (mounting plates and trunnions instead of pins). What's more, Anson & Deeley Patentees was still in business, presumably with Edwin Anson's inherited rights. Even the great Geoffrey Boothroyd considered hand-detachable locks to be a version of the original Anson & Deeley design.

In *Boothroyd on British Shotguns*, he put it quite plainly: *Although the principle of the hand-detachable lock is the same, it differs in that the limbs of the lock are not mounted on pins which pass through the action body, but on a separate plate which is removable... There is no doubt in my mind that this version of the Anson & Deeley system is one of the most practical and the most desireable.*

And for what it is worth, the patent reference to the hand-detachable lock in *Westley Richards & Co., In Pursuit of The Best Gun*, includes an addendum that references the original Anson & Deeley patent of 1875 as well as an enhancement of its cocking mechanism, (Patent No. 1833) patented in 1883. Both of these patents carry the names of William Anson and John Deeley, with no involvement by Leslie Taylor.

What fallout may have resulted from this situation is unclear. But if any existed, it may well have exacerbated the Anson family's "winter of discontent" with John Deeley and Westley Richards. This disgruntlement may have continued on its frosty course with another modification of the hand-detachable lock in 1907 with Patent No. 10,567, an alteration that moved the sear/notch engagement up on the tumbler, ostensibly to lighten trigger pulls through modified geometry. The patent also provides an enhanced means of securing the lockplates into the frame.

But let us return to our original timeline. The next chronological milestone is the death of Westley Richards on May 27, 1897. He was 83. As a result, George Dawson Deeley, second son of John Deeley, was appointed Director of the Company. With the future of Westley Richards & Co. thus secured, John Deeley may well have felt comfortable enough to retire and continue as "Chairman Emeritus."

John Deeley Retires to The Seaside

When he left his role as Managing Director of Westley Richards in 1899, John Deeley also closed the doors of Anson & Deeley Patentees. There is no clear evidence, but there are strong intimations from the Anson family that Deeley's move to shutter the company did not result in an equitable resolution for Edwin Anson, et al.

Clare Stride mused over this recurrent question in her Anson family research: *What was the relationship between William [Anson] and John Deeley and Edwin [Anson] and John Deeley? What happened at the cessation of Anson & Deeley Patentees? I am beginning to believe that Edwin and William were quite badly treated by John Deeley (Chairman of Westley Richards)... I know Edwin only left £507 which, compared to John Deeley and other prominent members of the gun trade, was derisory.*

It's all speculation, but over a century later, the answers to Clare Stride's questions are still unknown. Records show that even in retirement John Deeley continued to gain credit (and doubtlessly income) from new firearms patents managed by Westley Richards. On July 7, 1907, the names of both Deeley and Leslie Taylor appear on Patent No. 10,567, the salient aspect of which is a new hinged bottom plate for A&D guns with hand-detachable locks (an improvement of debatable merit). Previous bottom plates were removed entirely by pressing a spring-loaded catch, an arrangement probably engineered by Howard Davies at the onset of hand-detachable locks. Altogether, John Deeley held claim and interest in 19 patents related to firearm mechanisms throughout his career.

In other respects, it appears that John Deeley's retirement was rewarding and included an affinity for the seaside resort town of Rhyl in Wales. He had a small vacation residence there, and with this relocation, Deeley seems to essentially slip into obscurity. In fact, other than the patent mentioned above and a brief appearance before the assembled Westley Richards company at its 100th anniversary observance in 1912, we know very little about Deeley's life after retirement.

What is known is that, about a year after the Westley Richards company centennial, John Deeley died of "a brief

The "Christian Hunter" boxlock was introduced by Connecticut Shotgun Manufacturing Co. in 2015. Although it suggests a detachable lock/droplock iteration of the A&D gun, the locks cannot be removed by hand. *Photo — Courtesy of CSMC*

illness" at No. 8 Queen Street in Rhyl, on Saturday, July 5, 1913. He was 87. At the time, this property was listed as Holloway Confectioners. The address remains there today, about a block and a half from Parade Street and the sea, within easy sight of Rhyl's famous beach. In 1913, the address comprised a 10-room building, so it very likely contained private lodging along with the confectioner business. Upon Deeley's death, it is reported that his majority shares of the company, along with his post of Chairman, were inherited by his son, George Dawson Deeley.

Soon after his passing, public tributes to John Deeley began to appear. One Birmingham correspondent who knew Deeley well presented this perspective in *The Gunmaker*:

Everybody speaks of him as a master alike of the art of management and of mechanical detail, while his geniality and courtesy made him a general favourite.

It is agreed that he had a wonderful faculty for business, and his thorough knowledge and soundness of judgement on the Proof House Board made him a tower of strength in an emergency. The wide use of the various patents with which he has been associated are sufficient evidence of his share in the development of the modern gun trade.

I learn from Mr. Leslie Taylor that his death was quite unexpected, as he was understood to be quite well and having an enjoyable holiday at Rhyl.

Mr. Taylor states that three weeks ago he visited Mr. Deeley at his home and found him writing a letter without having to use his spectacles. They had a long conversation on various matters during which the veteran gave ample evidence of his undiminished intellectual vigour.

Not long before Mr. Deeley's departure for the seaside (Rhyl) he sat for a photograph to be made in a presentation to the Proof House in connection with the forthcoming Centenary celebrations.

Deeley was buried in the family plot on July 9, 1913, at Warstone Lane Cemetery, a facility now called Brookfields. It is located close to the Birmingham gun and jewelry quarters. Deeley's family marker commemorates him, his wife Elizabeth and two of his daughters, all of whom preceded him in death. Westley Richards & Co. was closed for the day in observance of his interment. The July 15, 1913, edition of *The Sporting Goods Review* described those in attendance at the services:

... There was a strong representation of gunmakers. In addition to those attending on behalf of Westley Richards & Co., the mourners were Messrs. G.D. Deeley (son) Mr. M.L. Drew (son in law) Mr. Joseph Rowlands (Law Clerk to the Proof House Guardians) Dr. Loxton, Mr. T.G. Deeley (grandson), Mr. A.J. Manton (grandson) Mr. Edward Taylor, Mr. Leslie B. Taylor, Mr. A.H. Gale, & Mr. D.J.P. Haines, the four last named being directors of Westley Richards & Co. The following employees of Westley Richards & Co. acted as bearers: Messrs. David Edge, Edgar Evans, Fred A. Hughes, Thomas Souls, Herbert Walker, and Joseph White.

On the occasion of Deeley's passing, Leslie B. Taylor eulogized his mentor in generous measure: *... Like his eminent predecessors in the firm, he has inscribed his name on the scroll of notable gunmakers. By his undaunted courage and his strenuous effort continued through half a century he has set a great example for us to cheerfully follow. I, for one who from youth have served under his leadership wholeheartedly acknowledge the gratitude I owe to him for teaching me the lesson of devotion to duty, and for the spirit which he daily inculcated of facing difficulties without fear. Small wonder that the burden of 88 [87] years sat so lightly on his shoulders who never turned his back, but pressed breast forward and in his beautiful old age faced the future with the same high spirit.*

Collateral with his management years at Westley Richards, John Deeley was active in the Birmingham community as a Freemason, Master of the Birmingham St. James Lodge, and a Past Officer of Provincial Grand Lodge, Chapter of Staffordshire. He was also a Guardian of the Birmingham Proof House and chairman of its finance committee.

It is likewise interesting to note that Deeley was a member of the Midland Club, the Midland Debating Society, and the Old Birmingham Book Club. His forensic fervor also extended to the Birmingham Liberal Club and the Edgbaston Debating Society. According to Leslie Taylor, it was at these organizations where Deeley often "shared in debates" with another local businessman, one Joseph Chamberlain.

Chamberlain was a radical liberal, who soon launched a political career and was elected Mayor of Birmingham.

In August of 1913, *Arms and Explosives* ran this obituary of John Deeley.

Chamberlain later became a member of Parliament. He was the father of Neville Chamberlain, the pathetically naive British Prime Minister who trusted the word of Nazi dictator Adolf Hitler at Munich in September of 1938.

Joseph Chamberlain was John Deeley's debating partner, a radical liberal, Mayor of Birmingham, an MP and father of Prime Minister Neville Chamberlain.

History records that when Neville Chamberlain flew back to England after meeting with Hitler, he waved a sheet of worthless paper and triumphantly declared "peace in our time." On the other hand, Hitler told his Foreign Minister, Joachim von Ribbentrop, "That piece of paper is of no further significance whatever." This was very true, as the Nazis invaded Poland a year later and launched WWII.

All that aside, John Deeley's name will certainly be remembered for decades to come because of one salient achievement — the Anson & Deeley action. Like the break-open shotgun itself, it was a seminal concept and one that would offer untold sporting opportunities to a vast new cohort of shooters.

In his book, *A Brief History of The Westley Richards Firm*, Leslie B. Taylor characterized John Deeley in these words: *Animated throughout by high principle Mr. Deeley invariably proved to be an honest rival in a fair field. He scrupulously respected the rights of others and uncompromisingly resisted the invasion of his own.*

History, and the facts we've presented here, may help to render a verdict on that. Fortunately, the House of Lords will have no say.

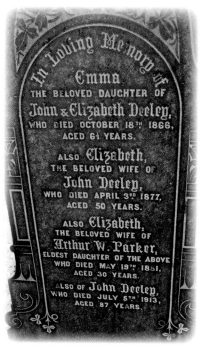

Recognition of John Deeley's passing and life accomplishments was made in *The Sporting Goods Review* on July 15, 1913. Seen above, the family grave marker still exists and tells their story.

Chapter Three
EDWIN ANSON

A Heritage of Invention...
and Dreams Unfulfilled

After William Anson's death, his son Edwin Anson, works manager at Cogswell and Harrison of London, made a concerted effort to carry on the family tradition. He took over his father's operations, changed the name to E. Anson & Co., listed at 14 Steelhouse Lane. Subsequent addresses for E. Anson & Co. include Egyptian Hall Slaney Street, 47 Great Tindall Street in 1895, 4 Steelhouse Lane in 1897, 46 Bath Street in 1899, 55 Bath Street in 1900, Upper Priory in Steelhouse Lane in 1903, 27 Durham Road in 1908, 14 Steelhouse Lane in 1912, and then 126 thereafter. Regardless of business location, Edwin pursued his own approach to the engineering and marketing of modern shotguns.

E. Anson & Co. Double Guns

When Harrington & Richardson ceased production of A&D double guns in the U.S., Edwin Anson might have seen an opportunity. At some point after 1885, it appears as though Edwin stepped in to at least partially fill the void via E. Anson & Co. and offered his own brand of double guns to the U.S. market. In doing so, Edwin apparently learned from H&R's experience and kept his sights focused on the upper tier of America's sporting clientele. From an empirical standpoint, his doubles are almost universally what H&R would have categorized as A-level or B-level guns.

As further insight into Edwin's venture, we've managed to encounter a very revealing case label that adds its own measure of mystery to the H&R/Edwin Anson double-gun saga. The backstory of this label hints that H&R may have assisted in U.S. distribution of Anson shotguns for some period of time after H&R doubles were officially discontinued.

The label in question comes from the defunct oak and leather trunk case of a 12-bore double gun that carries the identity "Harrington & Richardson, Worcester, Mass." on its top rib. The fascinating aspect of this label is that it has the trade name of E. Anson & Co. of Birmingham, England. Thus, we have an E. Anson & Co. gun...with Harrington & Richard-

This formal photograph of Edwin and Maud is undated but most likely commemorated their marriage in 1884.
Photo — Stride family

son identity...in an English trunk case, which was sold to a U.S. customer.

The gun is s.n. 1759 and coincides well with other H&R Anson & Deeley doubles we've examined. It is a 12-bore with original 28-inch Damascus barrels and light border engraving that was apparently used on Grade C guns. However, this double is blessed with a beautiful Grade B English walnut stock that was originally made with a 13¼-inch length of pull. One could easily imagine it as having been specifically ordered for a small man, or woman.

The original owner's family sold this gun to the late Oscar Gaddy, who ressurected the art of color case-hardening in the U.S. Mr. Gaddy honed this gun's bores back to a serviceable state, then sold it to author and retired English professor John Friedman of Ohio, who kindly passed it along to us.

Aside from being an artifact of gunmaking history, the label from this gun's case provides us with invaluable insight into the business relationships of Edwin Anson and, by extension, a potential agreement with Harrington & Richardson. The labels reads as follows:

E. ANSON & Co.,
(Late W. Anson, Established 1869).
Patentees and Manufacturers of Guns, Rifles and Sporting Accessories
Inventors of Anson and Deeley Hammerless Gun, Anson Snap Forepart,
Trigger Safety, Sear Safety, Tumbler Safety Cocking Lift "Peremptory" the latest
improvement in the A. & D. Hammerless Gun, "Peremptory" Ejector Gun,
Adjustable Fitting Gun and Double Rise Target Trap, & c.
EGYPTIAN HALL, SLANEY ST.,
BIRMINGHAM

Given that all marketing and promotion is imbued with a healthy measure of puffery, there are still worthy facts and information to be gleaned from the words of this label, along with a very intriguing mystery!

First, the date of 1869 in its "establishment clause" may, at first blush, be typically fanciful. English gunmakers were notorious for grasping at any "fact" that could become the basis for an early and enduring period of business. In 1869, William Anson had probably been in Birmingham for more than seven years and would live in those environs for the rest of his life. What's more, his son Edwin was five years old at the time.

However, there may be real truth in the 1869 date. It appears that William Anson established some form of independent operation that year at 123 Steelhouse Lane, and it is highly probable that this is where he made rifle sights, along with the Anson push-rod fore-end latches that he would patent in 1872. From a practical standpoint, one must assume that the latch concept itself took some time, followed by a reasonable development period, both taking place prior to 1872. Thus, there is some plausible rationale for an establishment date of 1869.

In reference to the case label once again, we can see that "Patentee" Edwin Anson could certainly claim much creativity for himself but not strictly the "Anson and Deeley Hammerless Gun, Anson Snap Forepart, Trigger Safety, Sear Safety, Tumbler Safety Cocking Lift "Peremptory" the latest improvement in the A. & D. Hammerless Gun."

All of that was the work of his father William. But through Edwin's inheritance of the business, he may have felt perfectly justified in a familial claim to those achievements.

On his own behalf, it is true that Edwin's first patent was for an ejector system (No. 12,402 of 1886), which was patented after Anson & Deeley ended its relationship with H&R. Unfortunately, the ejector never became popular.

In the early 1890s, the nascent sport of shotgun target shooting began to percolate in Edwin's mind. Perhaps this was spurred by an inventive relationship with a fellow named William Palmer Jones of Bath Street, Birmingham. We note this because Edwin and Mr. Jones shared Patent No. 6260 of May 16, 1891, which sought to protect a rather curious inflated aerial target of India rubber, along with the means to launch it. These targets were essentially weighted balloons. Predictably, this concept went over like the proverbial lead balloon.

The trade label of E. Anson & Co. affixed to the inside lid of trunk-style gun cases. The business location is specified as Egyptian Hall, Slaney Street.

Above, right: An undated British advertisement for E. Anson & Co. guns. The time frame must have been between 1923 and 1936, while Edwin's shop was at 126 Steelhouse Lane. Edwin himself is shown in the upper left corner.

This H&R double, ser. no. 1759, has dwelt for decades in a trunk case with an E. Anson & Co. label. It is a 12 bore with 28-inch Damascus barrels, B Grade stock, and C Grade border engraving. Odds are it was marketed by E. Anson & Co.

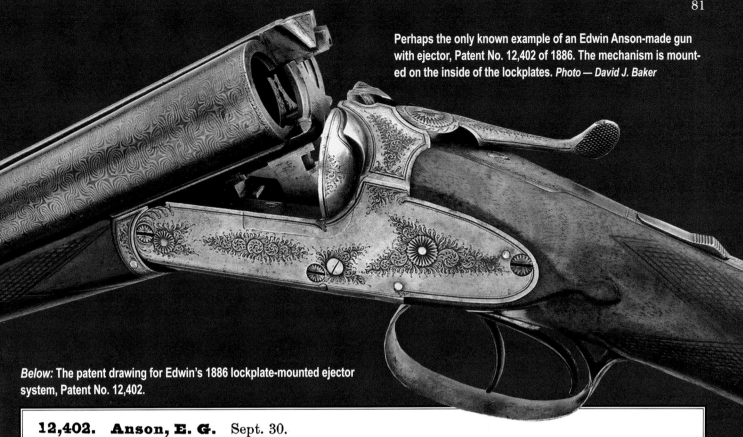

Perhaps the only known example of an Edwin Anson-made gun with ejector, Patent No. 12,402 of 1886. The mechanism is mounted on the inside of the lockplates. *Photo — David J. Baker*

Below: The patent drawing for Edwin's 1886 lockplate-mounted ejector system, Patent No. 12,402.

12,402. Anson, E. G. Sept. 30.

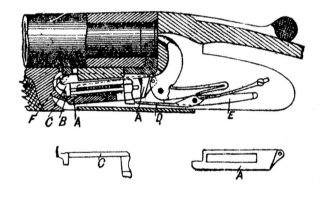

Breech actions, drop-down barrel.—Relates to the ejecting-mechanism of drop-down guns. A frame A is pivoted to the breast of the tumbler, and is forced back by the projection B on the fore-end, as the barrels fall, thereby cocking the gun. C is the ejector slide, between which and the frame A a spring is placed. As the frame A is being forced back for cocking the tumbler, the spring is compressed against the rear end of the slide C, which cannot move, as its way is blocked by the pivoted piece D. At the instant, however, of the tumbler being cocked, the downward movement of the sear E, before dropping into bent, depresses the piece D and releases the slide C, which, acted upon by the spring, at once strikes the ejector F and throws out the cartridge case.

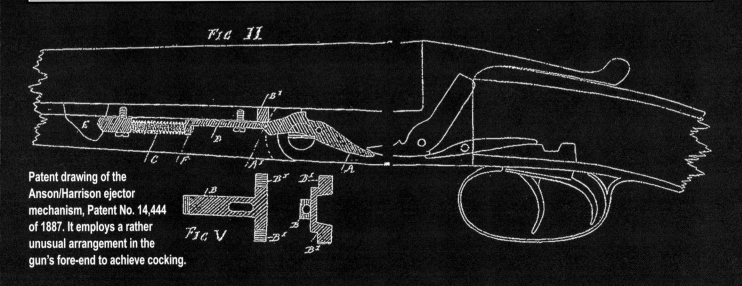

Patent drawing of the Anson/Harrison ejector mechanism, Patent No. 14,444 of 1887. It employs a rather unusual arrangement in the gun's fore-end to achieve cocking.

At some point in late 1891 or 1892, Edwin designed and introduced his own version of a try gun, the main sections of which were adjusted and secured by thumbscrews. This gun, along with a patterning target Edwin had dreamed up, were favorably reviewed in the October 1892 edition of *Arms and Explosives*:

We have recently had the opportunity of examining two inventions by Messrs. Anson & Co., of Birmingham, a short description of which may be of interest to some of our readers. The first is a simple and effective arrangement of an adjustable fitting gun, as shown in the accompanying illustration. The bend and cast-off being adjusted by means of screws the points of which are placed in grooves, screw 3 raises the face end of the butt, and screws 2 the heel end, screw 1 simply acting as tightening screw. The cast-off is arranged by the pointed ends of the screws being placed in grooves running parallel with the line of butt, and the length of butt is adjusted by means of the screw in the heel. The gun is actually lightened by the process, thus allowing for the adjustment of weight and balance. Any gun-maker can thus easily convert an ordinary gun.

The target illustrated...has marked upon it a 30-inch circle with a bird in the centre. The sportsman in our illustration has made but a very patchy pattern on the target, and has probably found out by this time the reason of his poor success in the field.

A close look at the barrels of Edwin Anson's ejector gun of 1886. *Photo — David J. Baker*

The top rib of Edwin's ejector gun carries a rather simple identity, perhaps in deference to the gun's singular status. *Photo — David J. Baker*

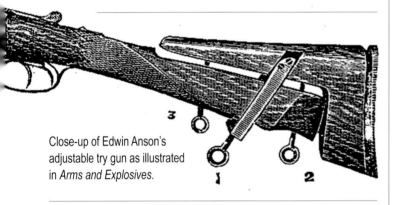

Close-up of Edwin Anson's adjustable try gun as illustrated in *Arms and Explosives*.

Below: The October 1892 *Arms and Explosives* review of Edwin Anson's adjustable try gun and pattern testing target.

In 1893, Edwin continued his foray into the realm of shooting improvement devices with a highly regarded double-rise trap. It was just in time to capitalize on the new clay target games that were catching shooters' attention. However, timing is everything, so we must accordingly refer once again to Clare Stride's research, which includes a letter from William Harding, Archivist of the Birmingham Proof House. In this letter, Harding discloses that, "I have also established details of the first Clay Pigeon Championship Meeting held in Britain... Note the date [of] August 1893, whilst [the] Anson trap appears in *The Ironmonger*, February 1893."

Harding goes on to note that Anson's trap design is nearly identical to a double trap introduced by the Eley firm, but that Anson's trap was patented first. Once again, this could be proof that great minds think alike — or that competitive minds think of schemes.

But let's return to the case label, and the "mystery" we referred to earlier. If Edwin Anson cites his ejector and double-rise trap on the trade label in our possession, then that label had to have been printed subsequent to his ejector and the introduction of his trap in 1893. However, the Harrington & Richardson double gun that was sold in this case was supposed to have been discontinued by H&R sometime around 1885. This raises a number of possibilities:

- The H&R double that we have may not have been originally paired with the case that carried the label. In other words, the gun may have been sold earlier by H&R, then placed into an E. Anson case at a later point. This is unlikely, however. Every previous owner of the gun, including the original purchasing family, recalls that the gun and case had always been together. It is equally unlikely that a perfectly matched E. Anson & Co. trunk case was just lying about in those days, unused and ready to accommodate a needy H&R double gun.

- Our double gun may have actually been sold by H&R to the original purchaser, in the labeled case, but on "special order" and at a date long after their A&D guns were formally dropped from general offer. This would possibly hint that H&R remained agents for Edwin Anson into the 1890s.

- In conjunction with the above, Edwin Anson may have continued a contingency relationship with H&R to help sell E. Anson & Co. guns in the U.S. on a limited basis. Perhaps H&R had a remaining supply of A&D doubles in their Worcester facility that they simply sold to Anson, who then retailed them in cases with his own trade label.

It is also our understanding that the family that owned our gun had another very similar Harrington & Richardson double in their possession for the same length of time. Potentially, both guns may have been ordered together. This lends credence to the fact that Edwin Anson's involvement in the U.S. double-gun market extended beyond a strict association with H&R.

In support of that, yet another E. Anson gun lends a bit more perspective. It is a high-grade boxlock, with spectacular wood, built on the classic Westley Richards Anson & Deeley action with its wide camming top lever and barrel extension bite. This gun, ser. no. 12088, is a 12-bore and has the name E. Anson & Co. inlaid in gold along the rear portion of the top rib. The gun, once offered by Kirby Hoyt of Vintage Doubles, is paired with its original case with the same E. Anson & Co. label we've mentioned previously.

Such an artifact lends more proof that Edwin Anson continued to market double guns in the U.S. for some period of time after his mainstream work for Harrington & Richardson had come to an end. This also dovetails with *The Birmingham Mail*'s characterization of Edwin in its 1936 obituary of the man:

He was head of the now defunct firm of Messrs. E. Anson & Co., Steelhouse Lane — one of the principle manufacturers of hammerless guns in the world. He previously won a high reputation in America where he was engaged in the

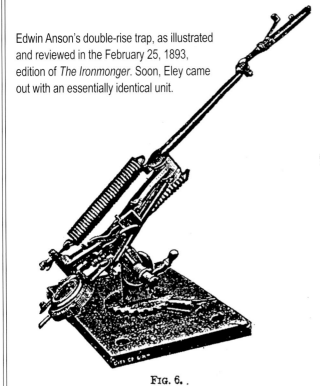

Edwin Anson's double-rise trap, as illustrated and reviewed in the February 25, 1893, edition of *The Ironmonger*. Soon, Eley came out with an essentially identical unit.

Stunning wood and beautiful proportions seem a hallmark of E. Anson guns, and ser. no. 1318 certainly underwrites that standard. *Photo - Kirby Hoyt of vintagedoubles.com*

Although its barrels have probably been rebrowned and some bluing reconstituted, ser. no. 1318 is impressive. The basic action appears to be a W. & C. Scott. *Photos — Kirby Hoyt of vintagedoubles.com*

In overall quality and trim, the ser. no. 1318 E. Anson & Co. gun closely parallels H&R's Grade B doubles.

Edwin painted this Worcester, Massachusetts, hunting scene in 1883, during the time he worked with H&R. *Photo — Stride family*

manufacture of sporting guns and rifles.

Like his father he was responsible for a number of important inventions in the field of gun manufacturing. Among them was the double rise target trap for clay pigeon shooting, which sport he claimed to have introduced to the Midlands.

From all indications, a good part of that reputation was acquired after Edwin had ceased to help H&R make double guns in New England. But again, the key question still arises: while Edwin Anson may have formally parted company with Harrington & Richardson, did he maintain their cooperation and access to their existing channels of distribution?

This possibility gains some traction as we return to Clare Stride's research. As we've already mentioned, her notes reveal that another son of William Anson, Claude Alonso Anson, had come to the U.S. to work for H&R with his brother Edwin. Claude then remained in the U.S. for the rest of his life, continuing on with H&R. According to Stride, Claude's son, Wilfred Alonso Anson, also worked for H&R.

Claude Alonso Anson was the son of William Anson. He traveled to the U.S. with his brother Edwin to work at Harrington & Richardson. Claude remained in the U.S. for the rest of his life. He worked at H&R, and he apparently played the banjo. *Photo — Stride family*

It's total speculation, but part of Anson's work with that company could have been involved with E. Anson & Co. double guns. Perhaps this included clearing out old stock or partially finished guns. After all, the name "Anson" must have still carried some prestige in the marketplace, even though it was not directly connected to "Deeley." This might well have been how H&R chose to wrap up their A&D gunmaking fiasco and recoup some costs, at least partially.

In any case, Anson's U.S. enterprise met with a formidable obstacle on October 1, 1890 — the McKinley Tariff. This legislation increased the average duties across all imports from 38 percent to 49.5 percent and added as much as $6 to every gun imported from Britain. The McKinley rates remained in force until 1894 when the Wilson-Gorman Tariff significantly lowered U.S. tariff averages. "The McKinley Tariff has practically closed the United States market for cheap guns..." lamented *The Ironmonger* issue of December 6, 1890.

Beyond the McKinley surcharge, the rising popularity of repeaters had already begun to change America's tastes in sporting guns. This transition began with Winchester's Model 1887 lever-action shotgun, designed by John M. Browning. Then, in 1897, Browning topped that concept with his Model 97 pump gun. The average hunter now had an affordable choice of shotguns with rapid multi-shot capability. Suddenly, two-shot double guns seemed like medieval technology, especially high-priced English doubles.

Edwin Charts His Own Course

On December 23, 1893, Edwin Anson was issued Patent No. 3789 for two designs. The first was a triggerplate action for sidelock guns with springs and key elements that look very similar to those in production even today. The second concept is for a double-gun grip safety that could be adapted to either the top or bottom tang. This safety did not gain acceptance.

It is also interesting to note that while Anson & Deeley Patentees continued on for a decade after William Anson died, his son Edwin shared absolutely none of his own patents with John Deeley. Nor did Edwin administer them under the aegis of Anson & Deeley Patentees. This seems curious indeed. Here was a company in which his father was a partner...a company that existed to patent gun mechanisms and then license the rights to those patents for the purpose of income. Why not take advantage of such an established entity, especially if you held a sustaining interest in the firm as the heir of one of its founders? There had to be good reason to eschew this opportunity.

To partially explain this, we can now reveal sensitive information regarding these times, provided to us by a deceased member of the Birmingham gun trade. Unfortunately, he must still remain an anonymous source. This is the allegation: [Upon his retirement] *John Deeley had managed to come away with the majority of his share holding capital* [in Westley Richards]: *On the order of £30,000 — a not inconsiderable sum... He had siphoned this money off for years without anyone knowing.*

There is absolutely no proof of this claim, and it may be a complete fabrication. However, it is difficult to understand

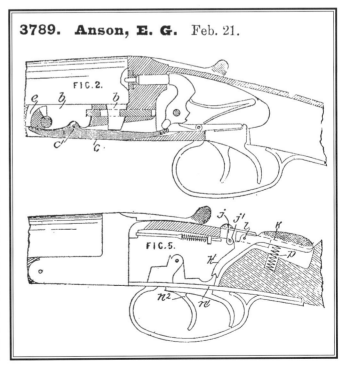

Edwin's patent for a top tang grip safety and yet another means to cock a double-gun action, Patent No. 3789.

why such a charge would be made up from whole cloth. And for the sake of context, £30,000 in 1899 would be worth approximately £1,796,700 in today's currency.

But there's more to consider. As we've pointed out, John Deeley remained as Managing Director of Westley Richards until 1899. Over that same period of time, Anson & Deeley Patentees continued on as a separate Birmingham business — 10 years after William Anson's death. It is very interesting that Anson & Deeley Patentees disappeared in 1899, the same year John Deeley retired.

It should also be noted that even in his retirement, Deeley maintained an unofficial role as "director emeritus" of Westley Richards. He also held and/or shared in at least 19 patents, one of which was issued post-retirement — Patent No. 10567 of May 7, 1907. These inventions undoubtedly generated substantial income for Deeley, especially the 1897 hand-detachable or "droplock" modification to the A&D action.

And..."ay, there's the rub," as Shakespeare's Hamlet once mused.

The Hand-Detachable Lock Affair

Upon reflection, this bit of ingenious engineering may have been a major bone of contention between the Ansons and John Deeley. How? Well, consider the possibility that certain parties could have viewed these detachable locks as simply a different means of mounting the established Anson & Deeley lock mechanism into the gun frame, and not so much a completely unique concept. Furthermore, such an interested party might view hand-detachable locks as a means to refresh value in (and generate new proceeds from) the A&D action. Thus, our interested party might accordingly

Some say the only salient improvement to the Anson & Deeley action was the hand-detachable lock (or "droplock") version of the mechanism. This 1897 patent is credited to John Deeley and Leslie B. Taylor, skirting Wm. Anson's inclusion.

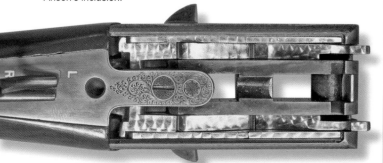

With this droplock's cover plate removed, the gun's sparkling lock units are exposed and can be plucked out by hand. But were they still A&D locks?

expect compensation. Indeed. The hand-detachable lock was patented, but it was under the names of John Deeley and Leslie Taylor.

So, just who might have been the "interested party" that was alluded to? I suggest Edwin Anson, et al., and here's why — even though patent protection for his father's action had lapsed in 1889, this 1897 "update" was patented anew and was most likely very profitable...but for patentees John Deeley and Leslie Taylor.

While we concede that the droplock patent was undoubtedly valid and legal, it may not have been particularly "cricket" under the circumstances. Especially in the eyes of Edwin Anson. Thus, it would be easy to see how Edwin may have viewed the patent as an effort to co-opt his father's genius for financial gain, but without due consideration to the Ansons. However, this is total speculation. An additional clue may be found in a reproduced instruction booklet on page 122 of *Westley Richards & Co., In Pursuit of The Best Gun*. In this booklet, a case containing two locks from a Westley Richards hand-detachable/droplock gun is shown. The promotional copy inside the case lid appears thusly:

DUPLICATE PAIR
Of
WESTLEY RICHARDS
PATENT DETACHABLE LOCKS.

Note that they are termed "Westley Richards Patent Detachable Locks" with absolutely no reference to "Anson & Deeley." However, the book *Westley Richards & Co., In Pursuit of The Best Gun* states that the hand-detachable lock was ginned up by Leslie Taylor and an unidentified Westley Richards shop foreman. Author Jeremy Musson describes its development this way:

It is said that the invention had been achieved almost by chance. Leslie Taylor had asked the then foreman if it was possible to conceal the various pins on the Anson & Deeley lock work, which showed through the side of the action body. He felt this was unsightly and that it would improve the elegance of a gun if this was concealed somehow. The foreman came up with the suggestion of fixing the lockwork to internal plates which, in their turn, were concealed and fixed into their positions by the action floor plate. Only after this had been achieved did Taylor and others realise that they had effectively invented the detachable gun lock action.

But this is also where things become a bit more confusing. Was it basically Leslie Taylor and "Shop Foreman X" who came up with the concept? Or was it Leslie Taylor, Shop Foreman X...and John Deeley? After all, John Deeley's name is on the patent, along with Leslie Taylor's. This inventive credit is supported in *Experts On Guns & Shooting*. There, G.T. Teasdale-Buckell attributes the new hand-detachable locks in this way, "The new improvement, [is] the invention of Mr. Leslie B. Taylor and Mr. John Deeley..." In *British Gunmakers, Vol. Two*, Nigel Brown also attributes invention of the "droplock" to Taylor and Deeley.

And as we've pointed out above, the names of these two men are specified on the 1897 patent itself and is correspondingly listed in the patents appendix of the Westley Richards book. We only suggest this in speculation, but John Deeley's name just might be on the droplock patent because (a) he was one of the original patentees of the A&D action, (b) because Leslie Taylor considered it as a wise political move to include "the boss," and (c) Deeley would certainly welcome a renewed financial benefit from the A&D action.

If this is so, Edwin Anson could have made the same claim in the name of his father William Anson. In addition, Edwin may have seen Deeley and Taylor's move as a disservice to his father's role in the seminal A&D concept and, by extension, a maneuver to avoid payment on its modification, i.e., royalties to the Anson family.

And if we again note the chronology, it appears as though this was the approximate time frame when Edwin Anson began to chart a completely independent course for himself, a full two years before Anson & Deeley Patentees was dissolved. So, if Edwin Anson held any inherited interest in Anson & Deeley Patentees, it may lend credence to the idea that the Anson family were ethically due some sort of compensation from the droplock patent. This may or may not be food for thought.

The Mystery of "Shop Foreman X"

For what it's worth, there may also have been some obfuscation going on with regard to the mysterious "shop foreman" and his role in the origins of the detachable lock.

First off, if this foreman was a Westley Richards employee, why not identify him per established format? William Anson was a Westley Richards shop foreman and got public credit for his inventions and patents as did James Edge. But for whatever reason, the detachable-lock collaborator remains anonymous. Except for recent revelations.

The Internet Gun Club contends that the mystery foreman's name was Howard A. Davies, head of the gun action department at the time. He later worked for Westley's in London, went on to join B.E. Chaplin in London, then established his own business in Winchester.

While there is no official confirmation, there is also a chance that this mystery man might have been a fellow named Frederick J. Penn. We broach this possibility because F.J. Penn was a noted Birmingham action maker of the same time period with whom John Deeley collaborated on a number of patents. For all practical purposes, these became Westley Richards patents. The ubiquitous Westley Richards "box ejector" is just one of them.

Nonetheless, the precise relationship between F.J. Penn, John Deeley, Leslie Taylor and Westley Richards remains unclear. Was Penn operating as a quasi-independent craftsman, much like William Anson after 1876? Was the detachable-lock concept so simple, coy and unique that it simply had to be represented as a Westley Richards trademark mechanism for purposes of company prestige and marketing? Would its glory be minimized if it were shared with a tradesman/outworker like Penn or a shopman like Davies? We may never know.

Edwin Anson's Air Pistol Legacy

By 1899, "Act One" of the Anson saga seems to have drawn to a close. The twentieth century loomed on the horizon, William Anson was gone, John Deeley's retirement was well monetized, and poor Edwin was left to establish his own niche in the trade.

This was also a time when England began to develop a measure of paranoia about private handgun ownership. So the British Pistols Act of 1903 was passed, entitled "An Act to Regulate the Sale and Use of Pistols or other Firearms." This act applied solely to pistols, and defined them as a firearm whose barrel length did not exceed nine inches.

In an effort to sidestep and capitalize on this legislation and to offer shooters a legal alternative, Edwin launched upon a series of air pistol designs. According to John Griffiths, author of *The Encyclopedia of Spring Air Pistols*, Edwin's air guns set new standards for the genre:

Edwin George Anson was one of the most innovative and influential of air pistol designers, and yet this fact is largely unappreciated, even by keen collectors of vintage air pistols... His contributions to air pistol design include:
- *First use of the pivoting grip handle cocking principle in air pistols (in his first Highest Possible pistol)*
- *Invention of the fixed barrel/moving piston concentric principle (in his second version Highest Possible).*
- *First use of a side lever pistol cocking system (the Warrior)*
- *Invention of the unique underlever cocking system of the Anson Star*
- *Introduction of the only radical modification of the push-barrel air pistol design principle ever attempted (in the Anson Firefly).*

The first of Edwin's air pistols was patented on November 9, 1907 (No. 24,837). According to the December 1910 issue of *Arms and Explosives*, it appeared to fall outside the provisions of the British Pistols Act by exactly half an inch: *The sample pistol under notice weighs 2 lbs., 12.3 ounces, and the length of barrel is a full nine-and-a-half inches, which means that the weapon is not a pistol within the meaning of the Pistols Act, and may, therefore, be sold without regard to the formalities which are ordained under that Act.*

The barrel itself was positioned above the air cylinder, and the pistol was cocked by its grip, which pivoted forward to actuate the air compressor. John Griffiths described the scheme more fully in his air pistol encyclopedia: *Anson had the ingenious idea of making the grip **push** the piston forwards, by a connecting lever under the cylinder, so enabling a longer compression stroke to be achieved. On firing, the piston was driven rearwards and the resultant compressed air was directed through a channel at the end of the cylinder where it made a 180-degree turn to propel the pellet located in a superimposed barrel.*

But creating this pistol was one thing. The challenge of making it in quantity and taking it to market was quite another issue. Here, Mr. Griffiths supplies us with more insight: *Anson showed little taste for personal bulk manufacture of his*

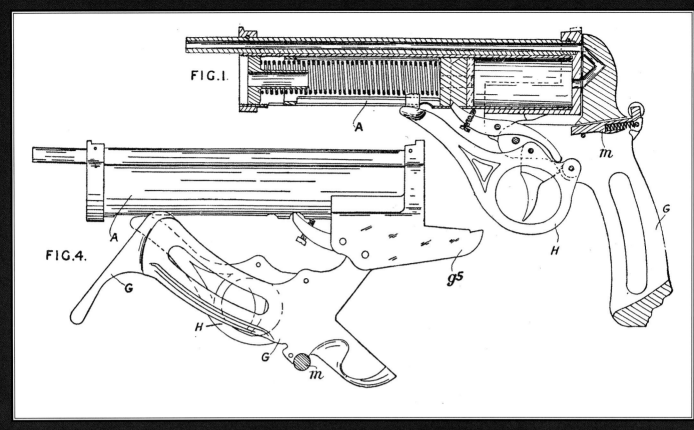

Above: The patent drawing for Edwin Anson's 1907 Highest Possible air pistol. It was cocked by pivoting the grip section forward.

Below: This page from the 1910 Westley Richards catalog features Edwin's Highest Possible air pistol and details its features.

The Westley Richards
New Patent Air Pistol—The "Highest Possible."

The Westley Richards air pistol is especially designed to remove the disadvantages of air rifle shooting; because pistol shooting requires greater skill, it is not so noisy, it makes accurate shooting more interesting because more difficult, it can be used in the smallest of rooms; moreover it provides an amusement in which ladies can join, as the air pistol is more easily manipulated and loaded than the air rifle.

In America and on the Continent of Europe the old-time sport of pistol target shooting by the wealthier classes, in shooting saloons, is fast reviving as a popular hobby. In England, saloon pistol or target shooting is also growing in popularity.

This air pistol is not a toy; it is a high class and accurate arm, as the name implies. It is made throughout by Westley Richards; the barrel, of steel, being bored, rifled, and set with the care and exactitude bestowed on this firm's world-renowned rifles.

It fires the ordinary No. 1 pellet, as used in standard air rifles. The air chamber and body are made of solid drawn steel, and the internal mechanism is of suitable steel, finely hardened and tempered. The handle or butt is beautifully finished off with polished horn plates. The sights are carefully adjusted, and any pattern of back or fore-sight can be supplied to order.

The length of the barrel is 9¾ in.; length of the pistol overall, 12 in., and weight 2¾ lbs. It is beautifully balanced, of handsome appearance, shoots well, and has no recoil.

The cost of this arm is **30/-**, black finish; and nickel plated. **35/-**

WESTLEY RICHARDS

The Westley Richards New Patent
Air Pistol—The "Highest Possible."

The Westley Richards Air Pistol is especially designed to remove the disadvantages of air rifle shooting; because pistol shooting requires greater skill, it is not so noisy, it makes accurate shooting more interesting because more difficult, it can be used in the smallest of rooms; moreover, it provides an amusement in which ladies can join, as the air pistol is more easily manipulated and loaded than the air rifle.

In America and on the Continent of Europe the old-time sport of pistol target shooting by the wealthier classes, in shooting saloons, is fast reviving as a popular hobby. In England saloon pistol or target shooting is also growing in popularity.

This air pistol is not a toy; it is a high-class and accurate arm, as the name implies. It is made throughout by Westley Richards; the barrel, of steel, being bored, rifled, and set with the care and exactitude bestowed on this firm's world-renowned rifles.

It fires the ordinary No. 1 pellet, as used in standard air rifles. The air chamber and body are made of solid drawn steel, and the internal mechanism is of suitable steel, finely hardened and tempered. The handle or butt is beautifully finished off with polished horn plates. The sights are carefully adjusted, and any pattern of back or fore-sight can be supplied to order.

The length of the barrel is $9\frac{3}{4}$ in.; length of the pistol overall, 12 in. and weight $2\frac{3}{4}$ lbs. It is beautifully balanced, of handsome appearance, shoots well, and has no recoil. It has been made to handle and balance like the officer's model regulation revolver.

The cost of this arm is	...	30/- black finish,
And, nickel plated ...	...	35/-

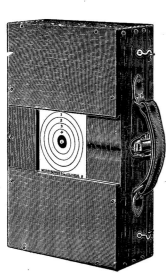

The . .
Westley Richards
Combined
Pistol Case, Target
Holder, and
Bullet Catcher.

An extremely useful and well made article.

Price ... **12/6** net.

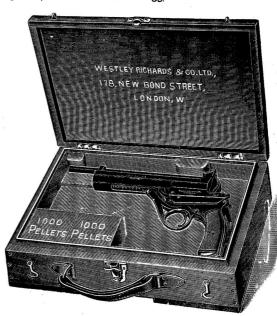

Westley Richards' catalog page of Edwin's Highest Possible air pistol states that the pistol was also available in nickel finish and was elegantly cased.

invention, and all manufacturing was transferred to Westley Richards Gun & Rifle Works, Bournbrook, Birmingham, who then made the gun in quantity (about 1200 were sold, between 1910 and 1915). The gun will therefore always be known, rather unfairly, as the "Westley Richards Highest Possible."

This rather inelegant looking pistol was featured in a Westley Richards advertisement in England's *Sporting Goods Review*, so it may have sold well enough to last for a decade or so. Also, existing stocks may have lingered for a while, and Westley's was compelled to continue marketing efforts.

Nonetheless, the "Westley Richards Highest Possible Air Pistol" was certainly well received in the December 1910 issue of *Arms and Explosives*: *To Messrs. Westley Richards, therefore, belong the very considerable credit of having well gauged public sentiment by placing on the market a properly worked out air pistol…that has been conceived on wonderfully ingenious lines.*

Note that Westley Richards & Co. gets credit for the pistol's invention. This may have been fine with Edwin Anson at the time, as long as the pistol sold and he got some income from it. In accordance with his Westley Richards reunion, it is well to keep in mind that Leslie Taylor was Director of the company at the time, not John Deeley. That could have made a big difference to Edwin.

As part of her Anson family research, Clare Stride discovered that there were actually two Edwin Anson Highest Possible Air Pistols. On this, she gained insight from William Harding of the Birmingham Proof House: *My specimen of the second version of Anson's patent air pistol, retailed by Westley Richards (the one with the barrel through the centre of the spring) is merely marked Anson's Patent & the related number.*

This detail of a Westley Richards Ovundo advertisement reveals the generally unknown 1921 update of the original Highest Possible air pistol with centrally positioned barrel. This is Edwin's Patent No. 178,048 of April 13, 1922.

This review of the Highest Possible air pistol appeared in the January 15, 1910, edition of *The Sporting Goods Review*.

The December 1910 *Arms and Explosives* review of Edwin's first air pistol, the Highest Possible, offered through Westley Richards.

There is no mention of Westley Richards on it. In contrast, my 1st version of this patent is stamped up Westley Richards.

Ms. Stride added this comment in a separate note: "Harding speculates that Edwin was bankrupt, tried to make the pistol himself, but went to Westley's to get it produced." Introduced in 1921, this was Edwin's second concept for air pistols and apparently carried the "Highest Possible" name for marketing continuity. Whether it was actually made up at Westley Richards is still an open question. Nevertheless, marketing was certainly carried out through Westley's.

Author John Griffiths offers these thoughts on the merits of Edwin's design: *Anson's second major invention came in 1921, with the introduction of his concentric Highest Possible design. In this instance he proposed the use of a piston that moved concentrically about a fixed central barrel. This brilliant idea was subsequently copied in many other pistol designs...*

While production and marketing of the second Highest Possible continued, the street directories from 1908 through 1915 record Edwin as living at Coundon, Warwick Road, Acocks Green. In about 1923, his workshop moved to the back of 126 Steelhouse Lane.

In 1918, the last year of WWI, Edwin launched into a flurry of mechanical achievments centered on sporting guns. For the most part, they didn't get much attention, probably because Britain and the various allied nations were a bit preoccupied with The Great War at the time.

On January 17, 1918, Edwin revisited his father's boxlock design and registered Patent No. 117,043. This was for an easily removable lever or cocking key intended for use in Anson and Deeley-type boxlock actions with a removable joint pin. Unfortunately, it was not popular.

On February 19, 1918, he registered Patent No. 122,299 for a

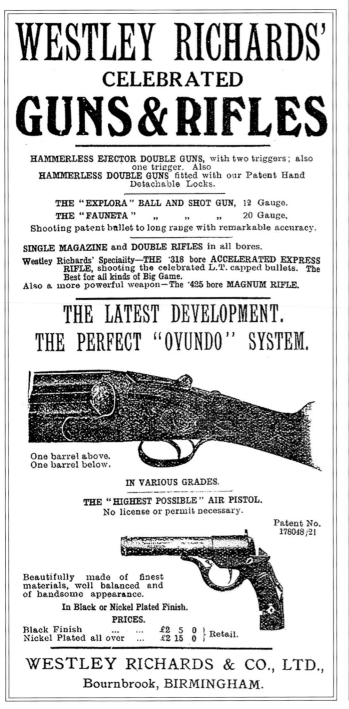

Photo — Courtesy of Andrew Orr, Holt's

Above: What might be dismissed as a 1920s advertisement for Westley Richards' Ovundo gun actually contains the revelation that there were actually two versions of the Highest Possible air pistol.

Right: This example of the original Highest Possible shows the pistol's curiously attractive inelegance.

The frame is stamped "Westley Richards & Co, London W."

Town center of Acocks Green, Birmingham, about the time that Edwin Anson lived and worked there at 968 Warwick Road.

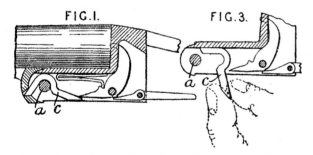

Breech actions, drop-down barrel.—Relates to guns of the Anson and Deeley type having a detachable joint pin, and consists in providing a loose cocking key or lever adapted to pivot on the joint pin, which is not cut away or grooved, and to be inserted from the underside of the body into its pivoted position. In the construction shown, the cocking-key or lever c, shaped as shown, is assembled by being passed forwards over the pivot pin a from underneath the body, as shown in Fig. 3.

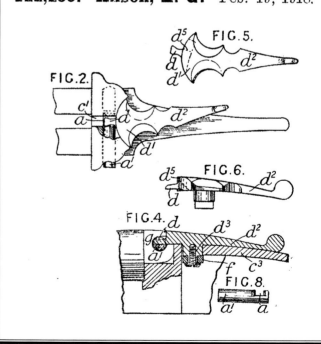

Above, left: In this Patent No. 117,043 dated January of 1918, Edwin provides yet another means to cock the A&D action via an easily accessible "key." It was not popular.

Above, right: Edwin's flurry of 1918 creativity included this alternative means of actuating a Greener-style top bolt. The claimed advantage was that it did not require a rather difficult cut in the frame for actuating arm travel. It was not popular.

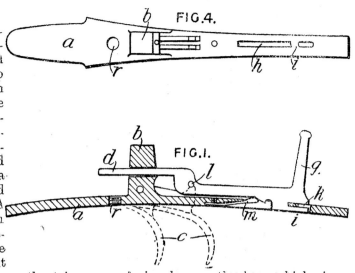

118,390. Anson, E. G. Feb. 21, 1918.

Breech actions, drop-down barrel.; safety-appliances; trigger guards.—Relates to safety mechanism of the type having a spring-controlled safety bar, adapted to be operated from the top of the action body, and consists in the provision on the bar of a part, working within a slot in the trigger plate, wherein is formed a slot for engagement with a part upon the plate. In the construction shown, the front *d* of the safety projects through a post *b* on the trigger plate *a* and a downward projection at the rear, entering a longitudinal slot *h* in the trigger plate, is formed with a slot *k* which engages a bridge-piece *i*. A spring *m* screwed on the underside of the trigger plate bears on the safety-bar and acts as a detent to retain it in either of its positions. The trigger guard (not shown) screws at the front into a hole *r* in the plate *a*. Manual operation of the safety-bar by means of the upstanding projection *g* determines the position, with regard to the trigger *c*, of pins *l* upon the bar, which, in the rear position shown in Fig. 1, locks the triggers.

top-lever operated Greener-style crossbolt. The big idea here was to eliminate the need to cut a slot for the top lever's operating arm that engages a cut in the crossbolt. It was a worthy endeavor, but found virtually no use in the trade. Probably because most gunmakers were already using the original system and already had tooling for the old-style slot, as well as the levers to fit it.

On February 21, 1918, Edwin registered Patent No. 118,390 for a trigger-bolting sliding safety. This scheme employed a guide rod that traveled through the trigger plate pillar to help move a crosspin/bolt overtop both trigger blades to prevent movement. With certain modifications, it was a design that did gain some use in both the English and Continental gun trades. Edwin's salient claim for this one was its exterior tensioning spring, which he claimed promoted ease of cleaning and lubrication via access from the triggerplate aperture. I've never seen a gun with this version of the safety.

On November 21, 1918, (ten days after the armistice) Edwin was issued Patent No. 120,668 for the redesign and repositioning of the A&D boxlock's sear springs. The salient advantage he claimed was that his approach obviated the need for separate sear spring cuts in the frame, which could weaken it. In addition, his design utilized existing machine cuts to mount vertically positioned flat springs, but still required a special cut to hold the spring tabs. This idea was not a success.

After WWI, Edwin returned to the air pistol arena. On April 13, 1922, he was granted Patent No. 178,048 for an air pistol mechanism that featured its spring around the barrel, just as William Harding described in his note to Clare Stride. This patent referred back to No. 24,837 of 1907, regarding the "Highest Possible" air pistol, only this one was marketed as the "Firefly." It had a distinctive "space gun" look to it, and virtually all examples do not have a triggerguard. The pistol was cocked by placing its muzzle on a firm but sympathetic

Above: Another of Edwin's 1918 patents offered an alternative spring arrangement for the sliding bar safety as well as enhanced access for lubrication. It garnered virtually no takers.

Below: Here, Edwin Anson offers an alternative sear spring arrangement for the A&D action. Again, it was not received with enthusiasm.

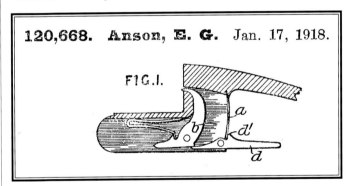

120,668. Anson, E. G. Jan. 17, 1918.

surface and pushing downward. The barrel then slid into the receiver to compress the spring.

As an aside, Clare Stride pointed out that Edwin was operating from 14 Steelhouse Lane at the time, which may have been a small component manufactory for these pistols. However, Ms. Stride also discovered that Edwin's name was crossed out in commercial directories of 1922, potentially because he may have attempted to manufacture the pistols at his Coundon, Acocks Green home address.

Note that Edwin had also made air rifles, including models like "The Ansonia" (apparently a play on his last name), "The Jewel" and "The Jem," which appear to have been made in Germany and were advertised from 1903–1907. However, this didn't work too well, since very few of these rifles were sold, and even fewer survive today.

On June 25, 1931, Edwin was granted his last patent,

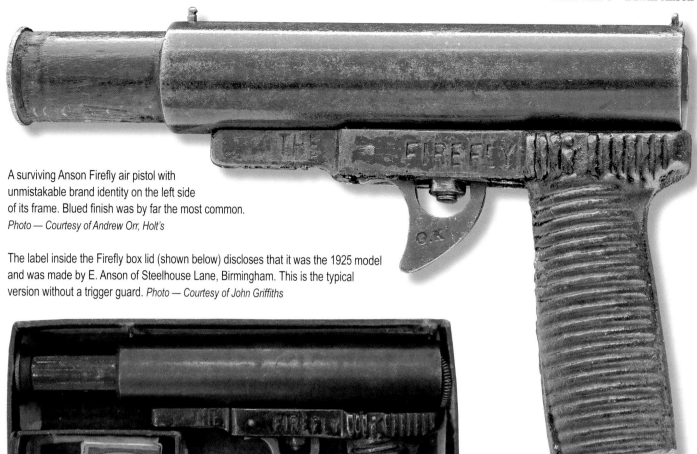

A surviving Anson Firefly air pistol with unmistakable brand identity on the left side of its frame. Blued finish was by far the most common.
Photo — Courtesy of Andrew Orr, Holt's

The label inside the Firefly box lid (shown below) discloses that it was the 1925 model and was made by E. Anson of Steelhouse Lane, Birmingham. This is the typical version without a trigger guard. *Photo — Courtesy of John Griffiths*

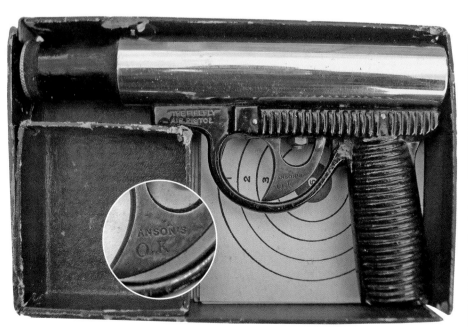

Left: This is the only known example of a Firefly with trigger guard. It also has the ultra rare nickel-plate finish. *Photo — Courtesy of John Griffiths*

Inset, far left: In close-up, the Firefly's identity is clear. Along with "Anson's O.K." on the trigger proper. This is thought to be related to final inspection. *Photo — Courtesy of John Griffiths*

Below: A 1922 German catalog listing for the Diana-Luftgewehr (air rifle). In England, it was marketed as The Ansonia.

A surviving example of the Ansonia air rifle in superb condition. The trigger unit is stamped "THE ANSONIA", with "E. Anson & Co 14 Steelhouse Lane Birm" on the left side of the frame. *Photo — Courtesy of Andrew Orr, Holt's*

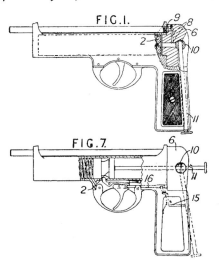

208,341. Clarke, F. Nov. 17, 1922.
Addition to 110,999. *No Patent granted (Sealing fee not paid).*

Pneumatic.—An air pistol of the kind described in the parent Specification, in which the spring plunger 2 is cocked by a sliding rod 11 mounted in a rotatable plug 10 so that it can be turned down against the handle, is provided with a breech-block 6 which is pivoted on a longitudinal axis so that it can be turned aside to open the breech, the rotatable plug being mounted in this breech-block. The breech-block is formed with a passage 8 connecting the air compression chamber with the barrel, and is mounted by being screwed into the rear of the air chamber. A leather or like washer 9 is provided at the junction between the block and the barrel. A safety device, comprising a slide 16, Fig. 7, engaging the trigger, and a cranked lever 15, is adapted to be released when the cocking rod is turned down against the handle.

No. 351,268, an update of his No. 178,048 "Firefly" air pistol. A fellow named Frank Clarke of 39-41 Lower Loveday Street, Birmingham, is listed as co-patentee on Patent No. 351,268. This design allowed for the pistol to be cocked via a long lever that ran along the entire right-hand side of the barrel. Initially, it was called "The Warrior" and was made up by the firm of Accles & Shelvoke of Birmingham. Collectors have determined that this air pistol went through two design permutations and was offered in both .17 and .22 calibers. Eventually, Edwin relinquished his rights to this pistol to Frank Clarke.

Later, Edwin reworked the concept yet again and came up with a significantly new air pistol called the "Star." In this design, Edwin moved the cocking lever under the barrel rather than alongside it. However, author John Griffiths contends there is evidence that Frank Clarke also had a hand in the Star's development. Advertisements for the Star appear for only one year, spanning 1932–1933, and less than 100 of them were made. Griffiths offers this overview in his book, *The Encyclopedia of Spring Air Pistols*:

The extremely rare Anson Star is as intriguing as it is innovative, and poses many unanswered questions. For example: Why is there no patent? Why are there are two distinct series of the pistol, one marked "Star" and the other marked "Anson's Star"? And why do all known examples have grip plates from Frank Clarke's last model Titan? The Star was based on Anson's concentric principle, but has a unique (though unfortunately not very user-friendly) underlever cocking system.

Years later, the remaining parts for the Star air pistol were sold to A.A. Brown, who made only 37 of them. Finally,

This air pistol was patented in 1922 by Frank Clarke, a gun quarter associate of Edwin Anson. It may well have been a mechanical forebear to the Firefly air pistol that Edwin and Clarke co-patented in 1931.

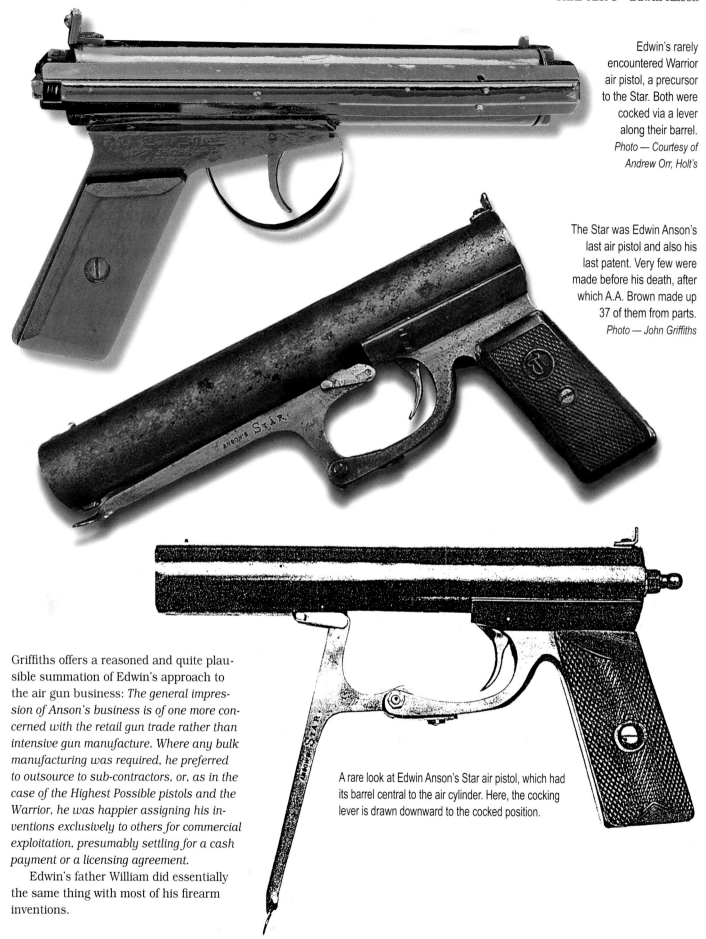

Edwin's rarely encountered Warrior air pistol, a precursor to the Star. Both were cocked via a lever along their barrel.
Photo — Courtesy of Andrew Orr, Holt's

The Star was Edwin Anson's last air pistol and also his last patent. Very few were made before his death, after which A.A. Brown made up 37 of them from parts.
Photo — John Griffiths

A rare look at Edwin Anson's Star air pistol, which had its barrel central to the air cylinder. Here, the cocking lever is drawn downward to the cocked position.

Griffiths offers a reasoned and quite plausible summation of Edwin's approach to the air gun business: *The general impression of Anson's business is of one more concerned with the retail gun trade rather than intensive gun manufacture. Where any bulk manufacturing was required, he preferred to outsource to sub-contractors, or, as in the case of the Highest Possible pistols and the Warrior, he was happier assigning his inventions exclusively to others for commercial exploitation, presumably settling for a cash payment or a licensing agreement.*

Edwin's father William did essentially the same thing with most of his firearm inventions.

Edwin Anson Dies, Followed by Maud

The air pistol seems to have been the final act in the Anson saga. Edwin Anson died on August 29, 1936, at Coudon, 968 Warwick Road, Acocks Green (a suburb of Birmingham). His daughter, Phyllis Hill (nee Anson), was present at the time.

Cause of death was listed as "hyperpiesis and myocardial degeneration," or heart disease/failure. He was 73, and he left a mere £507 to his wife Maud, along with all of his earthly possessions. We might assume this included the resources of E. Anson & Co. Sadly, Edwin's widow Jane Elizabeth Maud Anson would die intestate, virtually three years later on July 27, 1939. Her death came in a small one-bedroom walk-up flat at 19 Coppice Road, Moseley, Birmingham. The cause of death is listed as carcinoma of the liver, i.e., liver cancer. Maud left only £125 to her heirs. Maud was buried next to Edwin at St. Mary's Church of England, parish church, Acocks Green. Tragically, this area was struck by German bombs during WWII and all the headstones were destroyed, along with the remains of Edwin and Maud Anson.

The final disposition of E. Anson & Co. is unclear. The firm continued to be listed in *Gun, Rifle and Pistol Makers* at the "back of 126 Steelhouse Lane" through the year of Edwin's death, but his obituary in *The Birmingham Mail* clearly stated that he was no longer active at that time, reporting that: *Until his retirement, he was head of the now defunct firm of Messrs. E. Anson & Co., Steelhouse Lane — one of the principle manufacturers of hammerless guns in the world. He previously won a high reputation in America where he was engaged in the manufacture of sporting guns and rifles...* From this, we might assume that Edwin had officially retired at some indefinite point subsequent to 1933.

Adding to the story, Clare Stride references the late Geoffrey Boothroyd's contention that Edwin's shop, tools and trade name were purchased in 1945 by two fellows named Curry and Keen — possibly independent Birmingham gunmakers. If this was the case, Maud or Horace may have held on to Edwin's shop, tools and assets for a few years after his death. Still, nothing more is known about what happened to most of it. As mentioned above, the air pistol parts eventually ended up in the hands of A.A. Brown. In the final anaylsis, there is little doubt about one product of the Anson legacy: the Anson & Deeley Boxlock. It remains the "gold standard" for popular double guns, even today.

Like the original Lefaucheux break-action shotgun, the central-fire cartridge, or the barrel choke system, nothing else seems so simple, sensible and effective.

Thus, the Anson & Deeley action is not only timeless, but indispensible...and its inventors have become immortal.

Three generations of Anson ladies at the seaside. At left is Edwin's wife Maud Anson. Far right is their daughter, Phyllis Elaine Hill (nee Anson), Clare Stride's grandmother. In the center is young Joan Kathleen Hill, Clare Stride's mother. The photo is undated but appears to be from the 1920s–1930s.
Photo — Stride family

Below: An undated photo of Edwin and Maud Anson. From their appearance, it must have been taken not long after Edwin returned from the U.S. and wed Maud in April of 1884.
Photo — Stride family

Left: Gladys Buckley (nee Anson) was Edwin and Maud Anson's first child, born January 14, 1886. Gladys became an actress, as her photogenic flair might suggest. She died of an aneurysm on March 2, 1930, at the age of 44. *Photo — Stride family*

EPILOGUE

An old idiom holds that, "everything old is new again." This certainly applies to the Anson & Deeley gun, and although it's certainly old, the A&D action hasn't aged much at all in nearly 150 years. Thus, it remains perennially new. The reasons why center on its innate and timeless qualities:

- It is simple — based on mechanical principles virtually Newtonian in their primacy.
- It is robust — boxlocks are not prone to parts breakage, seemingly immune to dirt and fouling, and highly resistant to accidental discharge.
- It is versatile — the A&D concept can be used for side-by-side, over-under or single-barrel shotguns or rifles, all with equal satisfaction.
- It is compact — the entire mechanism takes up less space than any other comparable action.
- It is easier to stock and less prone to stock failure — the original vertical interface of the action frame with the stock head minimizes production time, preserves a large surface for recoil absorption, and helps extend the gun's useful life afield.
- It is economical to make — less human effort and fewer machine operations are necessary to create the boxlock than virtually any other action. This does not necessarily equal cheap. Top end boxlocks are highly refined sporting instruments and remain quite pricey.
- It is profitable — for all the above reasons, the boxlock lends itself wonderfully to traditional machine or modern CNC production, spark erosion, or investment casting techniques. All of this enhances profit margin.

The result of these qualities is that the A&D action has become the conceptual basis for more hammerless double-barrel shotguns than any other mechanism in history. This includes the Greener *Facile Princeps*, Parker, Fox, Stevens, Colt, Remington, Ithaca, Browning and many more.

Add to this the various boxlock permutations from around the world, and one fact stands inarguable: the A&D action is an invention that profoundly changed the sporting world. It continues on that course into this millennium and, with God's grace, it will do so into the next.

But, what of the men involved in the A&D story? How might they to be judged through the lens of history? The answer to that depends on how one measures them.

As a mechanical genius, William Anson stands above all. The legacy of his boxlock action is enduring proof of that. The Anson fore-end latch, "dickey bird" top tang safety, and the intercepting safety sear only add to his stature. However, as a businessman, he may not have been so adept.

On the other hand, John Deeley was a managerial superstar. He could not only produce profits but contrived the means to ensure their expansion, development, and continuation. As a mechanical engineer, he was a bit out of his comfort zone.

Then there was Edwin Anson. He tried valiantly to follow in his father's footsteps, but always seemed to end up short of triumph.

So, what might be the enduring lessons to be drawn from all this? It may well be that we do best in life when we follow our God-given talents and natural gifts. Another is that all men are mortal. As John Donne once said, "...never send to know for whom the bell tolls; it tolls for thee."

So, a man's most lasting legacy is his accomplishments. And how they helped us all to advance. Fortunately, the goodness of Anson and Deeley's boxlock gun has endured for far more than a century.

Few men could wish for a greater monument.

APPENDIX

NOTE: This section contains many of the full or expanded documents that have been referred to in Chapter texts. These include patents, key articles from periodicals, catalogue sections, advertisements and more. Please understand that some of the licensing contracts may be abbreviated in their central parts, simply because the core language and terms of the agreements are identical from one license to the other. In addition, some patents may not contain their full mechanical descriptions and have been reduced to their essential illustrations.

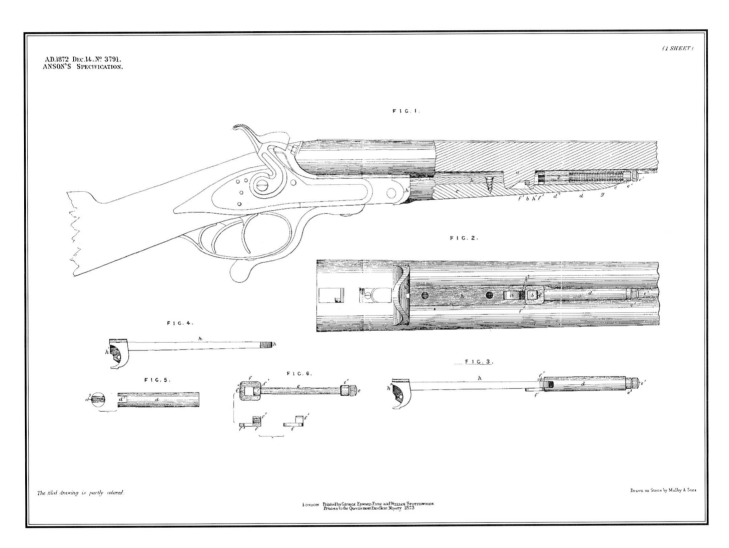

Original Anson Latch Patent Drawing No. 3791.

William Anson's 1872 Fore-end Latch Patent No. 3791

RESERVE COPY

A.D. 1872, 14th December. N° 3791.

Breech-loading Small-arms.

LETTERS PATENT to William Anson, of Birmingham, in the County of Warwick, Gun Maker, for the Invention of "IMPROVEMENTS IN BREECH-LOADING SMALL-ARMS."

Sealed the 30th May 1873, and dated the 14th December 1872.

PROVISIONAL SPECIFICATION left by the said William Anson at the Office of the Commissioners of Patents, with his Petition, on the 14th December 1872.

I, WILLIAM ANSON, of Birmingham, in the County of Warwick, Gun Maker, do hereby declare the nature of the said Invention for "IMPROVEMENTS IN BREECH-LOADING SMALL-ARMS," to be as follows:—

My Invention relates to breech-loading small-arms of the kind called drop down guns; that is, guns in which the barrels turn in a vertical plane upon a joint at the fore end of the body for the purpose of lifting their open breech ends from the face of the break off for charging, and for shutting down the said barrels against the face of the break off for firing.

My said Invention consists in constructing and connecting to the said drop down guns that part of the said guns called the "fore end" in the manner herein-after described. The said "fore end" consists of a prolongation of the body, which prolongation is fixed to the under side of the barrels and completes the joint on which the barrels turn, and also secures the barrels to the body. I dispense with the cross bolt and escutcheons ordinarily employed to connect the fore end to the body and barrels, and in place of the ordinary loop which is fixed at the under side of and between the barrels I make an undercut notch or hook, and I also make the extreme end of the "fore end" tubular. A bolt or rod working in the said tubular part of the fore end is provided at its outer end with a thumb plate, and at its inner end with a frame carrying a transverse bar, the said frame working in guides on either side a cavity near the middle of the fore end. A coiled spring around the bolt described tends to press it outwards or towards the muzzle of the gun. The rear part of the fore end is provided with the usual stop and abutment for completing the joint and securing the barrels to the body of the gun. In putting the said fore end in its place, its rear end is brought against the joint of the barrels in the ordinary manner, and the said fore end is pressed against the under side of the barrels. The undercut projecting notch or hook enters the cavity in the fore end, the cross bar coming in contact with the inclined side of the said notch or hook. The said cross bar is thereby forced back until the fore end is fully pressed to its seat, when the said cross bar snaps under the notch or hook by the action of the coiled spring, and the fore end is thereby secured in its placed.

In order to remove the fore end it is only necessary to press upon the thumb plate at the extreme end of the "fore end," when the cross bar is pressed back from under the notch or hook, and the fore end being thereby released may be lifted from the body of the gun.

SPECIFICATION in pursuance of the conditions of the Letters Patent, filed by the said William Anson in the Great Seal Patent Office on the 10th June 1873.

TO ALL TO WHOM THESE PRESENTS SHALL COME, I, WILLIAM ANSON, of Birmingham, in the County of Warwick, Gun Maker, send greeting.

WHEREAS Her most Excellent Majesty Queen Victoria, by Her Letters Patent, bearing date the Fourteenth day of December, in the year of our Lord One thousand eight hundred and seventy-two, in the thirty-sixth year of Her reign, did, for Herself, Her heirs and successors, give and grant unto me, the said William Anson, Her special license that I, the said William Anson, my executors, administrators, and assigns, or such others as I, the said William Anson, my executors, administrators, and assigns, should at any time agree with, and no others, from time to time and at all times thereafter during the term therein expressed, should and lawfully might make, use, exercise, and vend, within the United Kingdom of Great Britain and Ireland, the Channel Islands, and Isle of Man, an Invention for "IMPROVEMENTS IN BREECH-LOADING SMALL-ARMS," upon the condition (amongst others) that I, the said William Anson, my executors or administrators, by an instrument in writing under my or their, or one of their hands and seals, should particularly describe and ascertain the nature of the said Invention, and in what manner the same was to be performed, and cause the same to be filed in the Great Seal Patent Office within six calendar months next and immediately after the date of the said Letters Patent.

NOW KNOW YE, that I, the said William Anson, do hereby declare the nature of the said Invention, and in what manner the same is to be performed, to be particularly described and ascertained in and by the following statement thereof, that is to say:—

My Invention relates to breech-loading small-arms of the kind called drop down guns; that is, guns in which the barrels turn in a vertical plane upon a joint at the fore end of the body for the purpose of lifting their open breech ends from the face of the break off for charging, and for shutting down the said barrels against the face of the break off for firing.

My said Invention consists in constructing and connecting to the said drop down guns that part of the said guns called the "fore end" in the manner herein-after described. The said "fore end" consists of a prolongation of the body, which prolongation is fixed to the under side of the barrels and completes the joint on which the barrels turn, and also secures the barrels to the body. I dispense with the cross bolt and escutcheons ordinarily employed to connect the fore end to the body and barrels, and in place of the ordinary loop which is fixed at the under side and between the barrels I make an undercut notch or hook, and I also make the extreme end of the fore end tubular. A bolt or rod working in the said tubular part of the fore end is provided at its outer end with a thumb plate or head, and at its inner end with a frame carrying a transverse bar, the said frame working in guides on either side a cavity near the middle of the fore end. A coiled spring around the bolt described tends to press it outwards or towards the muzzle of the gun. The rear part of the fore end is provided with the usual stop and abutment for completing the joint and securing the barrels to the body of the gun. In putting the said fore end in its place, its rear end is brought against the joint of the barrels in the ordinary manner, and the said fore end is pressed against the under side of the barrels. The undercut projecting notch or hook enters the cavity in the fore end, the cross bar coming in contact with the inclined side of the said notch or hook. The said cross bar is thereby forced back until the fore end is fully pressed to its seat, when the said cross bar snaps upon the notch or hook by the action of the coiled spring, and the fore end is thereby secured in its place.

In order to remove the fore end it is only necessary to press upon the thumb plate at the extreme end of the fore end, when the cross bar is pressed back from the notch or hook, and the fore end being thereby released may be lifted from the body of the gun.

Having explained the nature of my Invention, I will proceed to describe with reference to the accompanying Drawing the manner in which the same is to be performed.

Figure 1 represents in side elevation partly in longitudinal section; and Figure 2 in plan of under side a drop down gun, the fore end of which is connected to the barrels according to my Invention; Figure 3 represents a side elevation of the fore end separately without the wooden cover; and Figures 4, 5, and 6 represent the metallic parts of which the fore end is made. In Figure 2, the wooden cover of the fore end is removed. The same letters indicate the same parts in the several Figures of the Drawing.

a is the loop on the under side of the barrels provided with an undercut notch or hook b; c is the wooden part or cover of the fore end. The muzzle end of the part c is made tubular, and in the said tubular part the metallic tube d is fitted. In the tube d a sliding bolt or rod e

William Anson's 1872 Fore-end Latch Patent No. 3791 — Cont'd.

Specification.　　　A.D. 1872.—Nº 3791　　　5

Anson's Improvements in Breech-loading Small-arms.

works. The said rod e has at its outer end a milled head e^2, and at its inner end a frame f, the part f^2 of the said frame constituting a cross bar for engaging with the hook or notch b of the loop a. Within the tubular part d of the fore end, and around the bolt or rod e is a coiled
5 spring g, by means of which the bolt is pressed outwards or towards the muzzle end of the gun. The coiled spring g takes a bearing at one end against the internal shoulder d^2 of the tubular part d, and at the other end against the collar e^3 on the end of the bolt e. The frame f, f^2, of the bolt slides on the under side of the bar h, the screwed eye f^3 on the
10 said frame working in the slot h^2 in the bar h. The bar h carries at its rear end the usual abutment and stop at h^3. In fixing the fore end to the under side of the barrels its rear end h^3 is placed against the joint on the barrels, and the said fore end is pressed against the under side of the barrels. As the fore end approaches the barrels the notch or hook b
15 passes through the opening in the frame f, and the bolt is pressed towards the breech end of the gun by the inner side of the bar f^2 of the said frame f, bearing against the inclined side of the notch or hook b. On the fore end being fully pressed to its seat the cross bar f^2 snaps upon the notch or hook b of the loop a by the action of the coiled
20 spring g, and the fore end is thereby securely connected to the barrels as illustrated in Figures 1 and 2. To remove the fore end the milled head e^2 of the bolt is pressed inwards or towards the breech end of the gun. The cross bolt f^2 is thereby removed from off the notch or hook b, and the fore end is released and may be lifted from the under side of the
25 barrels.

I manufacture the metallic parts of the fore end in the manner represented in Figures 4, 5, and 6 of the Drawing. I make the bolt part of the fore end of the rod e with its collar e^3 and milled head e^2 in one piece, and I secure to the said rod e the separate frame f, f^2, the end of
30 the said rod e being screwed into the screwed eye f^3 on the said frame. I make the tubular part d of a separate piece which I braze to the bar h, the end h^4 of the said bar taking into a cross slot d^3 in the end of the tubular part d. By building up the parts of the bolt in this way great simplicity of manufacture is secured, and the parts may conveniently be
35 made by machinery. As the tube d serves only as a guide for the rod e and an abutment for the spring g, the said tube d may be dispensed with, and the wooden cover c of the fore end may have in it the requisite tubular opening and shoulder to serve as a guide for the rod e, and an abutment for the spring g.

6　　　A.D. 1872.—Nº 3791.　　　Specification.

Anson's Improvements in Breech-loading Small-arms.

Having now described the nature of my Invention, and the manner in which the same is to be performed, I wish it to be understood that I do not limit myself to the precise details herein described and illustrated, as the same may be varied without departing from the nature of my Invention, but I claim as my Invention the improvements in breech-
5 loading small-arms herein-before described and illustrated in the accompanying Drawing, that is to say, connecting the fore ends of the said small-arms to the barrels, and disconnecting them from the said barrels by means of a sliding bolt, the parts of which are constructed, arranged, and combined, substantially as described and illustrated. 10

In witness whereof, I, the said William Anson, have hereunto set my hand and seal, this Seventh day of June, in the year of our Lord One thousand eight hundred and seventy-three.

　　　　　　　　　　　　　WILLIAM ANSON. (L.S.)

Witness,　　　15
GEORGE SHAW.

LONDON:
Printed by GEORGE EDWARD EYRE and WILLIAM SPOTTISWOODE,
Printers to the Queen's most Excellent Majesty. 1873.

RESERVE COPY

A.D. 1872 ...... Nº 3791*.

Breechloading Small Arms.

ANSON'S DISCLAIMER AND MEMORANDUM OF ALTERATION.

Filed 5th August 1879.

In the Matter of Letters Patent granted to WILLIAM ANSON, of Birmingham, in the County of Warwick, Gun Maker, for the Invention of "IMPROVEMENTS IN BREECH-LOADING SMALL-ARMS," bearing date the Fourteenth day of December 1872, No. 3791.
5 DISCLAIMER AND MEMORANDUM OF ALTERATION as proposed to be entered by the said William Anson, of Birmingham, in the County of Warwick, pursuant to the Statutes in that case made and provided.

WHEREAS Her Majesty Queen Victoria, by Her Letters Patent under the Great Seal of the United Kingdom of Great Britain and Ireland, bearing date at
10 Westminster, the Fourteenth day of December 1872, No. 3791, in the thirty-sixth year of Her reign, did give and grant unto the said William Anson, his executors, administrators, and assigns, the sole privilege for the term of fourteen years thence next ensuing, of making, using, exercising, and vending within the United Kingdom of Great Britain and Ireland, the Channel Islands, and Isle of
15 Man, the said Invention of "IMPROVEMENTS IN BREECH-LOADING SMALL-ARMS:"

And whereas in pursuance of a proviso in the said Letters Patent contained, I, the said William Anson, did within six calendar months next after the date of the said Letters Patent cause a Specification or instrument in writing under my hand and seal, purporting to describe and ascertain the nature of the said Invention, and
20 in what manner the same was to be performed, to be duly filed in the Great Seal Patent Office:

And whereas since the filing of the said Specification I have ascertained that certain parts of the Invention which at the date of my said Letters Patent I believed to be new had been used before the said date, and I now desire to confine
25 in the manner hereinafter indicated my claim in respect of the said Invention to those parts thereof that had not been so used;

2　　　A.D. 1872.—Nº 3791*.　　　Disclaimer, &c.

Anson's Improvements in Breechloading Small Arms.

I hereby disclaim and after the said Specification in manner following, that is to say:—

Referring to the Queen's Printers' copy of the said Specification, in page 5, line 26, between the words "end" and "in" I insert the words "with its
5 fastening;" at the end of line 27 of the same page I omit the words "part of" and I substitute therefor the word "for;" in line 31 of the same page between the words "I" and "braze" I insert the word "sometimes;" in line 35 of the same page I omit the words "as," occurring between the words "machinery" and "the," and also the word "only," occurring between the words "serves" and "as;" in the
10 same page, line 36, I insert the word "but" between the letter "g" and the word "the;" in page 6, lines 3 to 5, I omit the words "limit myself to the precise details herein described and illustrated, as the same may be varied without departing from the nature of my Invention," and I substitute therefor the words "claim generally the use of a sliding spring bolt for securing the fore-ends of drop down guns to the
15 barrels;" on the same page, line 9, I omit the words "of which are," and between the words "bolt" and "the" I insert the words "such as e sliding in a tubular guide such as d."

And the said Specification when so disclaimed, altered, and amended, will read as follows:—

TO ALL TO WHOM THESE PRESENTS SHALL COME, I, WILLIAM 20
ANSON, of Birmingham, in the County of Warwick, Gun-Maker, send greeting.

WHEREAS Her most Excellent Majesty Queen Victoria, by Her Letters Patent bearing date the Fourteenth day of December, in the year of our Lord One thousand eight hundred and seventy two, in the thirty-sixth year of Her reign, did
25 for Herself, Her heirs and successors, give and grant unto me, the said William Anson, Her special license, that I, the said William Anson, my executors, administrators, and assigns, or such others as I, the said William Anson, my executors, administrators, and assigns, should at any time agree with and no others, from time to time and at all times thereafter during the term therein expressed, should and lawfully
30 might make, use, exercise, and vend, within the United Kingdom of Great Britain and Ireland, the Channel Islands, and Isle of Man, an Invention for "IMPROVEMENTS IN BREECH-LOADING SMALL-ARMS," upon the condition (amongst others) that I, the said William Anson, my executors or administrators, by an instrument in writing under my, or their, or one of their hands and seals, should particularly
35 describe and ascertain the nature of the said Invention, and in what manner the same was to be performed, and cause the same to be filed in the Great Seal Patent Office within six calendar months next and immediately after the date of the said Letters Patent.

NOW KNOW YE, that I, the said William Anson, do hereby declare the 40
nature of the said Invention, and in what manner the same is to be performed, to be particularly described and ascertained in and by the following statement thereof, that is to say:—

My Invention relates to breech-loading small-arms of the kind called drop down guns, that is, guns in which the barrels turn in a vertical plane upon a joint at the
45 fore end of the body for the purpose of lifting their open breech ends from the face of the break off for charging, and for shutting down the said barrels against the face of the break off for firing.

My said Invention consists in constructing and connecting to the said drop down guns that part of the said guns called the "fore-end" in the manner herein-after
50 described. The said "fore-end" consists of a prolongation of the body, which prolongation is fixed to the underside of the barrels and completes the joint on which the barrels turn, and also secures the barrels to the body. I dispense with the cross bolt and escutcheons ordinarily employed to connect the fore end to the body and barrels, and in place of the ordinary loop which is fixed to the under side and
55 between the barrels I make an undercut notch or hook, and I also make the extreme

William Anson's 1872 Fore-end Latch Patent No. 3791 — Cont'd

Anson's Improvements in Breechloading Small Arms.

end of the fore end tubular. A bolt or rod working in the said tubular part of the fore end is provided at its outer end with a thumb plate or head, and at its inner end with a frame carrying a transverse bar, the said frame working in guides on either side a cavity near the middle of the fore-end. A coiled spring around the bolt described tends to press it outwards or towards the muzzle of the gun. The rear part of the fore end is provided with the usual stop and abutment for completing the joint and securing the barrels to the body of the gun. In putting the said fore end in its place in its place its rear end is brought against the joint of the barrels in the ordinary manner, and the said fore end is pressed against the underside of the barrels. The undercut projecting notch or hook enters the cavity in the fore-end, the cross bar coming in contact with the inclined side of the said notch or hook; the said cross bar is thereby forced back until the fore end is fully pressed to its seat when the said cross bar snaps upon the notch or hook by the action of the coiled spring, and the fore end is thereby secured in its place.

In order to remove the fore end it is only necessary to press upon the thumb plate at the extreme end of the fore end, when the cross bar is pressed back from the notch or hook, and the fore end being thereby released may be lifted from the body of the gun.

Having explained the nature of my Invention I will proceed to describe, with reference to the accompanying Drawing, the manner in which the same is to be performed.

Figure 1 represents in side elevation partly in longitudinal section, and Figure 2 in plan of underside, a drop down gun, the fore end of which is connected to the barrels according to my Invention; Figure 3 represents a side elevation of the fore-end separately without the wooden cover; and Figures 4, 5, and 6 represent the metallic parts of which the fore end is made. In Figure 2 the wooden cover of the fore end is removed. The same letters indicate the same parts in the several Figures of the Drawing.

a is the loop on the under side of the barrels provided with an under cut notch or hook b; c is the wooden part or cover of the fore end. The muzzle end of the part c is made tubular, and in the said tubular part the metallic tube d is fitted. In the tube d a sliding bolt or rod e works. The said rod e has at its outer end a milled head e^2, and at its inner end a frame f; the part f^2 of the said frame constituting a cross bar for engaging with the hook or notch b of the loop a within the tubular part d of the fore end, and around the bolt or rod e is a coiled spring g, by means of which the bolt is pressed outwards or towards the muzzle end of the gun. The coiled spring g takes a bearing at one end against the internal shoulder d^2 of the tubular part d, and at the other end against the collar e^3 on the end of the bolt e. The frame f, f^2, of the bolt slides on the under side of the bar h, the screwed eye f^3 on the said frame working in the slot h^2 in the bar h. The bar h carries at its rear end the usual abutment and stop at h^3. In fixing the fore end to the under side of the barrels its rear end h^3 is placed against the joint on the barrels, and the said fore end is pressed against the underside of the barrels. As the fore end approaches the barrels the notch or hook b passes through the opening in the frame f, and the bolt is pressed towards the breech end of the gun by the inner side of the bar f^2 of the said frame f, bearing against the inclined side of the notch or hook b. On the fore end being fully pressed to its seat the cross bar f^2 snaps upon the notch or hook b of the loop a by the action of the coiled spring g, and the fore end is thereby securely connected to the barrels as illustrated in Figures 1 and 2. To remove the fore end the milled head e^2 of the bolt is pressed inwards or towards the breech end of the gun. The cross bolt f^2 is thereby removed from off the notch or hook b, and the fore end is released, and may be lifted from the underside of the barrels.

I manufacture the metallic parts of the fore end with its fastening in the manner represented in Figures 4, 5, and 6 of the Drawing. I make the bolt for the fore end of the rod e with its collar e^3 and milled head e^2 in one piece, and I secure to the said rod e the separate frame f, f^2, the end of the said rod e being screwed into

the screwed eye f^3 on the said frame. I make the tubular part d of a separate piece, which I sometimes braze to the bar h, the end h^4 of the said bar taking into a cross slot d^3 in the end of the tubular part d. By building up the parts of the bolt in this way great simplicity of manufacture is secured, and the parts may conveniently be made by machinery. The tube d serves as a guide for the rod e and an abutment for the spring g, but the said tube d may be dispensed with, and the wooden cover c of the fore end may have in it the requisite tubular opening and shoulder to serve as a guide for the rod e and an abutment for the spring g.

Having now described the nature of my Invention, and the manner in which the same is to be performed, I wish it to be understood that I do not claim generally the use of a sliding spring bolt for securing the fore-ends of drop down guns to the barrels, but I claim as my Invention the improvements in breech-loading small-arms herein-before described and illustrated in the accompanying Drawing, that is to say, connecting the fore ends of the said small-arms to the barrels and disconnecting them from the said barrels by means of a sliding bolt, such as e, sliding in a tubular guide such as d, the parts constructed, arranged, and combined substantially as described and illustrated.

In witness whereof, I, the said William Anson, have hereunto set my hand and seal, this Seventh day of June, in the year of our Lord One thousand eight hundred and seventy three.

WILLIAM ANSON. (L.S.)

Witness,
GEORGE SHAW.

In witness whereof, I, the said William Anson, have hereunto set my hand and seal, this Seventh day of July, in the year of our Lord One thousand eight hundred and seventy-nine.

WILLIAM ANSON. (L.S.)

To the Commissioners of Patents for Inventions.

I hereby grant my fiat giving leave to the above named William Anson to file in the Great Seal Patent Office with the Specification to which the same relates the above written Disclaimer and Memorandum of Alteration. Dated this Second day of August, One thousand eight hundred and seventy nine.

JOHN HOLKER,
Attorney General.

LONDON: Printed by GEORGE EDWARD EYRE and WILLIAM SPOTTISWOODE,
Printers to the Queen's most Excellent Majesty.
For Her Majesty's Stationery Office.
1879.

The Original 1875 A&D British Patent No. 1756

RESERVE COPY

A.D. 1875, 11th May. N° 1756.

Breech-loading Small-arms.

LETTERS PATENT to William Anson, of Birmingham, in the County of Warwick, Gun Maker, and John Deeley, of Birmingham, aforesaid, Gun Maker, for the Invention of "IMPROVEMENTS IN BREECH-LOADING SMALL-ARMS."

Sealed the 9th July 1875, and dated the 11th May 1875.

PROVISIONAL SPECIFICATION left by the said William Anson and John Deeley at the Office of the Commissioners of Patents, with their Petition, on the 11th May 1875.

We, WILLIAM ANSON, of Birmingham, in the County of Warwick, Gun Maker, and JOHN DEELEY, of Birmingham, aforesaid, Gun Maker, do hereby declare the nature of the said Invention for "IMPROVEMENTS IN BREECH-LOADING SMALL-ARMS," to be as follows:—

Our Invention has reference to breech-loading small-arms of the kind commonly called "drop-down" guns and pistols, that is, breech-loading guns and pistols in which the barrels turn upon a joint, the open breech ends being raised from the break off for charging and shut down and fastened against the break off during discharge.

A.D. 1875.—N° 1756.

Anson & Deeley's Improvements in Breech-loading Small-arms.

Our improvements consist, first, of the following construction and arrangement of parts of the lock mechanism, whereby the cocking of the arm is effected by the raising of the breech ends of the barrels for charging. The fore end of the arm is prolonged backwards beyond the joint on which the barrels turn, the prolonged part entering into and working in a groove in the body of the arm. The fore end thus constitutes the long arm of a lever and the part of the said fore end prolonged backwards the short arm of the same lever, the ordinary joint of the fore end constituting the fulcrum of the said lever. The hammer or striker consists of a lever situated for the most part within the groove in which the short arm of the fore end lever works, the end of the short arm of the fore end lever bearing against the under side of the end of the hammer or striker lever within the groove described. The other end of the hammer or striker lever projects out of the body of the arm, and is turned upwards at the back of the brake off into a nearly semicircular form, its end entering into and working in a hole in the said break off in a line with the axis of the barrel, when the said barrel is shut down for firing. The said hammer or striker lever is provided with a a mainspring and a sear is pressed by a sear spring against the under side of the said hammer or striker lever, and takes into a bent in the said hammer or striker lever when the latter has been brought into a cocked position.

The action of the parts is as follows:—When on raising the breech ends of the barrels, the fore end is depressed, its short arm rises and lifts the end of the hammer or striker lever bearing upon it. The other or striking end of the said hammer or striker lever is thereby drawn back, the sear taking into the bent described and thereby retaining the hammer in its cocked position on the shutting down of the barrels for firing. The pressure of the finger on the trigger releases the sear from the bent in the hammer lever in the usual manner, and the hammer by the action of the mainspring discharges the gun or pistol.

Instead of making the end of the hammer lever strike directly on the primer of the cartridge, it may drive forward a loose striker, sliding in a hole in the break off.

Instead of making the hammer turn upon a joint it may have a rectilinear sliding motion in the groove described. In this case the mainspring may be either a coiled spring or an ordinary flat or V spring.

A.D. 1875.—N° 1756.

Anson & Deeley's Improvements in Breech-loading Small-arms.

When the barrels are fastened and unfastened by a lever on the under side of the arm, the cocking of the arm may be effected by the motion of the said lever, instead of by the motion of the fore end.

Our improvements consist, secondly, in the following arrangement of the lever mechanism situated on the tang of the break off for locking down and unlocking the barrels. We simplify and improve the said mechanism in the following manner:—The head of the lever is jointed at one side to the tang of the break off, a short link being jointed to the middle and under side of the head of the said lever. The other end of the link carries a pin, which passes through and travels in a slot in the tang of the break off. This pin is connected with a rod parallel with the slot and capable of a sliding motion, its rear end working through a fixed bearing. By means of a coiled spring the sliding rod is pressed towards the face of the break off, tending to bring the lever to its normal or locking position. On pressing the thumb plate of the lever aside, the unlocking of the barrels is effected, and on shutting down the barrels their locking is effected by a snapping action.

Our improvements are applicable to double and single barrel drop-down guns and pistols.

SPECIFICATION in pursuance of the conditions of the Letters Patent, filed by the said William Anson and John Deeley in the Great Seal Patent Office on the 10th November 1875.

TO ALL TO WHOM THESE PRESENTS SHALL COME, we, WILLIAM ANSON, of Birmingham, in the County of Warwick, Gun Maker, and JOHN DEELEY, of Birmingham, aforesaid, Gun Maker, send greeting.

WHEREAS Her most Excellent Majesty Queen Victoria, by Her Letters Patent, bearing date the Eleventh day of May, in the year of our Lord One thousand eight hundred and seventy-five, in the thirty-eighth year of Her reign, did, for Herself, Her heirs and successors, give and grant unto us, the said William Anson and John Deeley, Her special license that we, the said William Anson and John Deeley, our executors, administrators, and assigns, or such others as we, the said William Anson and John Deeley, our executors, administrators, and assigns, should at any time agree with, and no others, from time to

---

A.D. 1875.—N° 1756.

Anson & Deeley's Improvements in Breech-loading Small-arms.

time and at all times thereafter during the term therein expressed, should and lawfully might make, use, exercise and vend, within the United Kingdom of Great Britain and Ireland, the Channel Islands, and Isle of Man, an Invention for "IMPROVEMENTS IN BREECH-LOADING SMALL-ARMS," upon the condition (amongst others) that we, the said William Anson and John Deeley, our executors or administrators, by an instrument in writing under our or their hands and seals, or under the hand and seal of one of us or them, should particularly describe and ascertain the nature of the said Invention, and in what manner the same was to be performed, and cause the same to be filed in the Great Seal Patent Office within six calendar months next and immediately after the date of the said Letters Patent.

NOW KNOW YE, that we, the said William Anson and John Deeley do hereby declare the nature of the said Invention, and in what manner the same is to be performed, to be particularly described and ascertained in and by the following statement thereof, that is to say:—

Our Invention has reference to breech-loading small-arms of the kind commonly called drop-down guns and pistols, that is, breech-loading guns and pistols in which the barrels turn upon a joint, the open breech ends being raised from the break off for charging, and shut down and fastened against the break off during discharge.

Our improvements consist first of the following construction and arrangement of parts of the lock mechanism whereby the cocking of the arm is effected by the raising of the breech ends of the barrels for charging. The fore end of the arm is prolonged backward beyond the joint on which the barrels turn, the prolonged part entering into and working in a groove in the body of the arm. The fore end thus constitutes the long arm of a lever and the part of the said fore end prolonged backwards the short arm of the same lever, the ordinary joint of the fore end constituting the fulcrum of the said lever. The hammer or striker consists of a lever situated for the most part within the groove in which the short arm of the fore end lever works, the end of the short arm of the fore end lever bearing against the under side of the end of the hammer or striker lever within the groove described. The other end of the hammer or striker lever projects out of the body of the arm, and is turned upwards at the back of the break-off into a nearly semi-

The Original 1875 A&D British Patent No. 1756 — Cont'd.

Specification.   A.D. 1875.—N° 1756.   5

Anson & Deeley's Improvements in Breech-loading Small-arms.

circular form, its end entering into and working in a hole in the said break off in a line with the axis of the barrel when the said barrel is shut down for firing. The said hammer or striker lever is provided with a mainspring, and a sear is pressed by a sear spring against the under side of the said hammer or striker lever, and takes into a bent in the said hammer or striker lever when the latter has been brought into a cocked position.

The action of the parts is as follows:—When on raising the breech ends of the barrels the fore end is depressed, its short arm rises and lifts the end of the hammer or striker lever bearing upon it. The other or striking end of the said hammer or striker lever is thereby drawn back, the sear taking into the bent described and thereby retaining the hammer in its cocked position on the shutting down of the barrels for firing. The pressure of the finger on the trigger releases the sear from the bent in the hammer lever in the usual manner, and the hammer by the action of the mainspring discharges the gun or pistol.

Instead of making the end of the hammer lever strike directly on the primer of the cartridge it may drive forward a loose striker sliding in a hole in the break off.

The cocking of the arm may be effected by the motion of an under lever acting directly on the hammer lever instead of by the motion of the fore end.

Our improvements consist, secondly, in the following arrangement of the lever mechanism situated on the tang of the break off for locking down and unlocking the barrels:—

We simplify and improve the said mechanism in the following manner:—The head of the lever is jointed at one side to the tang of the break off, a short link being jointed to the middle and under side of the head of the said lever. The other end of the link carries a pin which passes through and travels in a slot in the tang of the break off. This pin is connected with a rod parallel with the slot and capable of a sliding motion, its rear end working through a fixed bearing. By means of a coiled spring the sliding rod is pressed towards the face of the break off, tending to bring the lever to its normal or locking position. On pressing the thumb plate of the lever aside the unlocking of the barrels is effected, and on shutting down the barrels their locking is effected by a snapping action.

6   A.D. 1875.—N° 1756.   Specification.

Anson & Deeley's Improvements in Breech-loading Small-arms.

Our improvements are applicable to double and single barrel drop-down guns and pistols.

We will now proceed to describe with reference to the accompanying Drawing the manner in which our Invention may be performed.

Figure 1 represents in side elevation, and Figure 2 in longitudinal vertical section a double barrel breech-loading drop-down gun containing cocking mechanism constructed according to our Invention, the hammer or striker lever being represented in its discharged position.

Figure 3 represents the said mechanism with the hammer or striker lever in its cocked position ready for firing.

Figure 4 represents in cross section, and Figure 4^A in plan of under side the body of the gun without the fore end lever.

Figure 5 represents in side elevation, and Figure 6 in plan the fore end lever detached.

Figure 6^A represents an arrangement of cocking mechanism worked by a lever on the under side of the gun.

Figure 7 represents in longitudinal section, and Figure 8 in plan our arrangement of lever mechanism for locking and unlocking the barrels.

Figure 9 is a plan of the under side of the body, and Figure 10 represents the bolt separately.

The same letters of reference indicate the same parts.

We will first describe the cocking mechanism represented in Figures 1, 2, 3, 4, 4^A, 5, and 6.

a, b, b, is the fore end lever turning on the joint c, the ordinary fore end marked a constituting the long arm of the lever, and each of the parts b, b, which are prolonged backwards beyond the joint c constituting the short arm of the same lever. The head of the fore end lever a, b, b, bears against the joint end of the body d in the ordinary way, the cross pin c forming the fulcrum of the said fore end lever passing through the sides of the body d, and also through the short arms b, b. The said short arms b, b, of the fore end lever work in the channels or grooves e in the body d, see the plan and cross section, Figures 4 and 4^A. The tail end of each of the short arms b, b, is inclined as represented.

Specification.   A.D. 1875.—N° 1756.   7

Anson & Deeley's Improvements in Breech-loading Small-arms.

f, f^2, is one of the hammer or striker levers of the gun, a hammer or striker lever being situated opposite each of the arms b, b, by which it is operated. The said hammer or striker levers turn on the centre g, and their short arms f^2 are pressed upon by the mainspring h. The hammer or striker levers f, f^2, are situated for the most part in the channels or grooves e, e, in the body, in which the short arms b, b, of the fore end levers work, the end of each of the short arms b, b, of the fore end levers bearing against the under side of the respective arms f^2 of the hammer or striker levers f, f^2, (see Figures 2 and 3). The other end of the hammer or striker lever projects out of the body of the gun, and has a nearly semicircular form, its nose or striking end working in a hole i in the break off k in a line with the axis of the barrel l when in its depressed position. In each of the hammer or striker levers f, f^2, is a bent f^3, with which a sear m engages, the said sear being pressed down by a spring n.

When the gun has been discharged the parts of the cocking mechanism occupy the respective positions represented in Figures 1 and 2, the hammer or striker lever being represented in its released position, and its nose end having been projected by the action of the spring h through the break off k, so as to strike upon the cartridge and discharge the gun. The barrels being unfastened their breech ends rise, and the fore end a is depressed. By the depression of the fore end a the short arms b, b, of the fore end lever turn upon the centre c, and their ends acting against the under side of the ends of the arms f^2, f^2, of the hammer or striker levers bearing upon them lift the said arms f^2, f^2, and draw back the opposite or striking arms f, f, into the break off, the sears m taking into the bents in the said hammer or striker levers, and retaining them in their cocked positions, as illustrated in Figure 3.

After the barrels have been charged and shut down the acting arms b, b, of the fore end lever descend from the short arms f^2 of the hammer levers f, f^2, leaving the said hammer levers ready for the next discharge of the gun, as illustrated in Figure 3, the said hammer levers being released and the gun discharged by pressure on the triggers p, p, in the usual way.

For the purpose of holding the hammer or striker levers f, f^2, in a position of safety when the gun is not required to be discharged we

8   A.D. 1875.—N° 1756.   Specification.

Anson & Deeley's Improvements in Breech-loading Small-arms.

combine with the gun a safety bolt for each hammer lever. The said safety bolts are marked g, g. Each of the said safety bolts consists of a cylinder working in the break off k. The opening in which the said bolt g works crosses the striker hole, through which the nose of the striker lever acts to discharge the gun. A portion of the bolt is cut away, so that when the bolt is turned in one position the striker hole is closed as represented in Figure 3, but when turned at a right angle to that position the striker hole is open, as represented in Figure 2. The said bolt has at its end a small lever g^2, by which it can be turned as herein-after explained, the weight of which lever brings the bolt into the position, Figure 3, in which it closes the striker hole when the said bolt is at liberty to move.

The action of the safety bolt is as follows:—On depressing the barrels to open the breech ends the short arm of the fore end lever withdraws the hammer, and the safety bolt being no longer supported by the said hammer, the said bolt turns into the position, in which it closes the striker hole by the weight of the lever at its end. The gun is now in a position of safety, for the striker hole being closed the hammer cannot reach the cartridge. In order to discharge the gun the thumb or finger presses the said lever g^2 upwards, when the changed position of the bolt brings its cutaway part opposite the nose of the hammer, which advances a short distance and engages with the sear, at the same time supporting the bolt in the position to which it has been brought. By pulling the trigger the gun may now be discharged.

The position of the safety bolts is best seen in the gun represented in Figures 4^A, 8, and 9.

When the hammer or striker levers f, f^2, are used for actuating loose strikers the nose ends of the said levers are shortened, the said loose strikers working in holes in the break off and being forced forward by the action of the nose ends of the said hammer levers upon them.

Figure 6^A represents our arrangement of cocking mechanism for cocking the hammer by the operation of a hand lever on the under side of the gun. r, r^2, is the hammer or striker lever turning on the centre r^3, the said centre being situated in a line with the face of the break off k. r^4 is the spring of the hammer lever. s is the bent in the hammer, and t is the sear, which on the cocking of the gun takes into

The Original 1875 A&D British Patent No. 1756 — Cont'd.

Specification. A.D. 1875.—N° 1756. 9

Anson & Deeley's Improvements in Breech-loading Small-arms.

the said bent and holds the hammer lever in its cocked position. u, u^2, is the hand lever for operating the hammer or striker lever r, r^2. The said hand lever turns on the centre u^3, and its short arm u^2 bears against the under side of the short arm r^2 of the hammer or striker lever r, r^2.
5 When the hand lever r is moved in the direction of the arrow the short arm r^2 of the said hammer lever is lifted by the short arm u^2 of the hand lever, and the hammer lever is cocked and held in its cocked position by the sear t engaging with the bent s. The gun is discharged by pressure on the triggers v, v, as usual. By arranging and jointing the two levers
10 r, r^3, and u, u^3, in the manner represented the cocking of the gun is effected with great ease.

The safety bolt herein-before described may be applied to the cocking mechanism Figure 6^A.

We will now describe our arrangement of lever mechanism for locking
15 down and unlocking the barrels represented in Figures 7, 8, 9, and 10. w is the hand lever on the tang x of the break off, the said hand lever being connected to the sliding bolt y by a screw pin w^2, the head of the screw pin w^2 being capable of a rotatory motion in the hole in the said hand lever. On the tang x are two cheeks y^2, y^3, against which the
20 head of the hand lever w bears. The cheek y^2 constitutes a fulcrum or bearing about which the hand lever w turns when moved aside to withdraw the bolt as indicated in dotted lines, and the cheek y^3 constitutes a stop. The front end of the sliding bolt y is connected by the screw z to a strong pin or bar 1 sliding in the slot 2 in the tang of the
25 break off. This pin or bar 1 is connected with a sliding rod 3 working through a fixed bearing 4 on the under side of the tang. A coiled spring 5 is situated around the said sliding rod 3, the said spring taking its abutment at one end against the fixed bearing 4, and at the other end against the pin or bar 1.

30 By means of the said coiled spring the snapping action of the bolt y is effected, and the hand lever w returned to its normal position. On pressing the thumb plate end of the hand lever w in the direction of the arrow, Figure 8, it turns on the fixed fulcrum at y^2, and thereby withdraws the bolt y from the prolonged rib 6 between the barrels and
35 unfastens the said barrels, the hand lever being carried with the said bolt. On the withdrawal of the bolt y, the bar 1 slides in the slot 2, and

---

10 A.D. 1875.—N° 1756. Specification.

Anson & Deeley's Improvements in Breech-loading Small-arms.

the rod 3 in its bearing 4, and the coiled spring 5 is compressed. By loosing the hand lever w the coiled spring 5 forces the bolt y towards the face of the break off, and its front end snaps into the prolonged rib 6 and fastens down the barrels, the hand lever w at the same time being
5 returned to its normal position, as shown in the Drawing. The sliding bolt works in a channel or cutaway part in the tang of the break off.

Instead of connecting the hand lever directly to the pin or bar 1, as represented, it may be connected by a link.

Having now described the nature of our Invention, and the manner in which the same is to be performed, we wish it to be understood that
10 we do not limit ourselves to the precise details herein described and illustrated, as the same may be varied without departing from the nature of our Invention; but we claim as our Invention of improvements in breech-loading small-arms of the kind called drop down guns and pistols,—
15
First. The construction and combination of the parts of lock mechanism herein-before described and illustrated in Figures 1, 2, 3, 4, 4^A, 5, and 6 of the accompanying Drawing, for cocking the said guns and pistols by the raising of the breech ends of the barrels for charging, that is to say,
20 converting the ordinary fore end into a lever by prolonging the said fore end backwards into the body of the gun or pistol, the said prolonged part constituting the short arm of a lever, which short arm on the raising of the breech ends of the barrels acts upon and cocks a hammer or a striker lever, substantially as described and illustrated, whether the
25 said hammer or striker lever act directly upon the cartridge or upon a loose striker.

Secondly. The arrangement or combination of the parts herein-before described and illustrated in Figure 6^A of the accompanying Drawing, for cocking the hammer or striker lever by directly acting on the said
30 hammer or striker lever by means of a hand lever on the under side of the gun or pistol.

Thirdly. The combination or arrangement of parts of the safety bolts herein-before described and represented in the accompanying Drawing.

Fourthly. The arrangement or combination of the parts herein-before
35 described and illustrated in Figures 7, 8, 9, and 10 of the accompanying

---

Specification. A.D. 1875.—N° 1756. 11

Anson & Deeley's Improvements in Breech-loading Small-arms.

Drawing, of lever mechanism situated on the tang of the break off for bolting and unbolting the barrels of the said guns and pistols.

In witness whereof, we, the said William Anson and John Deeley, have hereunto set our hands and seals, this Second day of
5 November, in the year of our Lord One thousand eight hundred and seventy-five.

     WILLIAM ANSON. (L.S.)
     JOHN DEELEY. (L.S.)

Witness,
10 HENRY SKERRETT,
  Clerk to George Shaw,
   Birmingham.

LONDON:
Printed by GEORGE EDWARD EYRE and WILLIAM SPOTTISWOODE,
Printers to the Queen's most Excellent Majesty. 1875.

Original Drawing of British Patent No. 1756

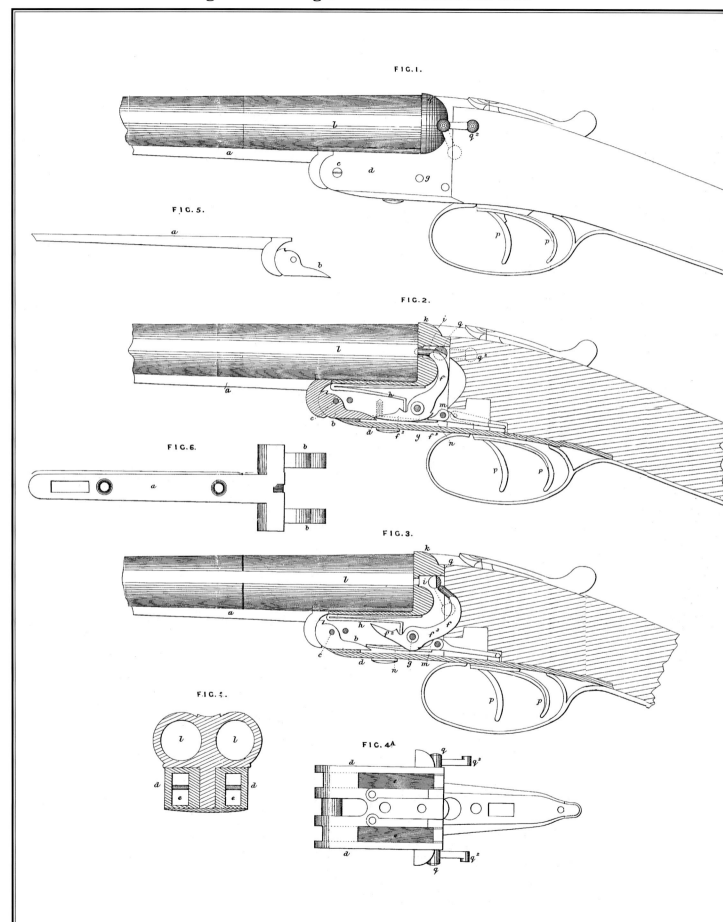

Original Drawing of British Patent No. 1756

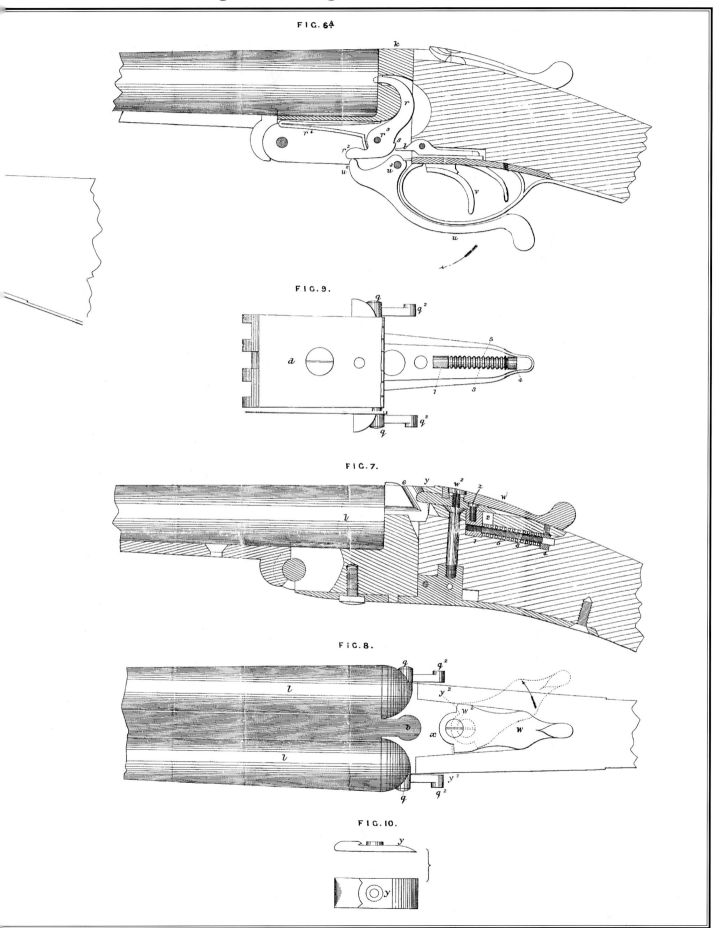

Anson & Deeley 1876 U.S. Patent Drawings, Patent No. 172,943

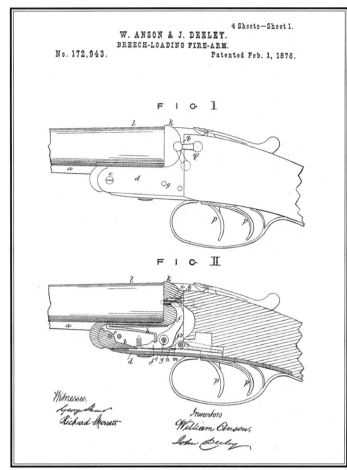

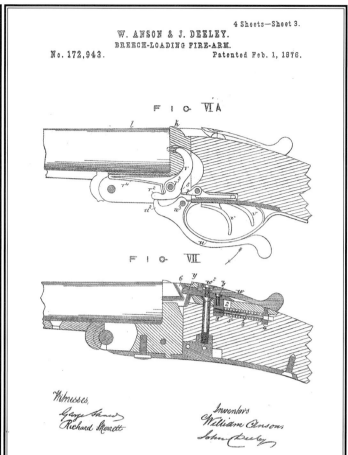

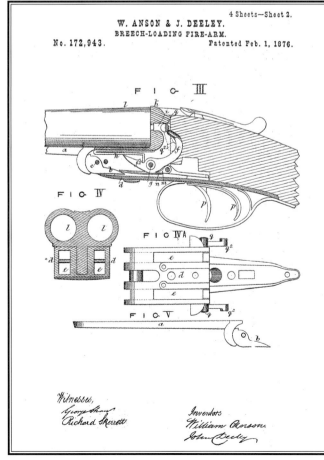

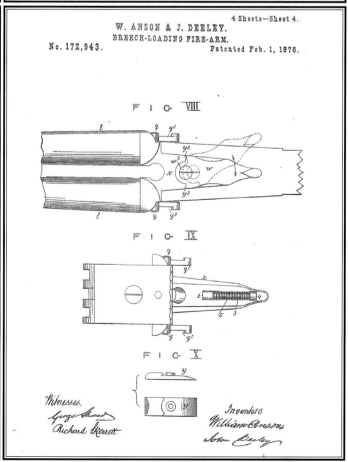

Robert Couchman's License to make the Anson & Deeley Gun (see also pages 47–49)

present Manufactory at High Street Birmingham or in any other premises the Licensees may occupy in Birmingham or elsewhere in the United Kingdom and not otherwise the said Invention for which the said Letters Patent were granted and to vend sell and dispose of sporting guns and double rifles comprising the said patented Improvement or any part or parts thereof subject nevertheless to the conditions and stipulations hereinafter contained **To have** and **To hold** the said license power privilege and authority expressed to be hereby granted with all benefits and advantages from the exercise thereof unto and by the said Licensees and their successors henceforth for the residue now unexpired of the term of years granted by the aforesaid Letters Patent subject nevertheless to the covenants stipulations restrictions and conditions hereinafter contained on the part of the said Licensees **Yielding** and **Paying** unto the said Licensor his executors administrators and assigns the royalty or sum of fifteen shillings for each and every sporting gun or double rifle which shall be made or manufactured by the said Licensees or their successors either in whole or in part according to the said Invention and Letters patent accounts of all such royalties payable by the Licensees to the Licensor to be made up quarterly to the thirty first day of March the thirty first day of June the thirtieth day of September and the thirty first day of December in every year during the continuance of this license and to be rendered by the Licensees to the Licensor within seven days after each of such quarter days and payments of all such royalties to be made within fourteen days after the rendering of such accounts the first of such accounts to be rendered on or before the seventh day of October One thousand eight hundred and

seventy six and the first of such payments to be made on or before the twenty first day of the same month And in consideration of the premises the said Licensees do hereby for themselves their successors and assigns Covenant with the said Licensor his executors administrators and assigns in manner following (that is to say) That they the Licensees and their successors shall and will during the continuance of the said License render or caused to be rendered to the said Licensor his executors administrators and assigns within seven days next after each the said quarterly days hereinbefore mentioned a true account in writing (to be verified by Statutory Declaration if required) of the number of sporting guns and double rifles which shall have been made in the preceding quarter by the said Licensees or their successors at their said Manufactory or any other premises to be occupied by them as aforesaid in whole or in part under or according to the said invention or Letters patent And shall and will within fourteen days next after the time appointed for rendering of every such account as aforesaid pay to the said Licensor his executors administrators and assigns all moneys then due in respect of the royalty hereinbefore reserved And shall and will from time to time when thereunto required by the said Licensor his executors administrators or assigns produce and shew to them or him or to such other person or persons as they or he shall appoint at the said Manufactory for the time being of the said Licensees or their successors all books accounts and writings relating to sporting guns and double rifles so made at the said Manufactory for the purpose of enabling the said Licensor

his executors administrators or assigns to examine & check every or any such account as aforesaid And also shall and will in the manufacture of the sporting guns and double rifles comprising the said patented improvement or any part thereof use the best quality of suitable material and workmanship for that purpose And further that the said Licensees and their successors shall not nor will without the written consent of the said Licensor his executors administrators or assigns use or employ any alteration or modification of the said Invention And also that they the said Licensees and their successors shall and will mark or stamp or cause to be marked or stamped the sporting guns and double rifles or parts thereof made by them under or by virtue of the License hereby granted and by means of the said Invention or some part or parts thereof with such mark or marks as the said Licensor his executors administrators or assigns shall from time to time designate and require and number them consecutively in the order in which they are made beginning with the No 1 And also that it shall be lawful for the said Licensor his executors administrators or assigns and for any other person or persons authorized by them or him as aforesaid to enter into and upon the said Manufactory or works and premises for the time being of the said Licensees or their successors at any time during working hours that the said Licensor his executors administrators or assigns shall think proper to view and inspect the method and materials used and employed by the said Licensees or their successors in manufacturing the said patented improvements comprised in this license and also to examine and test or prove by such ways or means as the said Licensor

his executors administrators or assigns shall think proper any part or parts thereof which may be then and there found either complete or in process of manufacture according to the said patented improvement and any part or parts thereof there found which shall be rejected by the said Licensor his executors administrators or assigns or by his or their Agent or Agents as being inferior in quality or workmanship or unsatisfactory from any other cause shall be mutilated in such way as to render the same incapable of being used and the same shall not be sold or disposed of by the said Licensees or their successors And also that the said Licensees and their successors shall not nor will without the Consent in writing of the Licensor make any assignment of the License hereby granted And also that in case of any wilful breach non-observance or non performance by the said Licensees or their successors of any of the Covenants conditions stipulations or agreements herein contained on their part or in case the said Licensees or their successors constituting the said Company shall be ordered or resolved to be wound up under any Act for the time being in force relating to Joint Stock Companies then and in any such case it shall and may be lawful for the said Licensor his executors administrators and assigns by any notice or Instrument in writing to be within six months after such breach shall have come to the knowledge of the said Licensor his executors administrators or assigns deliver to the said

The John Deeley/Robert Couchman "Parker Letter" to H&R • January 1883

82 High Street
Birmingham
England.

Mess Harrington & Richardson
Worcester
Mass. U.S.A.

Jan 2 1883

Gentlemen,

We have an application from Parker Bros. Meriden. Conn. asking us to give them a license to make our hammerless action. This of course we are unable to do as you are our sole licensees for the whole of the United States. We have written to them & asked them to communicate with you. As the sale of this gun is likely to increase very much in the States we think it worth your while considering the advisability of supplying actions & barrels to gunmakers in the United States as by this means you would not only create a very large trade in actions & barrels upon which you may secure a remunerative profit but keep the said gunmakers from bringing other guns into competition with yours. We shall have some improvements to bring under your notice shortly as we have patented a great improvement in the present hammerless gun dispensing with the dogs. It is of course on the same lines as the old one, exactly the same lockwork & the same principle of leverage but one central lever instead of two dogs. With this invention the gun can be put together with perfect ease when the hammers are down. We hope your trade is increasing & wish you a happy & prosperous New Year

Yours very truly
Anson & Deeley
per John Deeley

H&R License to make the Anson & Deeley Gun in the U.S.

United States of America.

COMMONWEALTH OF MASSACHUSETTS.

Worcester, ss., April 12 1886

Then personally appeared before me, a Notary Public, duly commissioned and sworn, in and for the said County of Worcester, William Augustus Richardson well known to me as the person who subscribed the foregoing instrument, and acknowledged the same to be his free act and deed, and desired that the same might be observed and recorded as such.

Witness my hand and Notarial Seal, at the City of Worcester, the day and year last above written.

Notary Public.

H&R License to make the Anson & Deeley Gun in the U.S. — Cont'd. (see also page 55)

of the said agreement and in consideration of the payments covenants clauses and agreements hereinafter reserved and contained on the part of the said Licensees He the said Licensor **Doth** hereby give and grant unto the said Licensees and their successors **The** license power privilege and authority to make use execute and put in practice but in connection with Guns and Rifles or Breech actions and improved Safety apparatus manufactured by them in whole or in part at or in their present manufactory at Worcester Mass. United States of America aforesaid or in any other premises which the Licensees may occupy in the United States of America and not otherwise the said Invention for which the said Letters Patent were granted and to vend sell and dispose of Guns and Rifles or Breech actions and improved Safety apparatus comprising the said patented Improvements or any part or parts thereof subject nevertheless to the conditions and stipulations hereinafter contained **To have and To hold** the said license power privilege and authority expressed to be hereby granted with all benefits and advantages from the exercise thereof unto and by the said Licensees and their successors henceforth for the residue now unexpired of the term of years granted by the aforesaid Letters Patent subject nevertheless to the covenants stipulations restrictions and conditions hereinafter contained on the part of the said Licensees **Yielding** and **Paying** unto the said Licensor his executors administrators and assigns the royalty or sum of Fifteen Shillings Sterling British currency for each and every Gun Rifle or Breech Action when the number sold during one year shall not exceed in the aggregate One thousand but in the event of the number sold during one year exceeding

One thousand the royalty paid for each and every Gun Rifle or Breech action shall be Twelve shillings and six pence which shall be made or manufactured by the said Licensees or their successors either in whole or in part according to the said Inventions and Letters Patent. A Statement of all Guns Rifles or Breech actions made by the Licensees and accounts of all such royalties payable by the Licensees to the Licensor to be made up quarterly to the thirty first March the thirtieth June the thirtieth September and the thirty first December in every year during the continuance of this License and to be rendered by the Licensees to the Licensor within seven days after each of such quarterly days and payments of all such royalties to be made within one calendar month after the rendering of such accounts **And** in consideration of the premises the Licensees do hereby for themselves their successors and assigns **Covenant** with the said Licensor his executors administrators and assigns in manner following (that is to say) That they the said Licensees and their successors shall and will during the continuance of this License render or cause to be rendered to the Licensor his executors administrators or assigns within seven days next after each of the quarter days hereinbefore mentioned a true account in writing (to be verified by statutory declaration if required) of the number of Guns Rifles or Breech actions which they shall have made in the preceding quarter by the said Licensees or their successors at their said manufactory or any other premises to be occupied by them as aforesaid in whole

or in part under or according to the said Invention or Letters Patent **And** shall and will within one month next after the time appointed for rendering of every such account as aforesaid pay to the said Licensor his executors administrators and assigns all moneys then due in respect of the royalty hereinbefore reserved **And** shall and will keep Books in which all sales or manufacture of Guns Rifles and Breech actions sold by the said Licensees shall be entered **And** shall and will from time to time when thereunto required by the said Licensor his executors administrators or assigns produce and show to them or him or to such other person or persons as they or he shall appoint at the said manufactory for the time being of the said Licensees or their successors all such books accounts and writings relating to the said sale or manufacture of guns rifles or breech actions so made at the said manufactory for the purpose of enabling the said Licensor his executors administrators or assigns to examine and check every or any such account as aforesaid **And** shall and will consecutively number all Guns Rifles or some part of the Breech action commencing with 1 and to be marked Anson and Deeleys Patent **And also** all and any other mark or marks required by the United States Patent Law **And also** that in case of any wilful breach nonobservance or nonperformance by the said Licensees or their successors of any of the covenants conditions stipulations or agreements herein contained on his or their part Then and in any such case it shall and may be lawful for the said Licensor his executors administrators and assigns by any notice or instrument in writing to

be within six months after such breach shall have come to the knowledge of the said Licensor his executors administrators or assigns delivered to the said Licensees or their successors or left at their Counting House or usual place of business or manufactory to revoke and make void this License and thereupon this License shall cease and determine to all intents and purposes whatsoever subject nevertheless and without prejudice to the right of the said Licensor his executors administrators and assigns to recover all such moneys as shall have become due to him or them by virtue of this License up to and inclusive of the delivery of such revocation **Provided always** and it is hereby agreed between the Licensor and Licensees in order to insure the proper working of the said Inventions in the United States of America that if in any one year the number of Guns Rifles or Breech actions made and sold by the Licensees do not amount to Five hundred then the said Licensor is to be at liberty to grant licenses for the manufacture and sale of guns rifles or breech actions to any other Company firm or person he may think fit in the said United States but in order to give the said Licensees time to prepare for the setting up of machinery and tools for the production and manufacture of such Guns Rifles or Breech actions the number required to be made within the first twelve months after the date of this agreement may extend over Two years **And** the said Licensor doth hereby covenant undertake and agree with the said Licensees that he will take all necessary and legal means in his power for the purpose of protecting from infringement the said patented Inventions so granted by the United States as aforesaid **Provided always** and it is hereby further agreed and declared

LECTURES TO YOUNG GUNMAKERS.
LXXIV.—MEASUREMENTS OF ANSON & DEELEY GUN LOCKS.

Debate frequently turns on the relative properties of side lock guns and those constructed according to the Anson & Deeley principle. Side locks having been examined with some degree of care, the same form of attention will now be devoted to the alternative A. & D. system, as it is commonly described. Two guns have been taken for the purpose of the present demonstration. The first is a very early type of Anson & Deeley gun, which was specially sectioned by Messrs. Westley Richards & Co., Ld., for the purpose of exposing the interior mechanism. Being an exhibition model of gun it has remained unsold, and is, therefore, available to-day to show what the system was like nearly forty years ago. The gun from which the more modern limbs have been taken was one of the twenty-guinea models with which Messrs. Clabrough & Johnstone have enjoyed so much success of late. Generally, it may be explained that from the point of view of distance of centre from the various crucial working surfaces the early Westley Richards' model very closely follows side lock guns. The departure from side lock conditions has evidently been made since the first introduction of the A. & D. system, and its object was no doubt to diminish the depth of the action below the flats. The greater strength which is demanded in modern guns owing to smokeless powders might justify a return to the older dimensions, especially as balance would be assisted by a greater concentration of metal in the action than commonly exists with box lock guns. Taking first of all the early Westley Richards' gun, the following figures relate to the sear :—

Analysis of early A. & D. Sear.
Distance from sear nose to pivot .. .. ·64 in.
Distance from sear tail to pivot .. .. 1·19 „
Ratio equals 1·86 times.

A casual glance at the mechanism shows that the sear tail is shorter than usual, whilst the nose end is of about standard length. This implies a lower than ordinary degree of leverage, which fact must be borne in mind with reference to the measured value of 1·86 times. This compares with 1·69 for the Holland sear. Turning now to the tumbler, the following is its record :—

Analysis of early A. & D. Tumbler.
Distance of striker point of tumbler to pivot .. 1·15 in.
Distance of bent of tumbler to pivot .. .. ·28 „
Ratio equals 4·11 times.

This ratio implies that the face, or rather the striking point of the tumbler, is more than four times further from the pivot than is the bent. Bearing in mind that the side lock gun worked out at less than three times, it will be evident that some interesting comparisons may be made later on. Turning now to the Clabrough & Johnstone gun the following figures refer to the sear :—

Analysis of Clabrough Box Lock Sear.
Distance from sear nose to pivot .. .. ·63 in.
Distance from sear tail to pivot .. .. 1·45 „
Ratio equals 2·30 times.

Here at once is a striking comparison between a modern box lock and an early A. & D. gun. The early pattern had a leverage value well under twice times, and this has since been increased to well over 2¼ times. The explanation of this increase is to be found in the altered conditions of the tumbler, which is next dealt with :—

Analysis of Clabrough Box Lock Tumbler.
Distance from striker point of tumbler to pivot 1·17 in.
Distance from bent of tumbler to pivot .. ·22 „
Ratio equals 5·32 times.

Here then is the reason for the considerable increase of sear leverage. The closer the bent of the tumbler is brought to the pivot the greater is the thrust exercised against the sear nose. The large resulting extra friction increases the effort required for release, hence the introduction of a longer sear tail to give extra power. It goes without saying that the mainspring must exercise a standard pressure on the tumbler, also that the amount of pressure at the sear nose should lie within definite practical limits. The strength of mainspring in both guns was carefully measured by applying a spring balance to the nose of each striker in the bearer or discharged position. Both locks showed absolutely the same value, viz., 10 lbs. The A. & D. showed that this pressure is reduced in the cocked position to 9 lbs. No ready means existed for making the same test in the other gun, so that no figures can be given. Taking 10 lbs. as the force exerted on the striker nose in all positions, and assuming that the bent is a quarter as distant from the pivot as is the striker nose, this 10 lbs. will represent a thrust against the sear nose of 40 lbs. If the ratio is one-fifth the thrust will be increased to 50 lbs. Hence the need for the different sear leverage already referred to for the two sets of conditions.

To reduce the two sets of measurements to something approaching a common denominator a new process, not previously explained, must be resorted to. Any pair of levers, no matter what their measurements and properties may be, have the same leverage value as a single lever of appropriate dimensions. Mechanical design may necessitate dividing the functions of a single lever into parts, but when it is desired to examine their net effect they can be re-combined by arithmetic process, so that a new ratio is found to express their joint properties. The only thing to remember in joining up a pair, or for that matter a whole train of levers, is the function of each individual of the series, viz., whether it increases or decreases the power that it transmits. The sear for instance undoubtedly increases the power that is applied to it by the trigger blade. The tumbler diminishes it, in the sense that the power is applied to the short arm for delivery by the long or hammer arm at the striker point.

It is open to be objected that the leverage of the sear has nothing to do with the blow struck by the tumbler, the latter being due to the mainspring, and the sear acting solely as a releasing medium. That admittedly is true, but the 10 lbs. of the mainspring becomes 40 lbs. thrust on the sear nose, and the friction resulting from that 40 lbs. thrust is the resistance which the sear has to overcome. Friction no doubt bears some kind of proportion to mainspring pressure, but whatever may be the outcome of some future examination of that other question, the fact remains that there is every theoretical justification for tracing the mainspring back to the lifting effect required at the sear tail. Taking the sear as a multiplying lever and the tumbler as a diminishing lever the joint effect of the two is obtained by dealing with them as follows in the manner of ordinary vulgar fractions :—

Ancient and Modern Anson & Deeley Mechanism.

Analysis of early Box Lock Mechanism.
$\frac{\text{Ratio of sear lever}}{\text{Ratio of tumbler}} \quad \frac{1 \cdot 86 \text{ times}}{4 \cdot 11 \text{ times}}$ Joint ratio = ·452 times.

This value conveniently expresses the joint effect of the two measurements of the sear and tumbler respectively of the early type of box lock. The figure ·452 times will be most instructive when compared with a similarly obtained value for the more modern type of gun. The figures for the latter are now given :—

Analysis of Modern Box Lock Mechanism.
$\frac{\text{Ratio of sear lever}}{\text{Ratio of tumbler}} \quad \frac{2 \cdot 30 \text{ times}}{5 \cdot 32 \text{ times}}$ Joint ratio = ·432 times.

Considering the very large differences that exist in the detailed measurements of the two sears and the two tumblers, it is interesting to find that their resultants are so strikingly similar, as displayed by the values ·452 times and ·432 times. The difference lies within five per cent., which certainly suggests that the effect is the same after forty years of evolution, even though the means of arriving at it have been altered. Insufficient space now remains to deal exhaustively with the question of length of sear tail travel. It will of course be apparent that greater leverage of the sear tail implies greater length of travel to effect release from a standard depth of bent, but experience seems to show that long dragging pulls are not due to this cause, but rather to the failure of the first movement to continue the process of release by its own momentum. A dragging pull may be likened to a badly arranged launch of a vessel. When once the various surfaces in contact have started to move over one another, practically nothing can bring them to rest. With a well-arranged trigger the first movement is followed by an equally overpowering continuation of the process. A dragging pull by comparison would be represented by a launch where the frictionless glide gives place to a series of bumps and jerks every moment threatening to bring the movement to rest. A long trigger motion is immaterial so long as in practice it constitutes a frictionless glide. It is the slow dragging pull, which can be stopped half way, that gives trouble to the shooter.

More important of course is the distance of the tumbler between the bent and the pivot. In the Holland gun the tumbler ratio was 2·90 times, a figure that is increased to 5·32 times in a modern box lock gun. Assuming equal mainspring pressure the thrust released is in one instance 29·0 lbs. and in the other 53·2 lbs. Part of this large excess is explained by the difference from the pivot to the striker of a box lock tumbler as compared with the corresponding distance to the face of the side lock tumbler. That both sets have the same mainspring strength at their respective working distances suggests the necessity of such a condition. Therefore, the root fact remains that the thrust on the sear nose is nearly double with a box lock to what it is with a side lock. There are many incidental issues and ramifications in the matters discussed in this lecture which it would have been tempting to explore, but which had necessarily to be left in order to pursue the main enquiry.

One misprint in the last lecture, possibly it was a miscalculation, must be set right. At the top of the first column on Page 5, reference was made to 8 lbs. 2 oz. lift on the left sear. The sear leverage of 1·69 was spoken of as converting this into 16·9 lbs., though it should have been 13·7 lbs. The true value 13¾ lbs. could be realised under favourable conditions of pull, but it is doubtful whether 17 lbs. would not give a long dragging pull.

The Sporting Goods Review Interview with John Deeley • April 15, 1897 (see also page 44)

monstrated that, and we claim if no holding down bolt at all were used, and the barrels simply fastened with a bit of tape, the gun would still be safe to fire."

Presently we passed on to the subject of rifles, a branch in which Westley Richards & Co. have of course played a particularly prominent part.

"In 1858," said Mr. Deeley, "Mr. Westley Richards introduced the first breech-loading arm used by theGovernment. That was thecapping carbine. Several were issued experimentally, and afterwards 20,000 were made by the Government for cavalry use."

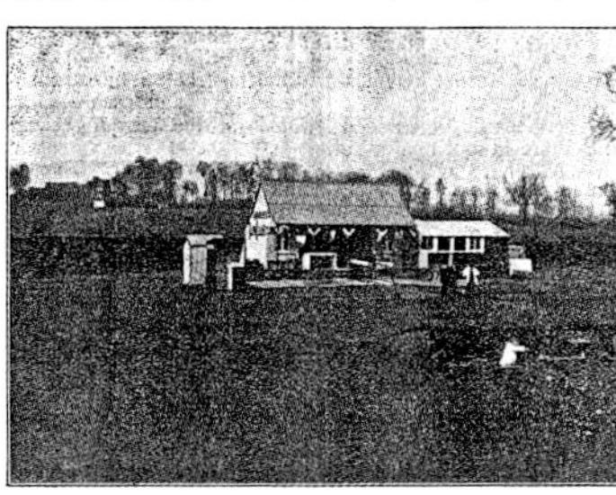

THE SHOOTING GROUNDS AT HENDON.

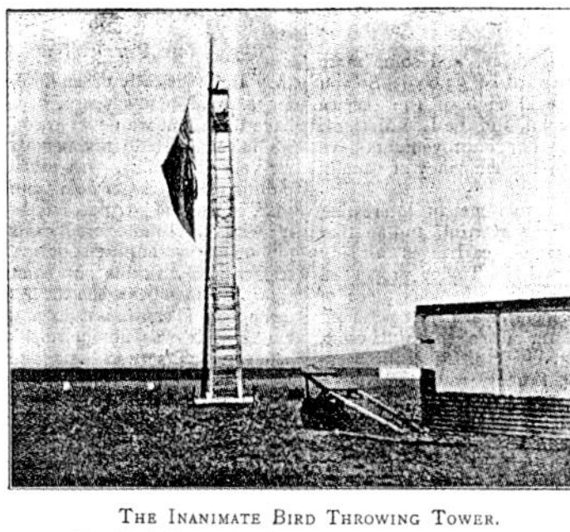

THE INANIMATE BIRD THROWING TOWER.

These illustrations are from Snap Shots by Mr. PERCY NEWTON.

"And what small-arm were the Government then using?"

"The Enfield, which had taken the place of the old Brown Bess. The Enfield was the invention of Captain Minié, or, rather, it was introduced by him, but the improvements of Mr. Westley Richards had a good deal to do with its success. The Government awarded him, Mr. Richards I mean, £1,000 for his improvements, and Mr. Newdigate, at that time M.P. for Warwickshire, stated in the House of Commons that the name of the rifle ought to have been the "Westley-Richards" instead of the "Enfield." Next, as perhaps you know, the Whitworth rifle made its appearance."

"Yes," said I, quite pleased with my historical knowledge, "the invention of Sir Joseph Whitworth, of Manchester."

Mr. Deeley smiled. "Well, not exactly," said he, "the production, not the invention. The real inventor was Brunel, the engineer of the Thames Tunnel. He, of course, was not a maker of rifles, and he mentioned this hexagonal bored barrel to Mr. Westley Richards, who made several rifles on the system, and afterwards communicated it to Whitworth. Ultimately the rifling with its pitch of one turn in 20" was patented by Mr. Whitworth, as he then was; but we got a free licence to manufacture, and were the only firm who had that right except the patentee."

"There was, however, a small royalty on sporting rifles, a shilling a rifle, I think," added Mr. Taylor, to which Mr. Deeley agreed, and then went on to tell me of the invention of the Falling Block rifle, the predecessor of the Martini, which, in some respects, anticipated that arm, so that Messrs. Westley Richards & Co. were paid a royalty in respect of the Martini, whilst at least ten thousand of the Falling Block rifles have been sold for sporting purposes.

"We come now," resumed Mr. Deeley, "to an improvement in hammerless gun locks, which has had very important effects on the trade. I mean, of course, the Anson and Deeley action introduced by the foreman of our machine shop, and myself, in 1875. Nobody before had succeeded in making an action with so few parts, and of such great strength. It was, too, the *first* gun in which the cocking was done by the dropping of the barrels, and the first really successful hammerless gun. I should think there are now twice as many guns of this type as there are of all the rest put together. Practically, everybody makes it, and, as regards principle, it remains the best to-day. It will, perhaps, interest you to know that the patent runs out next month, so the mechanism will become public property in a few days now. You know the gun, of course?"

I did; but, with none the less pleasure, I followed

a practical demonstration of its qualities, with which Mr. Leslie Taylor favoured me.

Resuming, Mr. Deeley next told me of the invention by Mr. Westley Richards of the solid metallic cartridge for use in his own Falling Block rifle. The first invention of this type was made by a Mr. Jones. Westley Richards's improvement was adopted by the Government and a royalty paid. This metallic cartridge was largely used for the Gatling gun. Next touched upon was the Deeley-Edge rifle, an arm with sliding block action and Metford rifling introduced for use at Wimbledon, where it achieved notable success.

"Then as concerns the latest service rifle," continued Mr. Deeley, "we have had our share in that too. We patented an attachment for the bolt head by screwing it right on to the bolt instead of using the weak pin attachment employed in the Mark I. rifles. The Government adopted it and awarded us £3,000 for the improvement. I had twelve month's correspondence with the authorities before I got the matter settled. Of course there was the usual tedious routine to go through, and at last we had to appeal to the Lords of the Treasury. Sir William Harcourt was in the chair, and witnesses were called to attempt to depreciate the value of the invention. I pointed out the inconsistency of the attitude, seeing the improvement had been adopted and awards of £500 and £1,000 had already been refused. Sir William concluded that as the validity of the patent was not in question, and the utility of the improvement clearly admitted, there was very little to be said about it. The matter will be considered, he remarked, and you will hear from us."

"And you did hear?"

"Yes; after a further long delay, and some more correspondence, we got our award of £3,000. So you see we have had our share in each of the service rifles—the Enfield, the Martini, and the Lee-Metford, and I think I may say that our improvements have contributed very materially to the efficiency of each of the arms."

Apropos of this, Mr. Deeley told me an interesting story of the manufacture of the Martini, and another about the solid-drawn metallic cartridges already referred to, after which he and Mr. Taylor proceeded to add to my knowledge of that ingenious piece of mechanism, the Deeley box ejector, which was patented in 1884. The various incidents of the lengthy lawsuit, well known to my readers as the Ejector Litigation, were briefly touched upon by Mr. Deeley, who displayed a moderation and good-humour in his reminiscences of that hard-fought fight which I could not but admire. With reference to the mechanism itself he pointed out that it had stood the test of nearly thirteen years' use with most conspicuous success. "The principle," he said, "is simply an adaptation of that employed in a gun lock, a mechanism perfected by centuries of mechanical ingenuity and skill. It has very few parts, and they so strong that it is almost impossible for the ejector work to get out of order; in short, we contend that ours is the best ejector which has yet been introduced; that it combines the greatest simplicity with the highest mechanical efficiency, and that the parts cannot be reduced without additional friction."

At this time I was standing with an Anson and Deeley Hammerless Ejector in my hands—a masterpiece of the gunsmith's craft. Before I put it down, Mr. Taylor called my attention to another point about it—the Westley Richards's safety mechanism.

"Ah, yes," said Mr. Deeley, "I intended to tell you about it. You know, particularly when a very light pull off is used, there is just a possibility of one lock being jarred off when the other barrel is fired. To prevent this, or any other like accident, it has been usual to fit tumbler safeties to block the fall of the hammers. These have to be moved by the action of the triggers, and we contend that, as anything which would jar the triggers would also jar the tumblers,

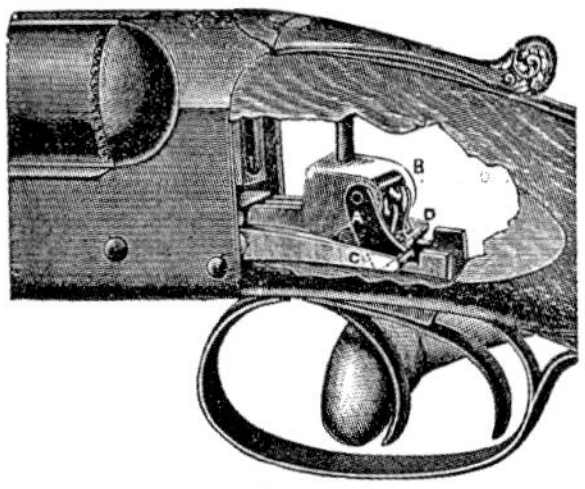

THE PATENT SAFETY MECHANISM.

they are practically useless. We made tumbler safeties for a good many years, because sportsmen liked to have them, but we never recommended them, and now we have adopted this new safety of ours altogether for very light pulls. Its principle is very simple, the pulling of one trigger being caused to bolt the opposite sear, so that no jarring can possibly have any effect on it; with our hammerless guns of the ordinary weight of pull-off we use simply the ordinary top safety, bolting the trigger, and with this our hammerless gun is absolutely safe. I remember when the A and D Hammerless first came out I showed it to a well-known Birmingham maker. He was not quite satisfied as to its absolute safety I could see, so I suggested a test to him. 'Hold it up at arm's length in the air,' I said, 'and let it drop butt down on the floor.' He took me at my word, and did it. The fourth time the stock broke across, but even then the locks remained absolutely unaffected."

"If it would stand that," said I, with conviction, "it ought to stand anything."

"Exactly. Take another instance. We had a gun returned to us from a client who had rolled from top to bottom of an embankment with it."

"And a ghastly state it was in, too," remarked Mr. Taylor.

"Yes; barrels bent, gun smashed nearly all to bits. It had no tumbler safety fitted, nothing but our ordinary trigger safety, and even with such an accident as that it did not jar off."

In the course of further conversation I gleaned some

interesting particulars of the new Westley Richards single trigger gun, and later on had the pleasure of trying it. I saw also the patent single rifle with detachable barrel, the invention, I believe, of Mr. Leslie Taylor. Barrels of two or three different calibres can thus be used with one stock. The attachment is simplicity itself, consisting of two lugs on the part of the barrel fitting into the breech, which lock into slots provided for the purpose on giving the barrel a quarter turn. The barrels each carry their own extractor, and the ordinary fore end is used. A new arrangement is also provided, so that two pulls off are obtained by means of a double bent. Altogether this rifle is one which represents the maximum of convenience and efficiency in a single loader. It is in every way worthy to take rank amongst the many improvements with which the name of the firm stands identified.

Before my talk with Mr. Deeley concluded, I elicited from him an interesting expression of opinion concerning the work turned out by gunsmiths in the early days of the century. Whilst, with Mr. Taylor for my cicerone, I had been visiting one or two departments in the factory, Mr. Deeley made his promised search for specimens of the "primes" referred to in the early part of this article, with the result that a sample of them is before me as I write.

"They are interesting," said Mr. Deeley, "as relics of a stage in the progress from the old flint lock to the hammerless of to-day."

"And yet," said Mr. Taylor, "it is only a few weeks since we had an inquiry from abroad for these very things."

"As for that," supplemented Mr. Deeley, "there are still to be found people who prefer flint locks. I remember we had some Moorish officials down here. They came from London to inspect work we were doing for their Government. They brought their own food with them in baskets; wouldn't touch anything we could offer. They had curious ways of eating, too, and used no knives; also they washed and prayed before and after each meal. When they were going away I thought I would give them a little present, so I told their interpreter to offer them a revolver each. If you'll believe me, they asked if we had any flint pistols, as they preferred them! We happened to have an old pair in stock, so they got what they wanted."

"Strange the views some people hold," quoted I, laughing.

"Yes; but there was reason in it," said Mr. Deeley. "I think they had a good deal of difficulty in getting percussion caps, and it struck me afterwards that very likely they were pleased to be able to snap the locks off, and see the sparks fly."

"Anyway, it was fortunate you had the old pistols on hand for them."

"Well, yes; but there is nothing strange in that; for we were established here whilst the flint lock was still in favour. To be exact it was in 1812, the year before our Proof House started, and our factory has never been removed. We have, of course, extended all we could, and the place where we are sitting was then a green in front of the works. Here, on this very spot, the men used to have their annual dinner—a tent being put up for it. We do not have any tent now, but the dinner goes on just the same, and has never been missed in all these years. Then our London house is the oldest gunmaker's establishment in Bond-st. We have our shooting grounds in London too—at Hendon—and have just introduced a new tower there for throwing inanimate birds as well as other conveniences for the members of the Middlesex Gun Club who hold their meetings on the ground. You see we do our best to keep up to date."

"And yet you have as many claims to rank with the old order as with the new, and can go back to the days when Joseph Manton was a power in the land," I said, and then, on the impulse of the moment, added, "I have often wondered how it came about that he made for himself a name which still stands a synonym for good work?"

"That *is* the reason," said Mr. Deeley quickly; "his work *was* good, and for that he deserved his reputation. He used the best materials, too. All his touch-holes were of gold; and his fitting was exquisite. Old Joe Manton was worthy of his title—the King of Gunmakers. And the locks he used—made by Braziers, of Wolverhampton, I believe—the work in them was simply lovely. There was music in those old locks: they rang like bells when discharged. Ah, *yes*; there have been wonderful advances since old Joe Manton's time, but the work he and some of his *confrères* did will always entitle them to be held in honour by those who follow in their footsteps."

A good word to make an end. As such let it stand.

TYNTAX.

It is stated, says the *Johannesburg Standard* and *Diggers' News*, that certain importers in Cape Town have been doing a brisk trade lately in supplying guns to up-country customers. Rifles are more probably meant, for the *Cape Times* declares that the weapon mostly in demand is the Martini-Henry, whilst the Lee-Metford is also frequently called for.

In the Court of Bankruptcy, on March 30th, a sitting was held for the examination of F. Hobson de Bearn, trading as F. Hobson and Co., gun and ammunition merchants. The debtor stated he had advertised, as a leading line, a gun which, with 100 cartridges, cost 7s. 6d., payable in advance. He had sold over 9,000 of these guns, but admitted that over 260 persons who had sent their money had not received the goods. He denied that the majority of his customers were of the labouring class.—Mr. Grey: But wealthy people do not buy guns at 7s. 6d. each, including ammunition.—The Debtor: I sold a better class of gun.—Mr. Grey: So I see from your advertisement—at 32s. 6d. (Laughter.)—The debtor added that he could not remember how much money he had received since the execution at his office in February, 1896, and the examination was adjourned to April 28th, to enable him to file such account.

One of the latest single-trigger mechanisms is that of Messrs. E. C. Green & Son, of Cheltenham. In the *Field*, of 3rd inst., a notice and description of the gun appears.

William Anson's Last Will and Testament Dated May 28, 1889

BE IT KNOWN that at the date hereunder written the last Will and Testament of *William Anson* late of *No 6 Church Road, Moseley, in the parish of Kings Norton, in the County of Worcester, Gun Maker* deceased, who died on the *28th* day of *May* 188*9* at *No 6 Church Road aforesaid* and who at the time of *his* death had a fixed place of abode at *No 6 Church Road aforesaid* within the District of *the County of Worcester*

was proved and registered in the District Probate Registry of Her Majesty's High Court of Justice at *Worcester* and that Administration of the personal estate of the said deceased was granted by the aforesaid Court to *Caroline Anson of No 6 Church Road aforesaid, Widow, the Relict of the said deceased, one of the Executors*

named in the said *Will. she* having been first sworn well and faithfully to administer the same. *Power reserved of making the like Grant to John Harris and Edward (in the said Will written "Edwin") James Harris the other Executors named in the said Will.*

Dated the *20th* day of *July* 188*9*

Gross value of Personal Estate £ *598 - 6 - 1*
Net value " " £ *471 - 7 - 9*

Extracted by *Reece, Harris & Harris, Solicitors, Birmingham*

205

This is the last Will and Testament of me William Anson of No 6 Church Road Moseley in the parish of Kings Norton in the County of Worcester Gun Maker I give devise and bequeath all my real and personal estate whatsoever and wheresoever of and to which I am now or may at any time hereafter become seized possessed or entitled in reversion remainder or expectancy or over which I have now or may at any time hereafter have any disposing power unto my Executors hereinafter named Upon trust at their discretion at any time or times after my decease to sell and realise the same in any manner they may deem expedient or to allow my dear Wife Caroline Anson to receive the income thereof for her life for her sole and separate use and benefit absolutely And from and after her decease to pay and divide the principal and the income to arise therefrom equally between and among all and every of my children who shall attain the age of twenty one years share and share alike the shares of my Daughters to be for their own sole and separate use and benefit absolutely In case my said Wife should die before the youngest of my children comes of age then I declare that the whole of the income of my estate if necessary shall be applied for the maintenance support and education of such of my children as shall be then under age until he she or they shall respectively attain the age of twenty one years anything hereinbefore contained to the contrary notwithstanding I declare that if any or either of my children or anyone claiming under them shall commence or prosecute any proceedings with reference to this my Will or the trusts thereof or in anywise relating thereto then such child or children shall immediately thereupon cease to take any interest whatever under this my Will anything hereinbefore contained to the contrary notwithstanding and the trusts hereof shall be administered in all respects as if such child or children had never been born I appoint my said Wife and John Harris of Birmingham in the County of Warwick Solicitor and Edwin James Harris of Smethwick in the County of Stafford Ironmaster to be Trustees and Executors of this my Will And I appoint my said Wife during her Widowhood Guardian of my infant children

1.

And I hereby revoke all Wills by me at any time heretofore made and declare this alone to be my last Will and Testament In witness whereof I have hereunto set my hand this tenth day of April One thousand eight hundred and eighty nine

Signed and declared by the said William Anson as and for his last Will and Testament in the presence of us present at the same time who at his request in his presence and in the presence of each other have hereunto subscribed our names as witnesses.

William Anson

G. Pearsall Locker, Clerk to Messrs Reece Harris & Harris, Solicitors, Birmingham.
Julia Rooker, 106 Nechells Place, Nechells, Widow, Birmingham.

6/6

Proved at Worcester the twentieth day of July 1889 by the Oath of Caroline Anson Widow the Relict one of the Executors to whom Administration was granted Power reserved of making the like Grant to John Harris and Edward (in the Will written "Edwin") James Harris, the other Executors.

The Testator William Anson was late of No 6 Church Road Moseley, in the parish of Kings Norton in the County of Worcester, Gun Maker, and died on the twenty eighth day of May 1889 at No 6 Church Road aforesaid.
Gross value of personal Estate £598 - 6 - 1
Net £471 - 7 - 9
Reece, Harris & Harris Solicitors, Birmingham.

2.

Taken from *The Sports Argus*, dated Septemer 17, 1904

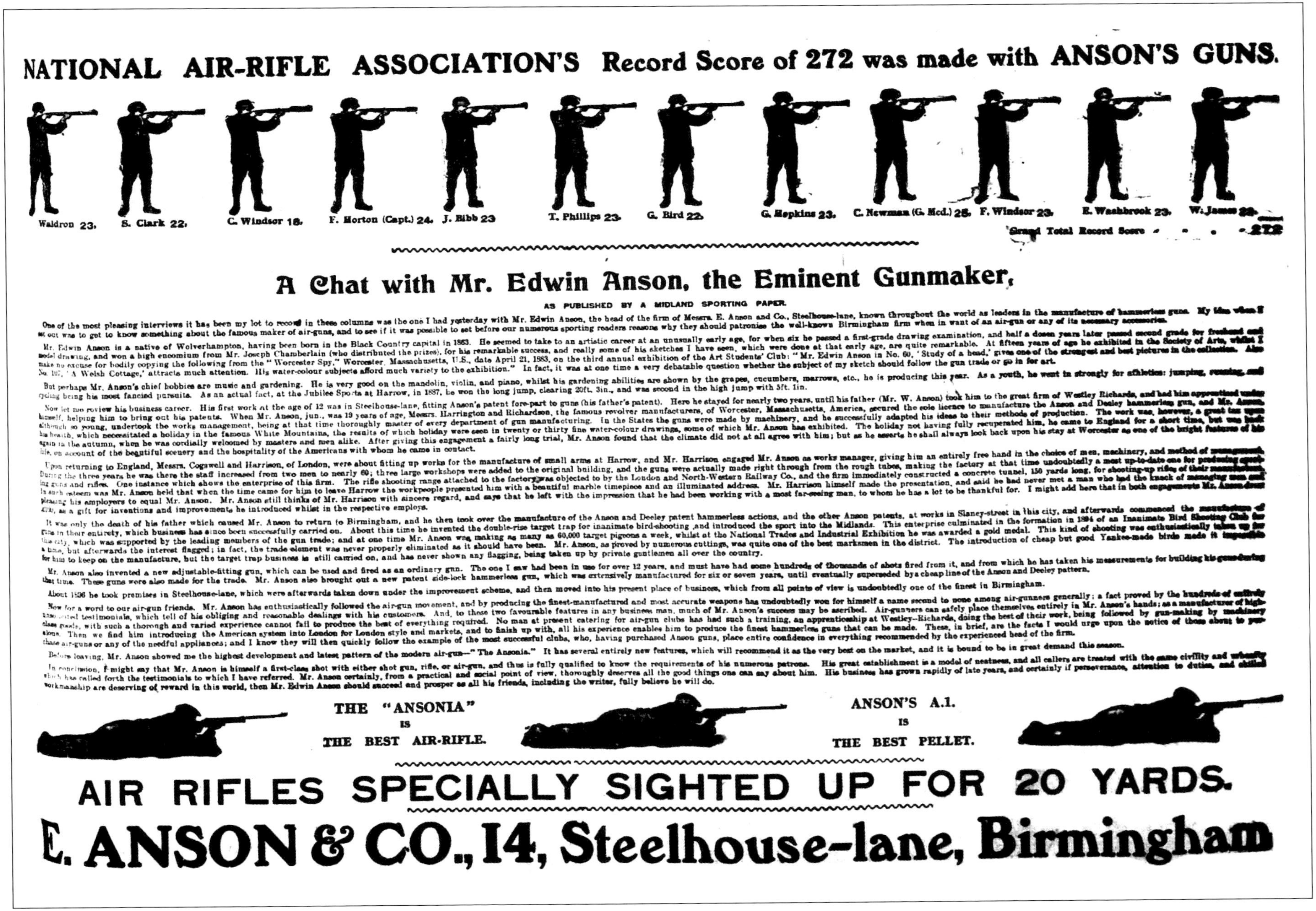

NATIONAL AIR-RIFLE ASSOCIATION'S Record Score of 272 was made with ANSON'S GUNS.

Waldron 23. S. Clark 22. C. Windsor 18. F. Horton (Capt.) 24. J. Bibb 23 T. Phillips 23. G. Bird 22. G. Hopkins 23. C. Newman (G. Med.) 25. F. Windsor 23. E. Washbrook 23. W. James 23.

Grand Total Record Score - - - 272

A Chat with Mr. Edwin Anson, the Eminent Gunmaker,

AS PUBLISHED BY A MIDLAND SPORTING PAPER.

One of the most pleasing interviews it has been my lot to record in these columns was the one I had yesterday with Mr. Edwin Anson, the head of the firm of Messrs. E. Anson and Co., Steelhouse-lane, known throughout the world as leaders in the manufacture of hammerless guns. My idea when I set out was to get to know something about the famous maker of air-guns, and to see if it was possible to set before our numerous sporting readers reasons why they should patronise the well-known Birmingham firm when in want of an air-gun or any of its accessary accessories.

Mr. Edwin Anson is a native of Wolverhampton, having been born in the Black Country capital in 1863. He seemed to take to an artistic career at an unusually early age, for when six he passed a first-grade drawing examination, and half a dozen years later passed second grade for freehand and model drawing, and won a high encomium from Mr. Joseph Chamberlain (who distributed the prizes), for his remarkable success, and really some of his sketches I have seen, which were done at that early age, are quite remarkable. At fifteen years of age he exhibited in the Society of Arts, whilst I make no excuse for bodily copying the following from the "Worcester Spy," Worcester, Massachusetts, U.S., date April 21, 1883, on the third annual exhibition of the Art Students' Club: "Mr. Edwin Anson in No. 60, 'Study of a head,' gives one of the strongest and best pictures in the collection. Also No. 107, 'A Welsh Cottage,' attracts much attention. His water-colour subjects afford much variety to the exhibition." In fact, it was at one time a very debatable question whether the subject of my sketch should follow the gun trade or go in for art.

But perhaps Mr. Anson's chief hobbies are music and gardening. He is very good on the mandolin, violin, and piano, whilst his gardening abilities are shown by the grapes, cucumbers, marrows, etc., he is producing this year. As a youth, he went in strongly for athletics: jumping, running, and cycling being his most fancied pursuits. As an actual fact, at the Jubilee Sports at Harrow, in 1887, he won the long jump, clearing 20ft. 3in., and was second in the high jump with 5ft. 1in.

Now let me review his business career. His first work at the age of 12 was in Steelhouse-lane, fitting Anson's patent fore-part to guns (his father's patent). Here he stayed for nearly two years, until his father (Mr. W. Anson) took him to the great firm of Westley Richards, and had him apprenticed under himself, helping him to bring out his patents. When Mr. Anson, jun., was 19 years of age, Messrs. Harrington and Richardson, the famous revolver manufacturers, of Worcester, Massachusetts, America, secured the sole licence to manufacture the Anson and Deeley hammerless gun, and Mr. Anson, although so young, undertook the works management, being at that time thoroughly master of every department of gun manufacturing. In the States the guns were made by machinery, and he successfully adapted his ideas to their methods of production. The work was, however, a great tax upon his health, which necessitated a holiday in the famous White Mountains, the results of which holiday were seen in twenty or thirty fine water-colour drawings, some of which Mr. Anson has exhibited. The holiday not having fully recuperated him, he came to England for a short time, but was back again in the autumn, when he was cordially welcomed by masters and men alike. After giving this engagement a fairly long trial, Mr. Anson found that the climate did not at all agree with him; but as he asserts he shall always look back upon his stay at Worcester as one of the bright features of his life, on account of the beautiful scenery and the hospitality of the Americans with whom he came in contact.

Upon returning to England, Messrs. Cogswell and Harrison, of London, were about fitting up works for the manufacture of small arms at Harrow, and Mr. Harrison engaged Mr. Anson as works manager, giving him an entirely free hand in the choice of men, machinery, and method of management. During the three years he was there the staff increased from two men to nearly 60; three large workshops were added to the original building, and the guns were actually made right through from the rough tubes, making the factory at that time undoubtedly a most up-to-date one for producing sporting guns and rifles. One instance which shows the enterprise of this firm. The rifle shooting range attached to the factory was objected to by the London and North-Western Railway Co., and the firm immediately constructed a concrete tunnel, 150 yards long, for shooting-up rifles of their manufacture. In such esteem was Mr. Anson held that when the time came for him to leave Harrow the workpeople presented him with a beautiful marble timepiece and an illuminated address. Mr. Harrison himself made the presentation, and said he had never met a man who had the knack of managing men and pleasing his employers to equal Mr. Anson. Mr. Anson still thinks of Mr. Harrison with sincere regard, and says that he left with the impression that he had been working with a most far-seeing man, to whom he has a lot to be thankful for. I might add here that in both engagements Mr. Anson drew [illegible], as a gift for inventions and improvements he introduced whilst in the respective employs.

It was only the death of his father which caused Mr. Anson to return to Birmingham, and he then took over the manufacture of the Anson and Deeley patent hammerless actions, and the other Anson patents, at works in Slaney-street in this city, and afterwards commenced the manufacture of traps in their entirety, which business has since been successfully carried on. About this time he invented the double-rise target trap for inanimate bird-shooting, and introduced the sport into the Midlands. This enterprise culminated in the formation in 1894 of an Inanimate Bird Shooting Club for this city, which was supported by the leading members of the gun trade; and at one time Mr. Anson was making as many as 60,000 target pigeons a week, whilst at the National Trades and Industrial Exhibition he was awarded a gold medal. This kind of shooting was enthusiastically taken up for a time, but afterwards the interest flagged; in fact, the trade element was never properly eliminated as it should have been. Mr. Anson, as proved by numerous cuttings, was quite one of the best marksmen in the district. The introduction of cheap but good Yankee-made birds made it impossible for him to keep on the manufacture, but the target trap business is still carried on, and has never shown any flagging, being taken up by private gentlemen all over the country.

Mr. Anson also invented a new adjustable-fitting gun, which can be used and fired as an ordinary gun. The one I saw had been in use for over 12 years, and must have had some hundreds of thousands of shots fired from it, and from which he has taken his measurements for building his guns during that time. These guns were also made for the trade. Mr. Anson also brought out a new patent side-lock hammerless gun, which was extensively manufactured for six or seven years, until eventually superseded by a cheap line of the Anson and Deeley pattern.

About 1896 he took premises in Steelhouse-lane, which were afterwards taken down under the improvement scheme, and then moved into his present place of business, which from all points of view is undoubtedly one of the finest in Birmingham.

Now for a word to our air-gun friends. Mr. Anson has enthusiastically followed the air-gun movement, and by producing the finest-manufactured and most accurate weapons has undoubtedly won for himself a name second to none among air-gunners generally; a fact proved by the hundreds of entirely unsolicited testimonials, which tell of his obliging and reasonable dealings with his customers. And, to these two favourable features in any business man, much of Mr. Anson's success may be ascribed. Air-gunners can safely place themselves entirely in Mr. Anson's hands; as a manufacturer of high-class goods, with such a thorough and varied experience cannot fail to produce the best of everything required. No man at present catering for air-gun clubs has had such a training, an apprenticeship at Westley-Richards, doing the best of their work, being followed by gun-making by machinery alone. Then we find him introducing the American system into London for London style and markets, and to finish up with, all his experience enables him to produce the finest hammerless guns that can be made. These, in brief, are the facts I would urge upon the notice of those about to purchase air-guns or any of the needful appliances; and I know they will then quickly follow the example of the most successful clubs, who, having purchased Anson guns, place entire confidence in everything recommended by the experienced head of the firm.

Before leaving, Mr. Anson showed me the highest development and latest pattern of the modern air-gun—"The Ansonia." It has several entirely new features, which will recommend it as the very best on the market, and it is bound to be in great demand this season.

In conclusion, I might say that Mr. Anson is himself a first-class shot with either shot gun, rifle, or air-gun, and thus is fully qualified to know the requirements of his numerous patrons. His great establishment is a model of neatness, and all callers are treated with the same civility and urbanity which has called forth the testimonials to which I have referred. Mr. Anson certainly, from a practical and social point of view, thoroughly deserves all the good things one can say about him. His business has grown rapidly of late years, and certainly if perseverance, attention to duties, and skilled workmanship are deserving of reward in this world, then Mr. Edwin Anson should succeed and prosper as all his friends, including the writer, fully believe he will do.

THE "ANSONIA" IS THE BEST AIR-RIFLE.

ANSON'S A.1. IS THE BEST PELLET.

AIR RIFLES SPECIALLY SIGHTED UP FOR 20 YARDS.

E. ANSON & CO., 14, Steelhouse-lane, Birmingham

APPENDIX

Edwin Anson's Last Will and Testament Dated August 29, 1936

In His Majesty's High Court of Justice.
The District Probate Registry at Birmingham

BE IT KNOWN that Edwin George Anson of 968 Warwick Road Acocks Green in the City of Birmingham

died here on the 29th day of August 1936

AND BE IT FURTHER KNOWN that at the date hereunder written the last Will and Testament (a copy whereof is hereunto annexed) of the said deceased was proved and registered in the District Probate Registry of His Majesty's High Court of Justice at Birmingham and that Administration of all the Estate which by law devolves to and vests in the personal representative of the said deceased was granted by the aforesaid Court to

Jane Elizabeth Maud Anson of 968 Warwick Road aforesaid, Widow the Relict of deceased, the sole Executrix named in the said Will

And it is hereby certified that an Affidavit for Inland Revenue has been delivered wherein it is shewn that the gross value of the said Estate in Great Britain (exclusive of what the said deceased may have been possessed of or entitled to as a Trustee and not beneficially) amounts to £697-0-0 and that the net value of the personal estate amounts to £ Nil

And it is further certified that it appears from a Receipt signed by an Inland Revenue Officer on the said Affidavit that £3-11-8 has been paid on account of Estate Duty and interest on such duty has been paid.

Dated the 17th day of September 1936.

District Registrar.

Extracted by J. C. James Solr, Birmingham

THIS IS THE LAST WILL AND TESTAMENT of me EDWIN GEORGE ANSON FIRST I desire that all my just debts funeral and testamentary expenses be paid and satisfied by my Executrix hereinafter named as soon as conveniently may be after my decease And SECONDLY I GIVE DEVISE AND BEQUEATH unto Jane Elizabeth Maud Anson my Wife All and every my household furniture goods chattels sum and sums of money which may be in my possession or due to me at the time of my decease also all monies invested in stocks funds and securities and all and every other my estate and effects whatsoever and wheresoever both real and personal whether in possession reversion remainder or expectancy to and for her own use and benefit absolutely AND I DO NOMINATE constitute and appoint Her to be EXECUTRIX of this my Will and hereby revoking all former or other Wills by me at any time heretofore made I DECLARE this to be my last Will and Testament IN WITNESS whereof I the said Edwin George Anson have to this my last Will and Testament set my hand the Eighteenth day of May in the year of our Lord One thousand nine hundred and Twenty.

EDWIN GEORGE ANSON

SIGNED AND DECLARED by the said the Testator as and for his last Will and Testament in the presence of us who at his request in his presence and in the presence of each other all present at the same time have hereunto subscribed our names as witnesses:-

WILLIAM FRANCIS HILL
MARION HELENA BURN
GLADYS BARNES

Affidavit of due Execution filed.

John Glaisyer
District Registrar.   17 SEP 1936

granted at BIRMINGHAM

IEV.

INDEX

A

Accles & Shelvoke, 95
Acocks Green, 92, 97
Anson, Caroline, 35
Anson, Claude Alonso, 24, 84, 85
Anson & Deeley (A&D), 9, 14, 17–23, 25, 26, 28, 35–39, 41, 44, 46, 47, 50–60, 62–66, 71–75, 78–80, 83, 85–87, 97
Anson & Deeley Patentees, 19, 20, 26, 36–38, 64, 66, 72, 74, 75, 79, 85–87
Anson, Dorothy, 36
Anson, (George) Edwin, 9, 19, 21, 24–26, 35, 36, 38, 65, 74, 79–84, 88, 92–97
Anson, Ellen, 9
Anson, Helen, 9
Anson, Jane Elizabeth Maud, 79, 97
Anson, (John) Albert, 11
Anson, Ronald George Kingham, 24
Anson, Titus, 9
Anson, Wilfred Alonso, 84
Anson, William, 9–14, 17–22, 24, 26, 35–39, 41, 44, 46, 47, 50–52, 54, 58, 60, 62–65, 70, 73, 75, 78, 80, 84–87, 98
Ansonia, The, 93, 95
Arbuthnot, G., 21
Archimedes, 14

B

Baker, Frederick (F.T.), 24, 25
Barens, Guillaume Lorent, 12, 13
Batley, John, 46, 47
Beesley, Frederick, 26
Bentley & Playfair, 51, 67
Bentley, Thomas C., 67
Birmingham Exhibition, 53, 54
Birmingham Museum of Science & Industry, 36
Bismarck, Otto von, 40
Bonehill, C.G., 30, 35, 56, 60
Braendlin Armoury, 51, 57, 66
Brazier, Joseph & Sons, 20, 47, 50
British Pistols Act of 1903, 87
Brown, A.A., 95–97
Browning, John, 85
Brussels, Belgium, 54, 70
Buckley, Gladys, 97
Buckley, Samuel, 26
Buttplates, rubber, 28, 30

C

Chamberlain, Joseph, 46, 77, 78
Chamberlain, Neville, 78
Chaplin, Bernard E., 73, 87
Christian Hunter boxlock, 76
Clabrough, J.P. & Bros., 30
Clarke, Frank, 95
Cogswell & Harrison (C&H), 35, 65
Colt, 22, 55, 57, 68
Connecticut Shotgun Mfg. Co., 76
Couchman, Charles, 20, 40, 44, 46, 65
Couchman Robert E., 19, 20 22, 23, 25, 26, 37, 38, 40, 44, 46, 47, 50, 52–54, 56, 57, 60, 62–66
Court of Exchequer, 62
Crystal Palace, 10

D

Daly, Charles, 54
Davies, Howard A. 72–75, 87
Deeley, Elizabeth, 51, 62
Deeley, Emma, 39
Deeley, John, 9, 11, 12, 14, 18–26, 31, 36–41, 44, 46, 47, 50–52, 56, 57, 60, 61–73, 75, 77, 78, 86, 98
Deeley & Edge, 12, 41, 52, 54, 58
Deeley, George Dawson, 66, 69, 70
Deeley & Hill, 64, 66, 70
Deeley, John, the Elder, 64–68, 70
Deeley, John, the Younger, 64, 66, 67, 69
Diana-Luftgewehr Air Rifle, 95
Dickey Bird Safety, 21, 22

E

E. Anson & Co. , 19, 25, 79, 83, 85, 97
Edge, James, 12, 41, 73, 87
Edwards, Henry, 39
Egyptian Hall, 18, 20, 79, 80
Elcho Shield, 69
Eley & Co., 82
Ellis, Charles Osborn, 52

F

Facile Princeps, 17, 35, 37, 51, 60–62, 66
FAMARS, 73
Firefly, 87, 93–95
Fore-end latch, 9, 11–13, 18, 30, 41, 52, 54, 58, 80
Foster, Ernie, 22, 23, 32, 58
Franco-Prussian War, 40, 46
Francotte, Auguste, 34, 54, 55, 63, 70

G

Gaddy, Oscar, 79
Great Exposition of 1851 (The), 10
Greener, Charles, 66
Greener, W.W., 17, 20, 21, 30, 35, 37, 50–52, 54, 57, 58, 60, 62–64, 66, 68, 69
Greenwood, Thomas, 46
Gutta Percha, 30, 32

H

Hand-detachable lock, 71–75, 86, 87
Harcourt, Sir William, 69
Harding, William, 82, 90
Harrington, Gilbert A., 22, 56
Harrington & Richardson (H&R), 21–32, 34–36, 55–60, 63, 65, 79, 80, 83, 84
Harrington & Richardson Gun Grades:
    Grade A, 28, 30–35, 59
    Grade B, 28, 30–33, 59, 79, 80, 84
    Grade C, 28, 30–33, 59, 79, 80
    Grade D, 28, 30, 31, 35
    Grade 1, 28
    Grade 2, 28, 33
Harrison, Edgar, 56, 65
Hemingway, Ernest, 17
Heym, F.W. , 54
Highest Possible Air Pistol, 87–91, 96
Hill, Joan Kathleen, 97
Hill, Phyllis, 97
Hill, Richard, 67
Hill & Smith, 67
Hodges, Edwin Charles "E.C.", 10
Holland & Holland (H&H), 21
House of Lords, 35, 37, 62

J

Jones, William Palmer, 80

K

Kenyon & Eckhardt, 24
King, Charles A., 58
Kirkpatrick, M., 54, 70

L

Ladougne, Jean Fructueux, 12, 13
Lang, Joseph the Elder, 10
Lee-Enfield rifle, 69
Lee-Metford rifle, 69
Lee, William, 67
Lefaucheux, Casimir, 9, 10
Lefever, 22, 55
Lichfield, Earl of, 9
Littlefield, Richard, 25, 26
Lindley, Lord Justice, 62
Lindner, Georg, 54
Lindner, H.A., 54
Lloyd's Banking Company Ltd., 46
London International Exposition, 10
Ludlow, Alfred, 46

M

Martini-Henry rifles, 70
Mauser rifles, 40
McKinley Tariff, 67, 68, 85
Meacham Hardware, 60
Metford, William, 69, 70
Mistrál a Marseille, 64

N

Napoleon III, 40
National Arms and Ammunition Co. Ltd., 46
Needham, Joseph, 14, 15, 41, 44
Nimschke, L.D., 31, 32

O

Oliver, Louis (photographer), 24–26
O'Neil, J. Palmer & Co., 26, 27, 30, 56
Ovundo gun, 91
Overbaugh, C.E. & Co., 60

P

Palmer, J., O'Neil & Co., 56
Parker, Arthur, 62
Parker Brothers, 23, 25, 57, 58
Parker Hammerless, 23
Penn, Frederick J., 37, 64, 65, 69, 60, 73, 75, 87
Perkes, Thomas, 21, 68
Pittsburgh Fire Arms Co., 26, 56
Playfair, Charles, 67
Playfair, Charles the Younger, 67
Pollock, Barn, 62
Powell, William, 51, 52 54, 60
Pryse, T. & L., 66, 67
Purdey, James, 11, 17, 26
Purdey underbolt, 17, 36
Push-Rod Latch, 80

R

Radcliffe, K.D., 72, 73
Radcliffe, Peter, 72, 73
Read, William & Sons, 60
Redman, Richard, 67
Reeves, Charles, 51
Reilly, E.M., 62
Rhyl, Wales, 75, 77
Ribbentrop, Joachin von, 78
Richards, Charles, 40
Richards, Westley the Elder, 39
Richards, Westley the Younger, 20, 39, 40, 46
Richardson, William A., 22, 56
Riley, William Spinks, 12, 13
Robertson, John, 11
Roosevelt, Pres. Theodore, 34
Rowe, Ted, 22, 32, 58, 60
Rowlands and Co., 64, 66
Royal Birmingham Society of Artists, 24, 36

S

Schaefer, William & Son, 54
Schoverling, Daly & Gales, 26–30, 35, 60
Scott, James C., 67
Scott, Martin, 67
Scott, W. & C. & Son, 20, 30, 67, 69
Scott, William Middleditch, 69
Smallman, Thomas, 68
Smith, John, 67
Smith, Joseph, 62
South African Republic (ZAR) , 70
Star Air Pistol (The), 95, 96
St. Mary's Works, 50, 60, 62, 97
Stocks, walnut, 28, 30, 31, 58, 79

T

Taylor, Caroline (Anson), 9
Taylor, Leslie B., 18, 41, 62, 71, 73, 75, 77, 78, 86, 87
Tranter, William, 51
Try Gun, 82
Tryon. E.K. Jr. Co., 60
Turner, James L., 67
Turner, Thomas, 67

W

Warrior, The, 95, 96
Warstone Lane Cemetery (Brookfield), 77
Waterlow and Saylor Ltd., 64, 66
Webley, Henry, 67
Webley, Thomas W., 67
Webley & Son, 67
Wesson, Frank, 22
Westley Richards & Co., 11, 12, 18–22, 24, 37–41, 46, 47, 50–54, 56, 58, 60, 62, 64, 66–68, 70, 73, 75, 77, 86, 90
Wilhelm, Kaiser, 34
Wilkinson, Edward, 52–55, 68, 69
Wilkinson, William, 52–55, 68, 69
William Read & Sons, 60
William Schaefer & Son, 54
Wilson-Gorman Tariff, 85
Worcester, Massachusetts, 21, 24–26, 36, 56, 79, 83, 84

X

"X", Shop Foreman, 71, 86, 87

About the Author

John Campbell is a writer, editor and former creative director of advertising. For over 40 years, he has been a contributor to shooting sports periodicals such as *Double Gun Journal, Rifle, Handloader, The Accurate Rifle, Precision Shooting, Field & Stream, Single Shot Rifle Journal,* and *Gun Digest,* where he was once an Associate Editor.

In addition, John is the author of two highly respected books on the Winchester Model 1885: *The Winchester Single-Shot, A History & Analysis* and *The Winchester Single-Shot, Old Secrets & New Discoveries,* both by Mowbray Publishing.

As an advertising creative director, John's past clients included Pontiac, Cadillac, GM Parts & Service, Bendix, Detroit Diesel Allison, Audi, Mercedes-Benz, Dow, Fruehauf, Budd, Michelob, Johnson Controls, Whirlpool, FUJI, and more.

Throughout his career, John has worked in all mediums, including film, television, print, and the internet. He has also won scores of awards for his work, including three Tellys and two Clio Awards — widely recognized as the "Oscar" of advertising.

John is presently retired and lives in the Grand Strand coastal area of South Carolina. He remains a freelance writer and a regular contributor to *Double Gun Journal.*